COLLECTING THE

MERCEDES-BENZ

1954-1993

Four Decades of Information on the Mercedes-Benz SL

Compiled from Ten Years of SL Market Letters

the SL Market Letter

John R. Olson,
Editor and Publisher

CORRECTIONS
COLLECTING THE MERCEDES-BENZ SL 1954 - 1993

Please retain this information with your book:

PAGE	SHOULD READ
vi	Correct credit for this photo is Mercedes-Benz of North America
9	The 380SLC was built from *May,1980 into September,1981.* The 190SL has a 4 cyl. engine. Line 17 is 220S/SE<u>b</u>: 16,902 built. USA sales unknown.
21	Caption error: Apply 4th and 5th italicized lines to Chart 21-C, omit "see next page" and change amount to *39¢ in 1992.*
113	Mr. O'Shea died in *August, 1990.*
209	The photo attributed to Mr. Hjeltness is actually of *Myron Reichert,* the '92/193 secretary of the Gullwing Group International. A narrative about Mr. Reichert was inadvertently lost. In frequent club service Mr. Reichert also vintage races an XK120 Jaguar, and has prepared his Gullwing in anticipation of a Mille Miglia pilgrimage.
211	Mr. *Pearce's* name is incorrectly spelled on this page.

INTERNATIONAL STANDARD BOOK NUMBER (ISBN) 0-9635394-1-8

COPYRIGHT 1993 BY THE *SL MARKET LETTER*, INCORPORATED
2020 GIRARD AVENUE SOUTH, MINNEAPOLIS, MINNESOTA 55405 USA
PHONE 612-377-0155. FAX 612-377-0157

OTHER BOOKS BY JOHN R. OLSON:
Collecting The Mercedes-Benz SL, 1954-1990, A 128 PAGE REPORT. 1990
Secrets of Buying and Selling Collector Cars, 96 PAGES. 1982
Make Money Owning Your Car (And Enjoy Every Minute), 178 PAGES. 1976

design:ericolson,nyc

PRINTED IN USA, WITH SOY INK IN FRUTIGER AND GARAMOND-THREE FONTS,
ON HEIDELBERG SORDZ/SPEEDMASTER 28.5 X 40 TWO AND FOUR-COLOR PRESSES.

If you don't yet own a Mercedes-Benz SL you may be pleasantly surprised by this book's premise. If you do own any of the rarer models that Mercedes builds every decade, the following may already be a part of your thinking:

- *Many Mercedes do become permanent assets; we have the power to halt their depreciation and in most cases make them re-appreciate.*

- *Collecting the right cars becomes a hobby that pays for itself.*

- *This century's most beautifully engineered automobiles are four(+) dimensional art forms every bit as brilliant as the two-dimensional paintings and static sculptures clogging most museums.*

- *The excellence of Mercedes Benz SLs is best measured in decades, not years, as their worth becomes even more obvious over time.*

- *The experience of owning a fine car is incomplete unless it is used in the manner originally intended. Merely possessing and/or enshrining a car without actual use is like living with the spouse of your dreams but having separate bedrooms.*

Consequently only half of this book is about the statistics and history and restoration. The other half is about using SLs and the people that use them, from simple comparison drives to racing across Mexico a 135 m.p.h. Collecting the Mercedes-Benz SLs is as much about enjoying motoring as it is about investing and polishing.

Germans by nature think everything they build is going to last forever. This is probably how we came to like Mercedes-Benz in the first place. Their "over-built" qualities are an insurance policy on our conviction that cars can be permanent assets. Add to this that Mercedes-Benz is not satisfied building good, sturdy "people's wagens." Their slogans, "Sacrifice Nothing" and "Engineered Like No Other Car in the World" describe something more grand. Mercedes-Benz cars are difficult to judge along side lesser marques because building a car to last decades is not apparent during new car tests. Most cars feel tight when they are new. In our garage are three Mercedes, one is 15 years old, the second 25 years old, and the third 35 years old. The older they get the more fun they've become as you shall see on these pages.

The first section of this book lists the surprising quantities built of some models, which makes other Mercedes-Benz quantities seem large. Hardly. To put Mercedes production in perspective, there were 35,567,728 new passenger cars built in the world during 1991! North America's share in this was also surprising... a weak third among the continents:

Western Europe:	13,286,020
Asia/Pacific:	11,949,734
North America:	7,230,499
Eastern Europe:	1,976,465
Middle East & Africa:	236,736
Central & South America:	888,274
Total new cars in 1991:	**35,567,728**

This means that even the 237,000 Mercedes-Benz SLs built from 1970 through 1989 (R107 Body) amount to less than 1/2200th of each year's new cars. Fairly elite company.

A subject you may look for in this book is current prices. Don't. We get into longer term value trends right away in Chapter 1, but specific shifts in prices from six months ago to now are left to the *SL Market Letter* (*SLML*) as it is published every three weeks. Every six months *SLML* does a major series of price trend issues on all SL models and other rarer Mercedes-Benz. The last page in this book has a discount *SLML* subscription offer for readers of this book.

A warm thank you to the many friendly Mercedes SL owners around the world that have reinforced my positive feelings about these cars. My thanks to this edition's chapter authors **Bruce Adams** (*Restorations*), **Robert Platz** (*Rare Accessories*), and **Alex Dearborn** (*Racing the 190SL*). **Michael Egan**, the United States' most ubiquitous resource on 230/250/280SLs, also was very helpful. Finally, a special thanks to **Eric Olson**, in whose good hands I've left this book's design decisions.

Happy investing in nostalgia,
SL Market Letter, Inc.

John R. Olson
Editor

Preface   iii
Dedication: Rudolf Uhlenhaut   vii

1 WHY PEOPLE COLLECT MERCEDES CARS
Collecting Cars: Some Fundamentals   3
The Importance of Numbers   5
What Makes a Car Collectible?   7
Choosing a Collector Car   15
Comparison of Collectibles   19

2 OVERVIEW OF THE MERCEDES BENZ SLs
350SL through 560 SLs   25
Four Decades of SLs: A Driving Comparison   33
230/250/280SLs   39
280SL/300SL Comparison   45
190SL Roadster and Coupe   53
300SL "Gullwing" Coupe   57
300SL Roadster   63
Prototypes and Special Cars   67
300/500/600SLs   73

3 PURCHASES & RESTORATIONS
Monitoring Price Trends   79
Cautions When Buying   81
Record Keeping and Insurance   89
Restoration:
A Customer's Perspective   95
Rare Accessories:
The Frosting on the Cake   105

4 SL's ARE FOR DRIVING
Why Rear Wheel Drive?   115
Four Days at the World's Best Driving School   119
Grand Touring, SL Style   125
Italy's Mille Miglia   133
Driving Rented SLs in Europe   143
Coast to Coast in 47 Hours   147
Long Distance Rallies   151
Vintage Racing: 153
At Lime Rock in a 190SL   157
At Laguna SECA in a 300SL   163
La Carrera Mexico in a 300SL   173

5 MERCEDES BENZ ART AND MEMORIBILIA   189
6 CLUBS, MAGAZINES & BOOKS   199
7 LEADERS IN THE SL COMMUNITY   207
8 MERCEDES BENZ TECHNICAL INFORMATION 215
224 Index

DEDICATION:
RUDOLF UHLENHAUT

1906-1989

During his 41-year career at Daimler-Benz, **Rudolf Uhlenhaut** had as much impact on Mercedes-Benz products as any man in the history of the company. Uhlenhaut's genius influenced the entire line of SL models covered in this book. In addition to SLs, Uhlenhaut was in charge of passenger car development and testing when the 3.5, 4.5, 600, 6.3 and 6.9 models and engines were conceived.

Long fascinated by suspension engineering, Uhlenhaut pursued several generations of swinging rear axles, insisting that good handling and softness of ride were not ir-reconcilable. These features remain a hallmark of Mercedes-Benz to this day.

Born in 1906 to an English mother and German father, Rudy learned English as a boy. He graduated in engineering from Munich University in 1931. The same year the handsome 24-year-old began work at Daimler-Benz as car testing engineer. It was not long before Rudy's uncommon abilities, both with engineering and with people, brought him to the attention of top engineering management. Only five years after being hired, Uhlenhaut became Technical Director of a new department at DBAG exclusively for race car building.

From 1937-39, this top secret department's cars became so successful that even after WW II the British Intelligence conducted special investigations on these designs, assuming that their undisclosed engineering was at the root of endless victories. According to the British "Investigation into the Development of German Race Cars, 1934-39," Uhlenhaut's department conducted successful tests of fuel injection in 1939, though the

leveraging. The production 300SL Coupe's frame weighed only 181 pounds.

Rudy's choices were original and audacious, from the Gull Wing's famous doors to the 600/6.3 engine and air suspension, yet his ability to make unorthodox designs work well and appear logical was equally impressive. Before funds were available for post WW II Grand Prix racing, Rudy was inspired by the

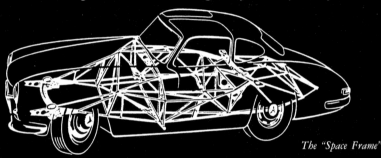

The "Space Frame"

technology was not utilized until the 1940s for German aircraft. (Fuel injection appeared later in the 1950s M-B 300s.) British Army Engineers brought Uhlenhaut to England as part of their post-VE Day analysis of enemy technology.

It was during this period that Uhlenhaut began work on a light-weight "space frame" that found its way into all 300SLs. He tested many miniature models, intentionally breaking them to determine where the small tubes would do the most good. The result was an exercise in triangles fastened together in such a way that most stress was push or pull in nature, rather than bowing or

racing version of Jaguar's XK120. He transfused the 115 horsepower 300 Sedan engine with 48% more horsepower without changing its displacement. Inside of six months he constructed the 1952 Le Mans, Nurburgring and Mexican Road Race winners. The Management Board then authorized the serious money necessary for the 1954/55 Grand Prix winning 300SLRs.

After Daimler-Benz withdrew from racing, Uhlenhaut moved back into production car development and testing. The concept of collapsible fenders absorbing the shock of higher speed accidents to protect the passenger zone was integral to all

Mercedes-Benz passenger cars by the 1950s. In the '60s we remember seeing a 230SL crashed from one side right up the hood seam, yet the hood opened and closed like nothing had happened. When the U.S. Department of Transportation announced its 1970s safety standards and pre-production crash tests, Rudy's engineers nicknamed their 1970s body designs the panzerwagens (armored cars).

Given his bent for fresh solutions, it is not surprising that Uhlenhaut took considerable interest in the Wankel engine and constructed several variants called the C111. For a while it was thought that the ultimate engine would be a turbocharged diesel Wankel. He reviewed turbines and electro/gas combinations, but in the end conventional piston engines remained his choice. We have been told that Uhlenhaut wrote at least one book which was also published in English, though we have not yet learned its English title or found a copy.

Uhlenhaut was hired in 1931 and retired in 1972. He died at age 82. During his last years, Uhlenhaut spent much time aboard his yacht in the Mediterranean. He retained his links to the company during retirement and was spotted several times by *SLML* subscribers at the Daimler-Benz Museum and restoration shop in the 1980s.

Uhlenhaut cut a dashing figure at the races shortly after being hired by DBAG in the 1930's.

Mercedes-Benz has remained the world's foremost passenger car, bus and truck manufacturer for 100+ years, with Uhlenhaut's influence contributing an extra thrill to many products. It almost seemed that there was an absense of special models for a few years after his retirement. During the 1980's Mercedes-Benz management gradually rekindled Uhlenhaut's audacity, and even went racing successfully! Happily, Mercedes-Benz's 1990's models show Uhlenhaut's spirit is still alive and well in Stuttgart.

JRO

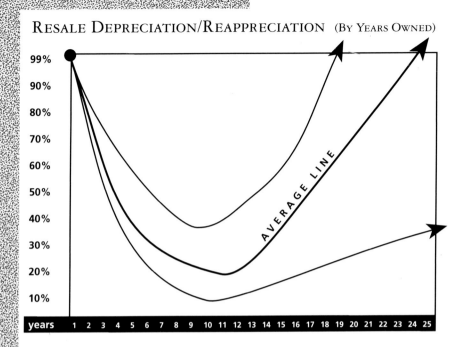

RESALE DEPRECIATION/REAPPRECIATION (BY YEARS OWNED)

99%
90%
80%
70%
60%
50%
40%
30%
20%
10%

AVERAGE LINE

years 1 2 3 4 5 6 7 8 9 10 11 12 13 14 15 16 17 18 19 20 21 22 23 24 25

I.

Why Do People Collect Mercedes-Benz SL's ?

COLLECTING CARS:
SOME FUNDAMENTALS

*"Contrary to what many
Americans think,
life begins at 10 for old cars,
and for appreciation,
the sky seems to be the limit."*

In determining the investment value of any collectible object, it is important to estimate its future scarcity. G. Marshall Naul did a fascinating study many years ago to determine how rapidly a given year's production of cars disappears from license registration statistics in various states of the USA. He found that on average, only 10% of all cars remained licensed in daily use twelve to fifteen years after they were built, and this figure dropped to 1% between the 20th and 25th years. As a result, attractive survivors, even among mass produced cars take on renewed value during their second and third decades of life.

This chart, from my 1970s book, *Make Money Owning Your Car (And Enjoy Every Minute)* is still the best way I know to describe how car values behave generally. The curve was developed by tracking prices of a dozen makes of cars, from zero to twenty-five years old. When our cars are under 10 years old, automobile dealers use Value *Guides* to show us how much our steeds have depreciated. If beyond ten years, we are often told that their *Guides* "just don't go that old."

Contrary to what many Americans think, life begins at 10 for old cars, and for appreciation, the sky seems to be the limit. When I did the original research for this chart my brother asked if it wasn't a bit indecent letting the arrows go off the top of the chart. "Not at all," was my considered reply, as we know the original base price is a very conservative base line. For Mercedes-Benz owners, the whole chart is conservative, as Mercedes-Benz last much longer and have appreciated more steadily than other makes.

The Mercedes SLs have regularly out-performed even the upper curve of this chart. Early 450SL purchasers, had the unusual experience of never seeing their cars drop below original base price. This extremely rapid rate of appreciation has never been common among the best of cars, including Mercedes-Benz.

Cars appreciate only when demand exceeds supply. This happens only when **a)** substantial numbers disappear through normal attrition,

b) supply gets restricted for non-automotive reasons, as happened when the dollar drops in relation to the Deutsch Mark, or **c)** the number of available buyers increases.

Factor "c" above plays into Mercedes-Benz hands due to its high public visibility as a brand symbol. Nostalgia can grow for things sought as well things we've had; as people prosper they sometimes go back and buy collector cars they could not afford earlier. These buyers accumulate while the number of vehicles decreases.

The chart on page 2 reflects how this balance switches normally, as each of these three variables occurs.

*Will Rogers once said,
"Buy land, they ain't
makin' the stuff any more."*

*They aren't making SSKs,
Gull Wings, or 190SLs
any more either.*

THE IMPORTANCE OF NUMBERS

"While all old cars eventually reappreciate, models with low production are often recognized as more 'collectible' from their first day of existence."

Limited edition cars disappear from the market less quickly than the average, but their rarity causes them to appreciate rapidly. For example, the Chevrolet Nomads (built in 1955-57) are still 20% accounted for by a club formed by their owners, and over 50% of all 300SL Gullwings & Roadsters still exist. With only 3,258 ever built, that world-wide owner group has become very elite.

Mercedes SLs are unique among cars costing more than Cadillacs both in steady growth in volume sold (see chart, page 6) and in the fact that their large numbers have not significantly harmed their resale value. Nevertheless, the maxim that lower production numbers enhance re-appreciation is evident, even for Mercedes Benz; the rarer models always fare better when comparison is made between SLs and sedans, or high volume sedans and lower volume sedans.

The following is a list of some very rare vehicles built back in the 1930s and 50s that have developed prominent reputations:

Car	Quantity Built
Duesenberg (all years)	488
Original Continental	5324
Mk II Continental	3000
DeTomaso Pantera (all years)	4000
Ferrari 365GT 2+2 V-12 (68-70)	800
Chrysler 300 Convts (57-65)	1356

MERCEDES			AVERAGE (PER YEAR)	
Model	Total Built	Years Built	World	USA
300SL	3,258	10	326	220
190SL	25,881	9	2,875	1,152
230SL	19,831	5	3,966	792
280SL	23,885	5	4,777	2,557
450SL	66,298	10	6,630	5,848
380SL	53,200	6	8,533	7,341
560SL	49,347	4	12,337	12,337

As we familiarize ourselves with the relatively modest production numbers of SL and SLC cars and other exotic brands, it becomes easier to recognize the importance of production quantities to collectibility. Knowing it takes Mercedes-Benz decades to manufacture and build up sales for each model, it becomes obvious how ridiculous was John DeLorean's widely publicized objective of selling 25,000 of his $28,500 cars annually, beginning with the first year. Trouble was assured.

The *SL Market Letter* monitors prices of most rarer Mercedes on a six month basis, and can spot trends in specific models, flat spots, and the brief surges that are typical. Most cars tend to appreciate unevenly, though if they are appraised every five years, the results are usually pleasing.

What Makes A Car Collectible?

*"It is arguable that finer
20th century automobiles,
highly complex,
mobile three-dimensional
objects, are a higher
form of art than mere
two-dimensional paintings
or sculpting
or architecture."*

We have seen million dollar prices for post-50s Ferraris and over five-million dollar prices for Bugattis. Mercedes-Benz owners seem to be going down the same path with 540Ks and 300SLs. What will be next? Making sense of the current scene would be easier if we looked back from another century. From the perspective of the 22nd century, our 20th century hobby of car collecting will seem to be in its infancy. A mere babe among collectibles. Yet collectors have already fixed their eyes on even newer subjects; high-tech collectibles... early TV sets and computers. Even Swatches (sick!).

Without denying the charm of each decade's greatest art and great automobiles, it seems clear that people in future centuries will look back on the first 100 years of the automobile differently than we do today. We already recognize the automobile as a leading factor in the modernization of civilization; it has helped us progress faster than in all previous centuries combined. One to two centuries from now, we suspect the importance of the "automobile century" will still stand out... even after future breakthroughs. If this is the case, which cars of our "first 100 years" of motorized history will be most prized?

We think the answer is those which had the most and/or longest impact on the public of their day, decade, or longer. They will often be examples of great engineering brilliance, not always the most expensive or complex. Modest Model-T Fords and Volkswagen Beetles and Mercedes-Benz 170s will be looked at with great amusement in one hundred plus years. Their place in history, plus inflation, may pull them above $100,000 in show condition. Hard to believe? When we predicted in 1968 that in twenty five years new VWs would be selling for over $10,000, it sounded equally unlikely.

The financial press finds it hard acknowledging the progress of any tangibles, long term. Paintings, antique furniture or automobiles are treated as oddities and flukes. Severe highs or lows get printed for their sensational value, but even handed 10, 20, or 30 year evaluations are rare.

The November **Forbes** (11/23/92) for example called car investments "popular delusions," sighting the see-saw history of the Ferrari GTO from $12,000 in 1963 to a proported $16 million in 1990. Today's value they suggest is closer to $3 million. Other horror stories were described.

What Forbes' **Christie Brown** over-looked (?) is that at $3 million the Ferrari has experienced over 20% compound annual appreciation for 30 years! That's awesome, and we've used your figures, Ms. Brown.

It is arguable that finer 20th century automobiles, examples of highly complex & mobile three-dimensional craftsmanship, are a higher form of art than mere two-dimensional paintings or sculpting or architecture. Are we too close to the trees in the forest to see complex engineering as the most sophisticated art form of this century?

Whether or not one accepts this view, the footprint of Mercedes-Benz on this century has been enormous, from beginning to end. We believe owning a 20th century Mercedes-Benz, any Mercedes-Benz, in the 22nd century will be as special as owning a promi-nent 20th century painting. And owning a very limited quantity, famous model, with show or competi-tion successes, will parallel Gauguin or Picasso status. It will be hard to make a mistake preserving any Mercedes-Benz long term; even the most mundane junior sedans will grow "special" as they become older. Having "allowed" all Mercedes, which models will be the *most* worth saving? Quantities built are extremely important. We've listed a post-1945 ranking of Mercedes-Benz, in order of their originally built quantities (see chart, page 9).

In general, car manufacturers build

more sedans than any other model. Fewer convertibles, even back in the 30s and 50s, were built than any other model. On the collector car scene today, vintage convertibles often command five times the price of sedans of the same make and year. Each marque has a few exceptions, such as the Avanti, the Mk. II Continental, the Ferrari 275 GTB, and of course, the Gull Wing. Age and specific model year can also be important. On some cars, the initial concept (first year) is cleaner than subsequent variants. Studebaker's stunning 1953 Starliner 2dr hardtop became more cluttered with tack-ons each following year. This phenomenon is less pronounced in Mercedes cars. The early 190SL was lighter, faster & gave better gas mileage than the last half of the series, but other refinements & a wrap around rear window in the '59-63 removable hardtops have neutralized any advantages of the earlier

20 Rarest Post-1950 2-Door Mercedes-Benz

Rarity	Model	Description	Yrs. Built	Quant. Built	US Sales	Sub-Quantities and Notes
1	300Sc	Fuel Injection	'55-'58	200	145	49 Convts, 53 Roadsters, 98 Coupes
2	300S	All variants	'51-'55	560	400	141 Roadsters, 203 Convts, 216 Coupes
3	300	4-dr. Cvtbl, all	'51-'56	640	350	591 types A & B, 51 type C, 65 type D
4	5.0 SLC	2-dr. Hrdtp.	'80-'81	1,299	20	4 speed automatic, 2.24 axle, ABS opt.
5	300SL	Gull Wing Coupe	'54-'57	1,400	1,100	29 all aluminum bodied cars
6	5.0 SLC	2-dr. Hrdtp.	'77-'80	1,470	40	3 speed automatic, 2.72 axle, ABS opt.
7	300SL	Roadster	'57-'64	1,858	1,440	offered w/ soft top or Hrdtp. or both
8	220	Cvtbl. A & B	'51-'55	2,360	300	"A": 3 window dsgn, "B": 5 window
9	170V	4 Cyl. Roadster	'49-'53	2,433	340	Seldom imported to USA
10	300 SE	6 Cyl. Cpe/Cvtbl.	'62-'67	3,127	2,100	Air Suspension
11	380 SLC	2-dr. Hrdtp., V-8	'77-'79	3,789	1,409	---
12	280 SE	3.5 Hdtop & Cvtbl.	'69-'70	4,502	1,609	USA: 801 Cvtbl., 808 Coupe
13	280 SE	6 Cyl. Cpe/Cvtbl.	'68-'72	5,187	2,055	USA: 902 Cvtbl, 1,153 Coupes
14	220 S/SE	6 Cyl. Cpe/Cvtbl.	'56-'60	5,196	1,744	USA recvd 33.6% A/C & 5 spd optns.
15	250 SE	6 Cyl. Cpe/Cvtbl.	'65-'67	5,371	1,100	2,081 Cvtbl, 3,290 cpes, 1,974 with FI
16	280 SLC	2-dr. Hrdtp., V-8	'74-'81	6,213	739	USA: 597 Cvtbls, 142 Coupes
17	220 SE	6 Cyl. Cpe/Cvtbl.	'60-'65	11,210	4,500	W111 body, Cpe, Cvtbl #s.not separate
18	190 SL	6 Cyl. 2pass Rdstr	'55-'63	25,881	14,000	
19	500-560SEC	2-dr. Hrdtop, V-8	'80-'92			
20	230-50-80SL	6 Cyl. 2pass Rdstr.	'63-'71	48,912	18,415	19,831 230SL; 5,196 250SL; 23,885 280SL

One of twenty-one 5 liter Rally-Racers built by
Mercedes-Benz and
Scuderia Kassel.
Man in picture is Robert Bayer, president of the
300SL Club in Europe.

years. Like-wise, LJK Setright's book *The Mercedes SL and SLC (now out-of-print)* favors drivability of the 230SL over 250 and 280SLs, yet larger engines, built-in headrests, etc. make '68 -'71 280SLs more valuable. All of this is not to say that engineering, statistics and finance rule the day; aesthetics and "nostalgia power" are important as well. Generally, the larger the passenger area of a car the harder it is to make a design exciting or stylish. Exceptions exist (some Bugati Royales), but just the step of adding four doors invites designs to be more bulky than two-door and convertible versions of the same model. Consequently two-door cars get more aesthetic "points" and are more appealing to enthusiasts. Open cars, with two or four doors are usually *the* most prized style. Exception; the Gull Wing coupe, one of the world's most photogenic cars.

Note in particular the lower-quanti-ties in the far right column (preceding chart). Also, a few 1952 300SL racers were sold, but M-B conscientiously rebodied them with production GW bodies & 1954 fuel injected engines ...which unwittingly diluted their pedigree. (More on engine switching in Chapter 3). Twenty-one 500SLC Rally Racers were built by Daimler-Benz and Scuderia Kassel, with up to 320 horsepower, 4.08:1 rear axle ratios, and often tires at 245/50 x 15 and larger.

300 SLR, Moss/Jenkinson, Mille Miglia 1955

50 Years...

of classic sports and racing cars from

Mercedes-Benz 1926-1976

the way
every car
should be built

Mercedes-Benz (United Kingdom) Ltd. Great West Road, Brentford, Middx.

Sought after 1976 Poster prepared by
Mercedes-Benz of England

SLML SUBSCRIBER'S POLL:
THE MOST
COLLECTIBLE
MERCEDES-BENZ

BY DECADE	1886-1920	1921-1930	1931-1940
	1914 Blitzen Benz: 73%	1929-31 SSK: 92%	1936-39 540K Special Roadsters: 78%
	1886 Patent Motor-Wagen: 15%	Other Compressor Models: 8%	1933-36 500K Special Roadsters: 14%
	All Other: 7%		1938-43 770, W125 & Other 8%

But rareness is not greatness. To be collected cars must also be respected by serious car enthusiasts. In 1990 the SL Market Letter polled its subscribers choices of the most collectible Mercedes-Benz cars of each decade (see chart). Certainly some models not on this chart will fair just fine... the 1960s SE Coupes & 230SLs come quickly to mind. Likewise 220 2dr. & 300 4dr. convertibles of the 1950s are hardly insignificant. Never-the-less, we take great stock in the "winners"... mostly because we take great stock in our subscribers. If John Stuart Mills were alive (professing "plurality of votes justly due for opinions grounded on superiority of knowledge") we think he would say *SL Market Letter Subscribers* are "grounded on superiority of knowledge" as a group for our poll.

We asked participants to do a "forced" rankings of their preferences, with rational and irrational reasons all lumped together. As you can see SLs faired very well. A conspicuous puzzle (weakness?) in the results is the absence of 190SL for the decade of the 1950s, and 230SL for the '60s. A 190SL subculture has been flourishing. It is evident that 1970s SLs have already left many positive impressions & fond memories, which may mitigate the higher quantities built. We think these "R107" SLs will be driven much longer than most "old cars", because of their toughness, modern look, & endless availability of repair parts...

1951-1960	1961-1970	1971-1980	1981-1990	1991-2000
1954-57 300SL Coupe: 50%	1969-71 280SE 3.5ltr Cnvtbl: 29%	1971-80 350/450SL: 39%	1956-90 560SEC: 26%	"no choices yet": 49%
1957-64 300SL Roadster: 32%	1967-71 250/280SL: 28%	1975-80 450SEL 6.9 39%	1988-90 300E/CE 26%	500 SL: 33%
1951-58 300S/Sc: 12%	1964-72 600: 18%	1977-81 5.0 ltr. SLC 19%	1990 (R129) 500SL: 24%	a V-12 in SL or SFC: 18%
all other 6%	1964-72 300SEL 6.3 16%	all other: 3%	1985-88 190E 2.3-16 18%	a 300 E V-8: (400E or 500E) 7%
	1961-67 6 cyl. cvtbls 8%		all other: 12.2%	

opportunity to accrue even more nostalgia. Regard for the current 560SEC is high... ditto for the 1970s 350/450SL.

The 1960s was a bountiful decade from M-B, providing four strong choices. Subscriber ranking of 250/280 SLs above the 600 bodes well for the SLs, but does not guarantee faster appreciation in the 1990s. We believe that even with 33% fewer votes, the good 600s will continue to sell for more money than good 250/280 SLs. Fewer 600s were built & technology more awesome.

Sentiment about the 1990's is guesswork, though two of the cars that SL Market Letter subscribers wished for have appeared, the 600SL V-12, and middle class V-8s... the 400E and 500E. Hopefully Mercedes will see a market for a 1990s 500CE Cabriolet too.

We think this is an important chart. If your "older Mercedes" aren't owned for personal nostalgia reasons, consider seriously picking from this list. It is an important estimate of which 20th century Mercedes will be most sought by collectors in the next century.

CHOOSING
A COLLECTOR CAR

"The search for collector caliber cars is national, even international."

The following is a summary of remarks and conventional wisdoms your author has presented in talks to car clubs and investment groups.

There are eight generic elements that affect the value & collectibility of all cars.

1. **Condition:** Just as location is paramount to the success of many retail businesses, in cars condition becomes more important even than rarity, *when* restoration costs are greater than the difficulty locating a high caliber car (more often than the seller wants you to believe). Originality (fewer owners & mechanics & a known history) can't be duplicated by restoration.

2. **Public acceptance** of a particular make and model. Well known marques such as Ford, Chevy, Cadillac, and Mercedes-Benz generate much stronger impressions in the contemporary mind than do minor or defunct marques. Nostalgia tends to die off with the generation that knew it. If a marque is strong today it's best past products are not forgotten. Enter Mercedes-Benz.

3. **Performance**, durability, and availability of parts and service. Engineering excellence takes many forms, and usually pays dividends.

4. **Tenure** in our depreciation/reappreciation chart (page 2). All cars reappreciate eventually, even parts cars. The more of these

more as a casual car enthusiast who would like to see your car appreciate enough to (maybe) be a free hobby... then, pick cars you truly admire. Unlike a stock certificate, you *will* have a relationship with all your cars. If your choice happens to appear on some expert's list, that may be a tribute to your good taste... but always try to like it yourself. You never know how long you will own it when you make the purchase. Treat your car like a pet; listen to it & become friends. Non-monetary dividends.

eight factors a car has going for it, the more apt it is to out-perform the chart's average line.

5. The more factory options

present on the car the better, even if they don't work. There is plenty of time to get them working. Looking back to the 1950s, a 300SL with Rudge wheels or disc brakes, a Becker Mexico radio and/or factory fitted luggage is worth many thousands of dollars more than one without them (all else being equal).

6. Your personal likes & dislikes.

IRS actually has definitions for "investments" which prohibit personal pleasure by the owner... If a painting is held as an investment you cannot put it over your fireplace while you own it. If you owned a group of "investment" cars you can be sure this criteria would apply. If you see yourself

7. Acceptance by auto experts

means a car will have an automatic and probably permanent PR department. Some flashy cars become fads of the moment, but if the automotive writers don't give good marks, the longer term is weakened.

8. Scarcity, based on original production numbers & attrition. Most companies build many sedans and few convertibles. Consequently even the best preserved sedans are slower to appreciate. Coupes fall somewhere in between. Of course there are exceptions, like the 300SL Gull Wing. Top of the line models are also prized, as they symbolize the best each marque offers, and are usually made in fewer numbers. With some marques (not so much Mercedes) the first year & last year a model is produced generate higher average sale prices (all else being equal).

Car shopping

Local vs. National. In our experience, the search for collector caliber cars must be national, even international in some cases. While your local market may contain the car of your dreams, even larger cities don't always give many choices for buyers *or* sellers. Mercedes-Benz dealers usually know the local market and will put you in touch with local M-B club members if they can not show you the "out-of-print" model you want. There are several ways to screen cars in another state before traveling to see it. Check out ads in other cities & states. After several phone calls a good step is asking the seller to bring the car to his local M-B dealer or to an independent auto diagnostic center for inspection (which *you* pay for so the inspectors know who they're working for!) Another alternative is hiring an appraiser or paying expenses of a fellow national car club member or an *SL Market Letter* subscriber who lives near the car. Ask him to drive the car (wavering his liability for courtesy assistance). This expands your shopping ground immensely before leaving your door step.

Selling *nationally* is sometimes also preferable for special cars. I have found that uncommon cars never generate heavy phone inquiries, even with national ads, but the people who do call tend to be more serious and qualified.

Don't be surprised if the person offering your dream car is not himself a car buff. A sizable group of Mercedes-Benz owners are "consumers" interested mostly in superior transportation from point-A to point-B. They do not place any special worth on the product as a permanent asset or investment; for them it is a consumable, but hearty means to travel about, and to look and feel good. These owners don't join car clubs or seldom renew if they do join. Use of their cars varies hugely: some put on 50,000+ miles per year, while others own three or four cars and accrue low miles.

Many a beautiful collector car has come from such a garage - original paint-and-all after fifteen years of under-use. Most of us know of cars like this lurking among our neighbors or acquaintances. Patiently state your interest to these folks. Don't let those cars get away! Hundreds of such cars are made available for sale to admirers posthumously by deceased owners' wills or widows. Just this past year I learned of a Gull Wing passed on to an admiring non-relative without cost via a will, but don't wait for that! Owners of unrestored originals of course expect a fair price for their cars, but having not personally gone through a costly restoration they may be easier to satisfy.

Another reason for going after originals is that most 1960s and 70s Mercedes-Benz models have been built in relatively large numbers compared to collector cars of the past. Along with the truly rare types are some equally famous higher production collector cars.

'55/'57 T-Birds	53,166
'54/'63 190SL	25,881
'63/'71 230-250-280SL	48,912
'71/'89SL (all)	237,287

Without lessening the splendor of major restoration work, production quantities such as these and the higher than average survival rate of Mercedes-Benz provide a good chance for you to locate unrestored, original paint cars. Finding a thirty or forty year old car that still has its original factory paint is rare, but keep a look-out for six to fifteen year-old originals. Shepherding such a car through its next couple of decades with minimal alteration is for my money a "higher" purpose than resurrecting a weathered bargain. I am not anti-restoration, but I like to see that art directed to twenty+ year olds that are truly rare.

The three most important things in determining price are 1) condition, 2) condition and 3) condition. Then come the other features mentioned here. The difference in price between "consumed" examples and well-preserved originals is huge (100%+ on cars over 10 years old), and usually justified. As cars move into the collector age group there are virtually two price scales for the same car, thousands of dollars apart, for collector vs. "ordinary" examples. The fastest way a car's price climbs is through an owner's restoration costs which he will never forget, ...and will never let you forget!

When you do find something close to your objectives, carefully add up any restoration you must do, and then double that figure or you probably allowed too little, or unfairly disregarded the worth of your own time. If the numbers still look attractive, you are probably on the right track. (See two page form in Chapter 3, in Cautions When Buying.)

A COMPARISON OF COLLECTIBLES

*"Pre WWII
American Paintings
were the overall winners,
but the 300SL
exceeded Sotheby's Aggregate Index
even after
removing inflation."*

The "prudent man rule," a standard for prudent investing by trust and estate managers, guides investors in taking risks with their clients' funds. What are considered "safe" investments vary with the size of one's estate and have changed over the course of time. During the first half of this century, many banks regarded mortgages as the most prudent securities. Gradually, the use of the blue chip stocks and bank CDs increased with definite preference for easily appraised, relatively liquid choices with low maintenance. More strictly regulated retirement accounts (IRAs) continued to favor shorter term equity and bonds. Research like the next few pages, however has prompted some trusts to include a percentage of art and collectibles.

Updated from the *SL Market Letter,* here is a comparison of old Mercedes-Benz SLs versus other kinds of assets, stocks, bonds, and fine art as reported by the Sotheby Index. Bearing in mind that the Sotheby Index tracks pre-1950 and in many cases pre-1900 objects, we chose the two oldest SLs, the 190SL and the 300SL, for our comparison. The Sotheby Index has included twelve categories since 1975. A thirteenth, Contemporary Paintings, was added during the mid-1980s, but we have excluded it here in order to preserve a consistent base.

Until 1989 Sotheby's Index was published in *Fortune* Magazine. We hope it finds an American forum again soon, as this work confirms the merit of all tangible investments.

None of our comparisons address taxes as that is best evaluated with

20-A

Item @ 14 years	W/Inflation	W/0 Inflation
300SL Gull Wing	19.99%	13.10%
Sotheby's Index1	15.99%	9.36%
190SL	12.95%	6.50%
DJI Growth and Div	12.17%	7.20%
IBM Growth and Div	11.41%	7.71%
US Gov. Bonds	8.5%	2.33%

THE SOTHEBY INDEX (1989)

20-B

Sotheby's Categories	9/'75	9/'82	9/'84	9/'87	11/'89	7/'92
Old Masters	100	199	251	349	660	811
19th Century European Paintings	100	183	220	303	575	643
Impressionist and Post-Impressionist	100	255	317	661	1525	913
Modern Paintings	100	245	301	666	1415	1,037
Pre WWII American Paintings	100	459	589	789	1371	1,179
Continental Ceramics	100	266	284	320	505	864
Chinese Ceramics	100	460	482	550	875	923
English Silver	100	183	237	349	420	440
Continental Silver	100	134	161	201	367	428
American Furniture	100	213	241	452	510	527
Continental Furniture	100	234	270	319	500	648
English Furniture	100	261	360	594	822	906

your accountant. Translated in compound annual returns, we get the figures you see in *Chart 22-A*.

Removing inflation can be an eye opener. The 190SL's real value actually fell backwards while its prices climbed between 1984 and 1987, though percentage-wise , it has been rivaling everything lately. Pre-WWII American Paintings are the current winners, however, the 300SL still exceeds Sotheby's Aggregate Index.

According to **Peter Mueller**, President of *Classic Automotive Investments, Inc.,* "It is best to read car values over 5 year periods to smooth out the peaks and valleys. For example, the worst completed 5 year period of recession in the last 15 years is 1981-1986. Many car values fell from 1983 through '85, but stayed on the plus side from '81 through '86! It has happened again recently... Gullwings dropped 30% from mid-1989 through mid '92, but the five years

Sotheby's and this book's analysis are historical and neither intended as advice or as prediction or guarantee of the future.

Using the same year of 1975 as the Sotheby's Index as our base of 100, we have the following figures for the 190SL
and 300SL in 1982, 1984, 1987, 1989 and 1992:

PRE-INFLATION

21-A

	1975	1982	1984	1987	1989	1992
Aggregate of twelve Categories of Art monitored by Sotheby's (our calculation)	100	251	302	463	795	777
190 SLs (1975: $3,706 = base of 100)	100	321	392	431	550	771
300 SLs (1975: $27,000 = base of 100)	100	288	296	465	1,273	810

These figures don't take inflation into account, however, which the value of the dollar has changed as follows:
see next page Since the value of the 1975 dollar equaled about 44 cents in late 1989, the appreciation of SLs, Dow
Jones Industrials, IBM, and fine art objects independent of inflation are as follows:

INFLATION ADJUSTED

21-B

	12/'75	12/'82	12/'84	12/'87	12/'89	7/'92
1. Effect on the dollar:	$1.00	$0.57	$0.53	$0.48	$0.44	$0.39
2. Aggregate of 12 Sotheby Categories:	100	143	160	222	350	303
3. 190SL (1975: $3,706 = base of 100)	100	183	208	206	242	301
4. 300SL (1975 SL: $27,000=base of 100)	100	164	157	223	560	316

OTHER "PRUDENT" INVESTMENTS

21-C

	9/'75	9/'89	9/'92
Dow Jones Industrial Average:	$794	$2,753	$3,250
DJI Average (Inflation Removed):	$794	$1,211	$1,300
DJI Cumulative Dividends:	$0	$890	$1,064
DJI Real Growth and Dividends:	$794	$2,105	$2,361
DJI gain (1975 as base year)	$100	$265	$297
IBM (adjusted for one stk. split):	$35	$105	$81
IBM 14 yrs. (inflation removed):	$35	$46	$32
IBM Cumulative Dividends:	$0	$53	$61
IBM Real Growth & Dividends:	$35	$99	$93
IBM gain ('75 as base year)	100	$283	$267

Footnote: Dividends are not subjected to inflation removal as they are spendable in the year received.

from mid-1987 to mid-'92 show a 100% gain. Mercedes owners seem to sense this without being told.

We see 600, 6.3 SEL and 6.9 SEL enthusiasts sifting through the best of these cars now. Only about 2,000 of each came to the USA. Allowing for attrition, above average examples are becoming scarce. We expect good Mercedes 600s to climb above $100,000 during the next five years, but be warned, they are strictly big-league machinery best reserved for folks with their own full-time technicians or mechanics. A 6.3 or 6.9 is a wiser first outing. When you've mastered that, graduate to a 600.

We need to remember tangibles have storage & insurance costs even when "pickled." We would estimate fire, theft and vandalism coverage, plus storage space as indicated below.

22-A

Item	Insurance	Space	Total
190SL at 15 yrs...	$3,000	$4,500	$7,500
300SL at 15 yrs	$6,000	$4,500	$10,500
Art Work at 15 yrs	similar	less	less
Stocks at 15 yrs	none	none	none

"Pickling" and unpickling an auto costs money too. This, plus a new battery and a few other surprises, would have a negligible effect on a 300SL's gains, but could pull a lower priced car to break-even quicker. Where does this leave us? If we are only talking investments and returns, with no hobby, fun, or associated friendships, then the list of cars eligible for our attention gets much smaller, and Chapter Four of this book becomes verboten!

As long-standing car enthusiasts, we see the hobby and investment issues as one benefit, not two: a hobby that pays for itself is like falling in love with someone who turns out to be financially independent.

MERCEDES-BENZ

Joie de vivre.

The 190 SL roadster,
available as a
convertible or with
removable hard top.

*Mercedes-Benz motor cars are distributed exclusively in the United States by the Studebaker-Packard
Corporation and sold and serviced through selected dealers franchised by Studebaker-Packard.*

 Studebaker-Packard
CORPORATION

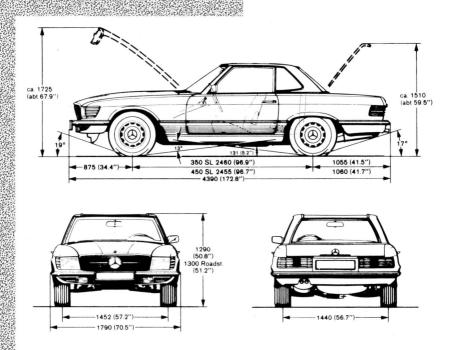

ca. 1725
(abt 67.9")

ca. 1510
(abt 59.5")

19°

13°

17°

131 (5.2")

875 (34.4")

350 SL 2460 (96.9")

450 SL 2455 (96.7")

1055 (41.5")

1060 (41.7")

4390 (172.8")

1290
(50.8")
1300 Roadst.
(51.2")

1452 (57.2")

1790 (70.5")

1440 (56.7")

2.
Overview
of the
Mercedes-Benz
SL

OVERVIEW:
350SL THROUGH 560SL

*"Never in the history of the
automobile have
so many two-passenger cars been
sold at 200%+ above the price
of an American Cadillac.
All the more impressive, its success
started during the
first great slump in the value of
the dollar; inflation drove
the window sticker price
up over 300% by 1989,
improvements notwithstanding."*

The R-107 body type has had the largest and longest production of any single SL (or SLC) body type. During its twenty years of production, each R107-type SL V-8 found larger per-year sales. They also experienced nearly 500% growth in price from at $10,540 (350SL E. Coast USA, 12/71) to $64,230 (560SL USA, 6/89).

After such unpresidented sales, we wonder if these cars will also defy our "fundamental" in Chapter 1 that lower production cars have the best chance for reappreciation. The other factors (positive nostalgia and/or supply of new buyers and rebuyers) will have to off-set the higher quantities. Fact is, the R107 SLs are extremely hearty cars. That means more SLs satisfying more owners longer, i.e. more nostalgia.

When Daimler-Benz began work on the Type R107 SL three decades ago, they knew that the USA's DOT crash test standards would stiffen progressively during the 1970s. No strangers to accident protection, D-B's "passenger cells" were highly impact-resistant even in the early 50s. D-B engineers nick-named their new SL the "Panzerwagen project" (armored car). The result was the strongest full convertible yet devised. Reviewers of styling unanimously ranked it below the designs of the 1960s and 1950s SLs; one *SLML* subscriber has called it an up-market, two-passenger Range Rover.

Model	Body	Engine	First Car	Last Car
280 SL	107	Twin Cam6	May '74	Aug '85
350SL	107	V-8 Iron	Nov '70	Mar'80
450SL	107	V-8 Iron	Mar '71	Nov '80
				Production Totals:

Model	Body	Engine	First Car	Last Car
280SL	107	Twin Cam6	May '74	Aug '85
300SL	107	Straight 6	May '85	July '89
380SL	107	V-8 Alloy	Feb '80	Oct '85
420SL	107	V-8 Alloy	July '85	May '89
500SL	107	V-8 Alloy	April '80	June '89
560SL	107	V-8 Alloy	June '85	June '89
				Production Totals:

Our first impression of the car, sighted on a Geneva, Switzerland street in 1971, was that it *did look* like an armored car. While it was technically advanced, we feared that its styling would hurt sales. How wrong we were! Demand exceeded the previous 280SL in 1971 and 1972 because it was a new model. How well M-B targeted this SLs market is driven home when we see at top of this page that sales flowed and flowed. Their best year (1986) was fifteen years after introduction! In retrospect, certain

R107 SL: Weight, Engine and Performance Variations

Model	Varient	Wheelbase	Weight	Length	Transmission
280SL	European	96.7"	3,300	172.4"	A or 4 or 5
380SL	USA	"	3,605	182.3"	A only
	European	"	3,392	172.8"	A only
350SL	USA	"	3,487	172.4"	A only
	European	"	3,487	172.4"	A or 4spd.
300SL	European	"	3.300	180.3"	A or 5spd
450SL	USA '72	"	3,780	172.4"	A only
	USA '80	"	3,750	182.3"	A only
	European	"	3,487	172.4"	A only
420SL	European	"	3,520	180.3"	A only
500SL	European	"	3,392	180.3"	A only
560SL	USA	"	3,780	180.3"	A only

(1970-1980)

1970	1971	1972	1973	1974	1975	1976	1977	1978	1979	1980	Totals
0	0	0	0	297	1,020	1,099	1347	1536	2,155	2,429	add '80-'90
3	4,802	4,778	1,647	574	390	540	650	743	934	243	15,304
0	2131	7473	8,654	6,093	6,011	6,625	8,110	7,434	8,184	5,583	66,298
3	6,933	12,251	10,301	6,964	7,421	8,264	10,107	9,713	11,273	8,255	91,485

(1980-1990)

1980	1981	1982	1983	1984	1985	1986	1987	1988	1989	1990	Totals
0	2,628	3,165	3,393	3,529	2,838	0	0	0	0	0	25,436
0	0	0	0	0	1,356	4,331	3,261	2,746	2,048	0	13,742
3,347	9,470	9,926	11,198	11,115	8,144	0	0	0	0	0	53,200
0	0	0	0	0	215	1,003	479	325	126	0	2,148
501	899	1,297	1,563	1,793	2,719	1,192	768	739	341	0	11,812
0	0	0	0	0	3,907	13,788	14,770	11,531	5,351	0	49,347
12,103	12,997	14,388	16,154	16,437	19,179	20,314	19,278	15,341	7,866	0	237,287

elements of the design, the roof and trunk lines, and tail light treatment, have proven to have an ageless quality not apparent (to us) in the beginning.

Never in the history of the automobile have so many two-passenger cars been sold at 200%+ above the price of an American Cadillac. All the more impressive, its success occurred during the most severe period of double digit inflation the USA has ever experienced. It has been successful during a period when the population generally has found it

Engine	Horsepower	Torque	Axle Ratio	0-60mph	Top Speed
Twin Cam 6	185@6,000	176@4,500	3.69&3.92	9.2 sec.	127mph
V-8 Alloy	155@4750	196@2,750	2.47:1	11 sec.	121mph
V-8 Alloy	218@4,750	224@4,000	3.27:1	8.8 sec.	134 mph
V-8 Iron	see 450SL	see 450SL	3.07:1	9.2 sec.	127mph
V-8 Iron	230@6,050	231@4,200	3.46:1	8 sec.	133mph
Strg. 6	188@5,700	192@4,400	3.46:1	9.2sec.	127mph
V-8 Iron	230@5,000	278@3,000	3.07:1	9.2 sec.	127mph
V-8 Iron	160@4,200	239@3,000	2.65:1	10.3 sec.	124mph
V-8 Iron	250@5,000	230@2,500	3.06:1	8.3 sec.	133mph
V-8 Alloy	218@5,200	242@3,750	2.47:1	8.5 sec.	133mph
V-8 Alloy	231@4750	297@3,200	2.72 & 2.24	7.4 sec.	140mph
V-8 Alloy	227@4,750	279@3,250	2.47:1	8 sec.	137mph

harder than past generations to build permanent assets and buy homes.

One key to the R107's success is the most successful portion of the baby boom , those generating $50,000 to $500,000+ annual income.
The number of people in this group has mushroomed. From 1972 through 1980 the number of the USA's millionaires grew 263% - up to 574,342! From 1980 to 1990 it grew again to 2.1 million people! These folks seek modern technology and a quality image; an identity with the here and now. Many are fast paced and achievement oriented. These consumers were quick to discover 1970's and 1980's SLs. During the last half of the 1980's they also re-discovered *earlier* SLs. There are three distinct owner groups here:

Daily drivers, owners who are buying utility - the finest utility they can find - to use and consume.
A car's ability to rise above these expectations comes later, with a long ownership, or even long *after* ownership, in one's memories.

Car collectors, hobbyists who like cars for their merit, a physical treasure of engineering, a piece of history, three dimensional art and nostalgia.

Investors, those placing first priority on appreciation of their investment, a small but growing minority. Lower production collector cars have out-performed other "tangible" invest-ments over the past 20 years. 1950's SLs (190SL and 300SL) are good examples.

If we look at how the majority of these cars are being used, in daily business and for family chores, with more than ever before on company leases, accruing high miles, accidents, engine rebuilds, and general "recycling" to further service, it becomes more apparent that the number of original paint, low mile, "show quality" examples is not that great in the five-plus year old category. The large majority (70% to 80%) are being consumed as in the past. After the majority of owners run the wheels off their SLs and sell what's left, some of those ex-owners will be infected by that sickness called nostalgia. Enough of the afflicted will compete for repurchase of the surviving cars to ensure demand and scarcity of the good examples.

We believe that with few exceptions (such as always perfect cream-puffs), most R107s will shift only slowly from the "daily driver" category to "collector" status. Those low mileage, original paint gems will move into an elite class that reappreciate above original 1980s selling prices. These are the cars "too good to drive" destined for life as an object of wonder. Some cars (some whole marques) escape to this status prematurely, as odd engineer-ing makes them un-dependable "drivers" anyway. This is certainly *not* the case for 1971-1989 SLs.

*Unquestionably the most
popular high-priced
sports car of all time, this
series struck a
responsive chord in America
and Europe
that continues today.*

*Safety will be one of the lasting
legacies of this series,
introducing such features as fuel tank
mounted over the rear axle
and computer designed windshield posts
(for maximum strength).*

There may be no tougher, more *usable* collector cars ever built. When service is needed, prompt Mercedes-Benz parts availability is legendary, even for twenty and thirty-year-old models. Mercedes SL salvage businesses are also prolific and cheerful in providing spare parts.

Picking the "best" engine variant of the R107 is somewhat personal, as each has unique benefits. The number in the car's label indicates the size of its engine in cubic centi-

meters. Even the smaller 280 (a twin cam 6 cylinder) and the 350 V-8 surprise most first time drivers with their pep as horsepower does not correspond directly to the label. Also, 280 & 350SLs can be found with 4 and even 5 speed manual transmissions. 420 and 500s are the rarest. Dealer support for the 450/380/560 is second to none since they sold most of them new.

Typical Dollar Range By Model (1993)

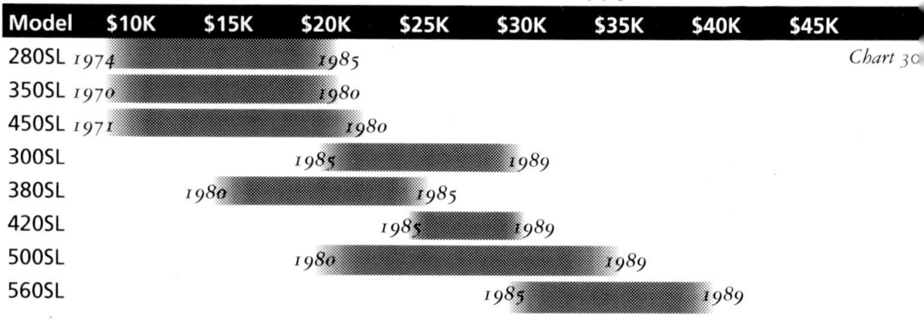

Chart 30

Model	Bar Range (approx. $ / years)
280SL	1974 ($10K) — 1985 (~$20K)
350SL	1970 ($10K) — 1980 (~$20K)
450SL	1971 ($10K) — 1980 (~$22K)
300SL	1985 (~$19K) — 1989 (~$30K)
380SL	1980 (~$15K) — 1985 (~$25K)
420SL	1985 (~$24K) — 1989 (~$32K)
500SL	1980 (~$18K) — 1989 (~$37K)
560SL	1985 (~$29K) — 1989 (~$40K)

(Estimated In 5 Years)

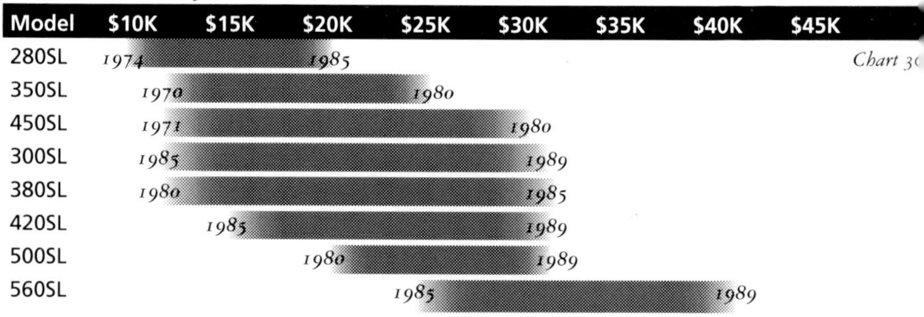

Chart 30

Model	Bar Range (approx. $ / years)
280SL	1974 ($10K) — 1985 (~$20K)
350SL	1970 (~$11K) — 1980 (~$25K)
450SL	1971 (~$11K) — 1980 (~$30K)
300SL	1985 (~$11K) — 1989 (~$30K)
380SL	1980 (~$11K) — 1985 (~$32K)
420SL	1985 (~$15K) — 1989 (~$30K)
500SL	1980 (~$20K) — 1989 (~$33K)
560SL	1985 (~$24K) — 1989 (~$42K)

(Estimated In 10 Years)

Chart 30

Model	Bar Range (approx. $ / years)
280SL	1974 ($10K) — 1985 (~$25K)
350SL	1970 (~$20K) — 1980 (~$33K)
450SL	1971 (~$20K) — 1980 (~$35K)
300SL	1985 (~$20K) — 1989 (~$35K)
380SL	1980 (~$20K) — 1985 (~$35K)
420SL	1985 (~$20K) — 1989 (~$30K)
500SL	1980 (~$24K) — 1989 (~$40K)
560SL	1985 (~$25K) — 1989 (~$45K)

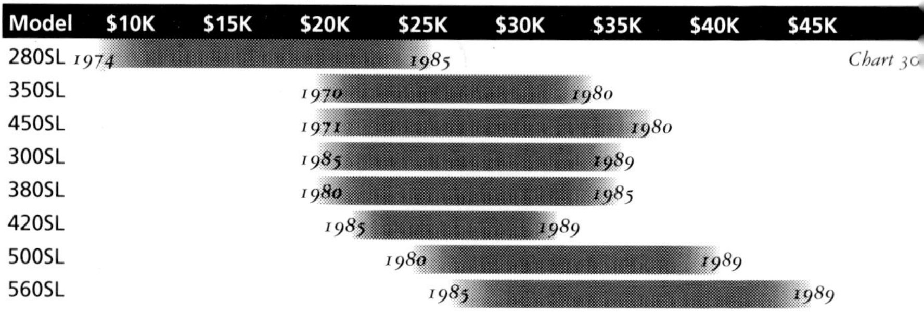

As you see from the charts, we think the prize of the litter, long term, is the 560SL. Generic rule: top of the line models always fair best. 560 SLs have it all. Latest technology, blazing performance, ABS, and MBNA dealer support. The whole R107 Group seems solid as the rock to us, almost too busy serving their owners to allow any time off to be history... yet.

The Mercedes-Benz 450SL.
Spoil yourself.

This is no conventional 2-seater. It's a Mercedes-Benz. So, you expect the extraordinary. You won't be disappointed.

Technological triumphs are the norm in sporting automobiles. Unfortunately, the same cannot be said for creature comforts. Happily, the 450SL breaks this convention.

Standard equipment includes electric windows, air conditioning, power-assisted steering and brakes, automatic transmission — even a central locking system.

Pure pleasure

Women who hate cramped sports cars will appreciate the ease of entry and exit of a 450SL. Whether in evening dress or a brief skirt, ladies remain ladies.

Orient yourself in the cockpit. Tailor the height and back angle of a formfitting seat to your body. Turn the key.

Listen.

wheel mates the standard radial tires to the road. Marvel at the road feel the variable-ratio, servo-assisted steering transmits. And drive secure in the knowledge that a double-circuit, 4-wheel disc braking system is at your disposal.

410-Mile cruising range

One more thing. You can enjoy the precision and response of a 450SL

Presence...and split personality

This extraordinary automobile has an undeniable presence. And a split personality.

With the convertible top in place, it takes on the lean look of a jet aircraft. With the removable hardtop on, instant coupe. With no top, the outdoors is yours. Practically three automobiles in one.

The no-gimmick styling is an exercise in function. The crisp lines of the rear deck accommodate your golf bag and enough luggage and miscellaneous gear for a holiday for two without difficulty.

There isn't another engine in the world like this alloy 4.5-liter, fuel-injected, overhead cam V-8 which powers the 450SL. A special 3-speed automatic transmission was designed to complement it. Shift it through the gears manually or let it do the changing automatically. The choice is yours.

Now challenge your favorite stretch of country road. Feel how a separate suspension system for each

without the annoyance of frequent fuel stops. According to the latest strictly supervised fuel mileage test results from *Motor Trend* magazine, the Mercedes-Benz 450SL averages 17.3 miles per gallon.

Motor Trend drove the car in a series of actual driving situations on a 73-mile course of regular city streets and highways. The figure they got gives the 450SL a cruising range of 410 miles. A truly remarkable automobile.

Mercedes-Benz

Four Decades Of SLs
A Comparison Of:

1950s 300SL
1960s 280SL
1980s 560SL
1990s 500SL

When M-B's first wholly new SL in 19 years was introduced in 1990, Mercedes-Benz of North America (MBNA) was kind enough to grant the *SL Market Letter* a week with their new crown jewel, the 500SL. Since our readers have SLs from the last four decades, we arranged to drive SLs from four decades together on the same three roads, and score them on that popular 1990s stuff... *how they felt*, to four different type of drivers. How the engines "felt" & sounded, how smoothly they shifted, steered & braked. How well they insulated away bumps, how well their suspensions carried these heavy-weights over a mixture of roads in comfort, and finally, overall ambiance.

We chose three severely different roads...

1. **An expressway** for cruising, higher speed maneuvering and passing.

2. **A very curved, hilly stretch** that would disadvantage sedans.

3. **A very rough, poorly maintained road** necessitating drops to under 15 mph.

In addition to this writer, test drivers included 2) *SL Market Letter* Advisor **Russ Leabch**, 3) automotive engineer & inventor of 25+ years **Bruce Kelly**, and 4) **Art Olson**, the author's twenty year old son who will be forever jaded by the experience. No one re-vealed their scores during testing and each criteria was given from 0 to 10 points by each tester. Our definition of a 10 is *"not improvable"* ...intentionally a tough though hypothetical standard; our testers were told that if they gave any 10s, it was to be *for results they could not imagine improving upon in the context of their knowledge at that time.*

Naturally the newest 500SL often scored high & became the unofficial benchmark, however all of these cars have "excelled" over the years ...each one has received rave reviews in many car tests. Most of their strong points have not become obsolete. We think we were tough graders; of a total of 352 votes we gave out only 30 "perfect 10s." And the 500SL received 25 of them! The 280SL received one 10 for *"engine smoothness & sounds"*. The original 1950s 300SL received three 10s for *"engine smoothness & sounds"* and one 10 for *"subjective ambiance"*.

500SL (Body #129)

The 500SL is clearly a star, but at close to 50% more cost than the 560SL we wondered just how much better it would be, and in what ways. Our first drives in the car, before the tests, drew attention to a lack of road feel through the steering column. The adjustable steering column eliminates direct feeling of the steering box in the driver's hands; at first we felt deprived of a basic message channel from the road to the driver. Later, when driving

each car, one after another, on the same roads, we realized that grand old steering column "feel" was the source of much negative road shock and vibration. An important contributor to the 500SL's high marks in insulation from bumps was absence of steering wheel resonance during bumps. The other thing we noticed before the tests was firmness of the ride... while entirely typical of cars as fast as the 500SL, it was stiffer than we've come to expect from Mercedes. This impression didn't go away during the tests. We suspected the firmness was a necessity to "manage" it's 4,150 pound weight under widely varying situations. No sooner did we give the car its only score under "9" for "overall suspension behavior," when we received 1991 model details describing the newest SL option, **Adaptive Dampening System (ADS)**. This automatically adjusts the hydraulic shock absorbers to the type of road & driving being pursued. We're sure our score for this category will rise for later SLs delivered with ADS.

Starting with highly adjustable memory seating including steering column & all three mirror & headrest & shoulder harness, the 500SL's interior seems to flow out from the driver's easiest reach. Under way, we've never driven a more gentle shifting, yet prompt automatic transmission. Sensitivity to accelerator pressure (down & up) and engine needs never once left *time to think that* shifting would have been faster

Tough duty by test drivers: (L-R)
John Olson, Bruce Kelly, Art Olson

manually. Our test vehicle had been driven 10,000 miles when we received it... and showed very little wear for it's service... a slightly loose driver's seat back, and the beginnings of a split at the edge of one of the soft top's rear windows. The soft top on the 500SL is an amusement center in itself. Demonstrating it in this press department car has probably raised & lowered the top as much as an owner would do in 100,000 miles. The 500SL's lowest scores were well above the other cars tested in these categories. Just how good this car is should be clear in the final scores. These are *all* good cars. Our scoring only went below "7" once. "8s" were frequent. The step upward to "9s" & "10s" came much harder due to our definition of a "10." We consider our final score of 93% for the 500SL a very high rating ...93% of perfection! We'd add it speaks well of Mercedes-Benz's self critique (& our test) that the 1991 ADS suspension option targets the only areas we ranked below a "9."

560SL (Body #107)

The closeness of the 21yr. old 280SL & 31yr. old 300SL scores to the 560SL was the biggest surprise of our test, though maybe it shouldn't have been. Of course the 560SL's V-8 exceeded the 280SL's acceleration at all speeds, though its 227hp & 3,750 weight did not intimidate the old 300. Its 250hp 6 cylinder engine retained a lower hp per lb. ratio, *and* acceleration times. A big change for all R107 bodied SLs (1989 back to 1970) was their "safety car" structure. Its styling has endured something like a colonial house, clean, straight-forward and hearty. Good objectives, though probably the least "exciting" of all five SL designs (count the 190SL). R107 engine insulation was not greatly improved from earlier SLs. Putting a 560SL in passing gear is no where near as quiet as the same engine in contemporary 560SECs or SELs... or the new 500SL. One of our drivers felt the 560SL only modestly quieter or better handling than a well preserved 1972 450SL! The *SL Market Letter (Issue 137)* predicted the 560SL will be the most valued R107 variant (1971 thru 1989 SLs) by collectors in the next century. We'll stick with this assessment, as all 560s have ABS, most have SRS airbags, and many other refinements, but early 450SLs (the ones with 225hp) should not be overlooked! Someday we will do a similar driving test exclusively among R107 variants; 450, 380, 560, with maybe a 280 or pre-1985 500SL thrown in.

280SL (Body #113)

The 280SL exceeded everyone's expectations. Styling is less aggressive than the others; there's a more perky, friendly look about it. Couple this with less horsepower and the softest suspension of the four, and we assumed it would come in a weak 4th in points. As you can see it was not that far behind, and delivered less uneven scores than it's famous predecessor.

The engine has a split personality. It can be driven all day without going over 3,500 RPM, moving about town more quietly than a sports car is expected to do. If there are any folks who drive their 280SL (or 250SL or 230SL) in this way they might be surprised to learn there is a suppressed rascal under their hoods. Americans as a group were not brought up on high RPM cars, and given a good one, half their owners don't know what to do with it.

The 280SL's "other half" is that 3,500- 6,500 RPM zone; engine & tach sweep so fast & smooth between 4,000 & 6,000 RPM that it is better than a turbo! The other thing we've learned is that this series' soft springs are misleading. Cornering grip is much better than body lean would lead a new driver to trust... what feels like excess suspension travel is positioning the rear wheels at an ideal negative camber for good adhesion. Grip actually digs in harder with increased gas pedal. The 280SL we drove was equipped with the 54% firmer compensating spring (This M-B option is now made in the U.S.A. after-market). In our opinion this alternative should have been the standard on all 230/250/280SLs.

There is no mistake the 280SL and 300SL are sixes... which run "busier" than V-8s while doing their work. Not to say the sounds are unpleasant (both got high marks for their wonderful sounds!), but we did give the 280SL higher marks in the insulation department over the 300SL. This includes both engine decibel count & road resonance. 300SLs (Coupe & Roadster) had increasing amounts of insulation each year, though the #113 body design and exhaust system are clearly more effective. This included rubber at all suspension points in the 280SL. This series stretched & began legitimizing a new definition of sports cars by offering automatic transmission, air conditioning & reclining seats. Mercedes clientele reacted

SLML Road Test Results:

Test A, B, C	300SL (1959) A Hwy	B Crv	C Bmp	ABC Total	280SL (1969) A Hwy	B Crv	C Bmp	ABC Total	560SL (1987) A Hwy	B Crv	C Bmp	ABC Total	500SL (1990) A Hwy	B Crv	C Bmp	ABC Total
Engine																
• smoothness & sound	93%	90%		183%	93%	90%		183%	90%	88%		178%	98%	96%		194%
• starting accel.	91%			91%	83%			83%	89%			89%	95%			95%
• mid-spd accel.	90%	91%		181%	78%	85%		163%	88%	89%		177%	95%	95%		190%
Shifting Up & Down	83%	80%		163%	76%	75%		151%	85%	78%		163%	95%	95%		190%
Brake Manners	83%	83%		166%	80%	80%		160%	85%	85%		170%	90%	90%		180%
Steering	79%	79%		158%	74%	79%		153%	00%	00%		150%	91%	91%		183%
Insulation																
• of engine & wind sound			68%	68%			78%	78%			78%	78%			98%	98%
• of bump sounds			75%	75%			70%	70%			78%	78%			90%	90%
• of road bumps from seats			75%	75%			80%	80%			80%	80%			93%	93%
• of road bumps from steering			80%	80%			80%	80%			83%	83%			95%	95%
Weight Control		80%		80%		77%		77%		83%		83%		94%		94%
Suspension behavior		80%		80%		75%		75%		84%		84%		89%		89%
Overall Visibility		84%		84%		84%		84%		84%		84%		89%		89%
Overall Interior Comfort	73%		83%	156%	80%		85%	165%	83%		90%	173%	91%		96%	188%
Subjective Ambiance	90%	95%	88%	273%	75%	79%	78%	232%	83%	83%	78%	244%	90%	96%	94%	280%
Total Score	682%	682%	549%	1,914%	639%	649%	554%	1,842%	683%	670%	571%	1,924%	745%	747%	654%	2,146%
Total Possible Score	800%	800%	700%	2,300%	800%	800%	700%	2,300%	800%	800%	700%	2,300%	800%	800%	700%	2,300%
% Max. Obtained	85%	85%	78%	83.20%	80%	81%	79%	80.07%	85%	84%	82%	83.63%	93%	93%	93%	93.28%

favorably & competitors followed with the same options. By the 1970s 450SLs were offered *only* with automatics world-wide (& *only* with A/C in America).

We discuss 280SL rear axle ratios & highway RPM on pages 51,52 and feel owners should examine their choices here, as well as the effect tire diameter has on RPM. Some relatively inexpensive changes to fit personal tastes can create one of the most drivable, affordable, collector cars. And a sports car at that.

Be careful, you might gain a lifetime pal.

300SL (Body #042)

Enter, Big Daddy. Public awareness of the 300SL is astounding considering only a few thousand (coupes *and* roadsters) were built 30 years ago. Roughly 75% came to the USA when new, though attrition & recent exports have trimmed the USA numbers back to 40% (an *SLML* guess; there are no hard numbers despite a well managed registry by the Gull Wing Group, International).

As our scores indicate, the 300SL still excels strongly in some key areas which thrill drivers and bystanders alike. Our "9+" scores generally occurred when one of the cars *thrilled* us... that feeling when something really touched our senses, just as one's favorite passage of music cuts through the thick skin we've built up to handle ordinary experiences. The 300SL and 500SL broke though this skin more than the other two cars. When choosing the "Overall Ambiance" score for the 300SL **Russ Leabch** was candid enough to admit, "Its hard to beat the feeling of watching other people watch me in a 300SL!" When this car excels, it really excels!

Styling is one of these areas. This car has the uncanny ability to look strong and soft at the same time. **Brooks Stevens**, the automotive designer once gave the 300SL an Aesthetics Award saying...

> "Its genius is the integration of bold mechanical lines (especially the stiff rocker panel & side vent holes) with soft, feminine upper fender lines. Autos usually look either angular & stiff or soft & sensuous. The 300SL has achieved both."

Conclusion:

Each of these SLs is quite special. While the total points of the 280SL are not higher than the 300SL, the fluctuation in its scores is smaller. The range of our scores show each newer SL delivering a tighter evenness of excellence. While the 300SL is still awesome today at some things, its range of scores span 27 percentage points. The 280SL dropped to 18%. The 560SL spanned 12%, and the 1990 500SL only 9% (and tighter still with ADS equipped '91s). Few cars would earn better scores for their respective decade. We drove good examples and tried to filter out normal wear & tear differences in the cars. Their evolution recognizes the growing demands in each decade toward safety, driving convenience, and expanding service intervals. During the new SL's first year both *Road and Track* (Dec., 1990) and *Motor Trend* (Nov., 1990) included the new 500SL on their "10 best Cars" lists. The subsequent arrival of the 600SL added a V-12 and ADS as standard equipment. If this pushed our scoring for the 600SL above 95% we wonder what car, if any, could deliver a higher overall score.

In addition to MBNA, our thanks to Don Sears, Mercedes-Benz dealer in Minnetonka, MN., for prompt loan of the 1987 560SL used in this test.

Overview:
230/250/280SLs

"230/250/280SLs fill a lot of
footsteps, entirely drivable, yet not
so expensive as to
prohibit street exposure,
distinctive marque & model with
low enough production
for future rarity, and
interchangeability of
mechanical parts with sedans."

The second largest production of a single SL body type is the Type "113," the two seat roadster/coupe body used for the 230SL, 250SL an 280SL. Production began in March 1963, and continued into March, 1971, for a total of 48,912 vehicles. The figures below separate the USA equipped cars handled through MBNA from those received by Americans at the factory for subsequent US destinations.

From the mid-'50s to mid-'60s Studebaker-Packard distributed M-B in the U.S.A. but their exact SL sales results were never revealed. Thanks to **Gunter Engelen's** late 1980's access to Stuttgart archives for his fine book *Mercedes-Benz 190SL-280SL* (only printed in German) we now know how many SLs were shipped to the U.S.A. before MBNA took over in 1965.

Examination of production data reveals that only 830 280SLs were built in 1971. However, MBNA marketed 2,539 280SLs in 1971, a large portion came from 1970 production that did not find its way to MBNA dealers and their clients until 1971. In my calculations, I have "drawn off" enough 1970 non-USA units to achieve the volume MBNA states that it sold in 1971. The same situation occurred in 1967; only 185 230SLs were built, yet more were sold.

Production of 230/250/280 SLs (PER YEAR/BY QUANTITY)

	230SL		250SL		280SL	
	Non-USA	**USA**	**Non-USA**	**USA**	**Non-USA**	**USA**
1963	1,289	176				
1964	6,221	690				
1965	5,218	1,107	0			
1966	2,266	1,717	17			
1967	85	1,047	3,434	1,255	143	0
1968	0	15	2	488	4,530	2,400
1969	0	0	0	0	4,227	3,820
1970					1,550	4,019
1971					650	2,539
1972					0	7
Totals:	15,079	4,752	3,453	1,743	11,100	12,785

The numbers above are developed from two forms of information:
1) world-wide production, and 2) USA marketing data.

The 1950s SLs were unusually civilized for their decade with tops and windows that did not leak, signal seeking radios, dual heaters, back-up lights, non-glare rearview mirrors, and quiet muffler systems. By the 1960s, "civilized" had broadened to include extensive options from power steering to air conditioning. Air conditioning wasn't offered in Europe and became a dealer installed option in the USA. See chapter on Rare Accessories.

ENGINES

All three engines were iron block, single overhead cam, in-line sixes; four main bearings for the 230SL and seven for the 250 & 280SL. The post 1965 engines used in the 250/280 are almost entirely interchangeable with 250SE and 280SE (108 chassis) engines of 1965-72. However for show purposes each was assigned a motor number which designated specifically that it was used in an SL or in a sedan. It is wise to change the oil filter every 3,000 miles or at 3 to 4 month intervals if driven regularly.

SUSPENSION

The #113 body and suspension unit is arguably the most significant single outgrowth of hte 300SL and the 190SL. Its size and performance characteristics were placed between the previous models with considerable attention given to suspension refinements. Tire and suspension technology was on everyone's mind: **Colin Chapman's** Lotus successes emphasized the point, and during the sixties, handling and road adhesion progressed faster than any other aspect of auto designing.

Rudolf Uhlenhaut (in charge of all car design and development) pooled vast suspension experiences (300SL, 190SL, and grand prix racing) These cars used progressively lower pivot points. The Type 113 body continued this evolution by extending the length of each axle, effectively expanding the radius of each rear wheel's swing path. This modification, together with progressive-rate springing (to govern closely the degree of swing), delivered handling more suitable for its broadening market without giving up the rough-road handling superiority of swing-axles. The wheelbase remained

grease points, some due every 2,000 miles on the 230SL) the 280SL utilized additional rubber bushings in the front chassis. This concurrently achieved a "boulevard ride" without reducing cornering abilities. While all #113 rear wheels drop nicely into negative camber on corners, the rubber bushings kept this good news from the 280SL driver. More on handling later.

identical to the 300SL and the 190SL at 94 1/2 inches, while the front and rear tracks both grew nearly 2 inches to 58 1/2 inches.

During the production life of the #113 SLs its suspension went from taunt and sure-footed in the 230SL to somewhat "soggy" in the 280SL. To avoid frequent greasing intervals (18

BRAKES
The 230 and 250SLs featured 10.8" diameter disc brakes in front with 2.5" rear shoe and drum brakes. The 280SL was given 10.8" diameter discs (Girling) in front, and 10.25" diameter discs at the rear. Power brakes on all models are by ATE (Bendix). Tires started out on 5 .5" wheels, which grew to 6" on the 250 and

280SL. Both were 14" diameter. This reflects the growth in weight from 2,855 pounds for 230SLs to 3,120 pounds for the last 280SLs..

TRANSMISSIONS

More #113 chassis SLs were sold with automatic tranmissions each year. This automatic starts in second gear when placed in "drive" position, but may be shifted as a manual if need be. The automatic is a somewhat "jerky" fluid coupled design (as opposed to a torque convertor) which can be made to work to your advantage once you get used to it. Both DB's manual & automatic tranmissions are robust and rarely need any work other than oil changes and shifting linkage rod bushing replacement (outside of the box). Neglecting these bushings when shifting gets sloppy or sticky, will lead to internal problems.

INTERIORS

The 230/250/280SL was generally trimmed in MB-Tex (Mercedes' version of vinyl). Leather was a special order option which could be specified separately for the seats, door panels, dash, or other trim items. Carpet material for the 230SL was square weave wool. Beginning in January 1968, A two-tone nylon loop carpet was used.

There were also numerous subtle changes to the interior during the nine years these SLs were being built. Most related to safety or for production savings on trim pieces. With the introduction of the 280SL stereo radios (always German, and most commonly the Becker Europa II or Becker Mexico) were available from dealers.

SOFT TOPS AND HARD TOPS

Neither the softtop or detachable hardtop for this series is available new any longer. In addition, restoration of them is highly specialized work, expensive and labor intensive. It takes an estimated 50 manhours to redo a hardtop (chrome, lining, gaskets, paint) Therefore, take this into account when evaluating a purchase.

PROSPECTS FOR THE 1990s

Despite builting nearly 50,000 230/ 250/280SLs, and approximately 60% of them coming to North America, their respective resale values still doubled during the 1970s. During the last ten years they've climbed again .... but the biggest 1980s growth was in 1950s SLs. The 1990s is certainly a different world, however #113 SL values have been pleasantly stable during the latest recession, while Jaguar & Ferrari sportscars tumbled 40% and more. It's hard for us to imagine a more reliable, "modern old" car for the discerning enthusiast to use and collect at the same time.

Styling *of each series of SLs is quite different. Their very similar size*
and the traditional SL heraldry makes their origin unmistakable,
but the integration of body shapes from one generation to the next
is not really obvious, as it is in Mercedes-Benz sedans.
Changes in the designs are nowhere more severe than between
the 190SL (also 300SL) and the 230/250/280SL
(nick-named the "pagoda SLs" for their concave hardtop roof lines).
The 190SL and 300SL have soft, human-like fenders, while the high-tech
machine-look took over many products and architecture by the 1960s.
All functional measurements improved with each series... passenger space,
trunk size, soft-top placement, etc., despite very similar overall lengths.
There is a hint of 1950s & '60s 220 sedans in the 230SL, and also
the look of a California channeled custom; it's low waistline adding
to the large window area and the car's pronounced width.
The result is a lighter appearance than previous SLs, belying a car
heavier and stronger than it appears. Each SL model
is accruing a following of enthusiasts that don't necessarily
embrace the genius of the previous or subsequent designs.
This is an inevitable consequence of the major changes between models
and the ageless qualities each possesses.

COMPARISON:
280SL AND 300SL

"There's more in common here than meets the eye.

Weight and wheelbase are identical, the suspension concept is the same, as are a choice of rear axle ratios, hard and soft tops options, and seating for two. The engines are also similar; most evident are their smooth, wide torque ranges."

We had an opportunity to drive a 1969 280SL 3,000 miles recently, and immediately after that trip drove a 1959 300SL Roadster 2,000 miles to the Gull Wing Group National Convention (from Minneapolis to Detroit and back). The 280SL trek was from New Jersey to Minnesota the long way, via Vermont, New Hampshire, Rhode Island, New York, Ohio, etc.

Comparing these cars was fun. They have more in common than meets the eye. Weight and wheelbase are identical, the suspension concept is the same, as are a choice of rear axle ratios, hard and soft tops options, and seating for two. The engines are also similar; most evident are their smooth, wide torque ranges. In-line sixes are inherently smoother than V-6s or V-8s due to their longer crank shafts. The silky purr of the 300 and 280 sixes at low (under 1,000 rpm) or high (both cars red line at an impressive 6,500 rpm), is more pleasure to this writer's ears than the fine Becker Mexico radio offered in both models.

Back in the early 1960s, engine designers in the USA were wrestling with two performance paths: large cubic inch engines with lower rpm and lower compression vs. smaller cubes, high rpms and higher compression. GM in Detroit introduced several creative small engines. The 215 hp 215 cu. inch aluminum V-8 in small Oldsmobiles is one example. A few even had turbo chargers.

Corvair's Corsa flat six with 180 hp from 164 cu inches was another. It was during this same period (and earlier) that Mercedes earned its way into post WW II garages with their highly reliable small six cylinder engines. These were the expensive but almost indestructible engines that Rudolf Uhlenhaut once said were the most important single component in renewing the company's credibility with 1950s and 1960s consumers. The 300SL race cars received glowing reports in the press, but it was the "meat and potatoes" 220 sedans that consumers experienced first hand. American engineers admired these small engines and felt that they had a future. They were right, but American consumers, spoiled by low gas prices, kept buying giant V-8s until Washington let oil seek its own price.

Mercedes sold many times more 190 and 220 engines than the powerful, expensive 300s. Fourteen 190SLs were sold for every one 300SL, so it was no surprise that they should blend features of both these cars into the next generation SL. Uhlenhaut had found weight and suspension design to be as important as further horsepower in the 300SLs, so he gave handling top priority in the new 230SL. While using the less costly and lighter 220 sedan drive train and suspension components, and a unique SL unitized body, Uhlenhaut retained the 300SL's proportions. The wheel track vs actually 3.5" wider in front and 1.5" wider at the rear with 11" less overall length. The 300SL's single pivot independent rear axle was still there, albeit much lighter in weight. Pounds saved in the drive train were quickly re-spent on unit body and interior features.

Following the 300SL's footsteps was no small feat even if it was billed with a smaller nomenclature. The same customers were watching and deciding if they should buy. A lot did. In a widely reported 1963 press demonstration of the new 230SL in France, Uhlenhaut lapped the Montroux track within .2 seconds of Ferrari designer **Michael Parkes** in a V-12 Ferrari 250GT Berlinetta. During its first year the 230SL also finished first in the very difficult and mountainous Spa Sofia Liege Rally.

Walking up to the two cars gives completely different impressions. Both reek the usual Mercedes quality, yet styling is totally different.

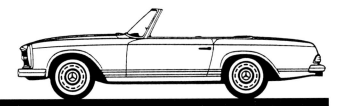

The 300SL's deeply rounded fenders and straight, broad rocker panels make a statement of strength seldom matched in post WWII auto designs. This "thick" hearty appearance is continued in the broad bumpers, large headlights, heavy, widely pleated leather seats, and an oversized steering wheel. Firing up the engine also sends muffled belching from the exhaust and air intake rams that fascinate even the most seasoned enthusiast.

The #113 chassis (230/250/280SL) body lines are far more civilized and subtle. There is no mistaking its Mercedes identity though the lithe, agile look follows more in the vein of a Ferrari Lusso or BMW 507. Bumpers are soft spoken. The gondola type roof conveys a perky openness inside and out. Seats are even more bucket shaped than in the 300SL. A thick, traditional steering wheel is well positioned, though not adjustable.

Starting the 230/250/280SL causes much less warm up commotion than the 300SL (though a high amperage battery is a good investment). Both engine and factory exhaust are rather quiet below 3,500 rpm. The clutch can be released below 1,000 rpm without regret, and gentle movement through traffic is enjoyably well mannered, especially with manual shift which gives the driver absolute choice of rpms. The automatic transmission has higher rpm shift points than most Americans are accustomed; as the engine's wider range of usable rpms is very Lotus or Porsche-like.

300SL Roadsters have a "sports cam" which puts out a pronounced second burst of power from 4,300 to 6,300 rpm; it feels for all the world like a turbo or supercharger. The 230/250/280SL (particularly the 280) has a similar surge above 4,000 reaching its peak torque around 4,500 rpm and quickly passing 6,000 even under heavy load (i.e. our scaling of Mount Equinox in Vermont). This remarkable "elasticity" is often misunderstood or wasted on American "cubic inch addicts." GM eventually gave up building its '60s small block high performance engines. Alas, even Mercedes succumbed to V-8s; the 600 and 6,3 achieving 75% of their peak torque at a mere 2,000 rpm. But not without a price: great weight and high fuel consumption. The 80's produced a serious revival of small

high output engines. Wonderful hindsight.

Driving the 280SL reminds us of the 300SL. Along with the engine, suspension behavior jumps out for comparison. When the 300SL went to a single pivot rear axle in 1957, it incorporated much longer, softer rear springs, calibrated to go into negative camber on corners, but set relatively vertical when driven straight. These characteristics remain in the 230/250/280SL, including a slight proneness to rear end steering (wander) when loaded down with a full trunk. The 280SL Service Manual (available from MBNA dealers) shows a wide variety of spring mounting pads plus two front and three rear spring rate options. Since M-B indicated their sport springs are no longer available, 5 spring sets have been duplicated by the after-market.

Two passenger sports cars are always designed with a narrower "pay load" range. If a full trunk,

frequently full gas tank, and two occupants are normal, thicker mounting pads and/or stiffer springs are in order. Firmer springs at the front also reduce the rather notice-able nose-dive in braking and sudden turns present in most 1960s Mercedes cars. M-B's quest for good handling & good ride is not helped by the reality of earth bound travel; lots of crummy roads. When the 280 arrived, added rubber suspension "insulators" muted subtle road cracks and feel surprisingly like 6.3s, 600s and 6.9s. The result: 230/250/280SLs are agile, yet "smoother" than their 94.5" wheelbase would suggest. Nevertheless, for our personal tastes, the standard 280SL springs are too soft. We were happy to see alternatives.

The first step to achieving crisp original handling is new Bilstein shock absorbers. Then adding the slightly stiffer and shorter sport springs will curtail nose-dive in braking general softness.

Four different rear axle ratios were used during the seven year 113 chassis run with a limited slip offered in later years.

WITH ORIGINAL DIAMETER TIRES (185 HR14):

Model	Torque	Orig. Ratio	RPM @60 MPH
230SL	159	3.75	3,067
250SL	174	3.69	3,019
	174	3.92	3,216
280SL	193	4.08	3,341
	193	3.92	3,216
	193	3.69	3,019

Mercedes engineers saw nothing wrong with 3,400 rpm at 60 mph on the 280SL, considering its 6,700 rpm red line. For rural and mountain roads found in so much of the world, the 4.08 along with the 280's higher torque, gives an aggressive manner not far removed from the 300SL. On American expressways 3,500 to 4,500 rpm cruising on a long trip gets a little old. Solutions are: a) pay an extra $5,000 for the rare but authentic ZF five speed stick shift (the ultimate SL option), b) locating 75 or 78 profile tires: 195/75 x 14, (never go under "70 Profile"on pre-1972 SL's)

or 185/78x 14, or c) switching rear axle ratios. The axle switch is easy as 1965-67 250S/SE; 1968-72 28S/SE (108 Chassis). The 1969-71 280SE 3.5 Coupe/Convertible (Chassis 111) rear axles will fit the 250/280SL. When checking junk yards, each rear end should have its ratio stamped outside, usually on the lower drivers' side. For highway cruising the 3.69 is the one to find. 230SL rears had drum brakes, and with their 3.75 ratios are too close to the 3.69 to warrant change. Opt for the limited slip variant if you get the choice. Finding parts brings up an important benefit for prospective 230/250/280 SL owners; many SL drive-train parts are shared with sedan, coupe and convertible (108,109 or 111 chassis bodies) models of their respective years. That spells availability and civilized prices. 230/250/280 total production as 48,912 world-wide, and we would guess over 50% have died of rust or accident. Compared to approximately 237,000 1971 to 1989 SL models (the #107 body), the 230/250/280SL is already quite rare.

These 230/250/280SLs fill many objectives. They are friendly to drive and (yet) not so valuable as to prohibit street exposure. It is a distinctive model with low enough production for future rarity, yet with exchangeability of mechanical parts with the more plentiful sedans. If you think this all makes sense for you too, you had better get with it; prices could double in the next five years.

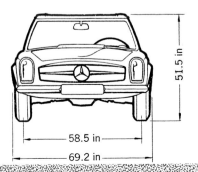

Mercedes-Benz announces a more potent 230SL –the 250SL.

If you like the Mercedes-Benz 230SL but would like it more if it had more torque, you can now buy the Mercedes-Benz 250SL.

250SL resembles the 230SL!

What's new?

Outside, the 250SL is identical with the 230SL because there was no reason to make it look different. But internally, it features these changes:

1. A 2.5-liter, single overhead camshaft, fuel-injected 6-cylinder engine.
2. Four-wheel disc brakes.
3. An oil-water heat exchanger has been added to help keep engine oil temperature low.
4. Gasoline tank capacity has risen to 21.6 gallons.

And since the 250SL costs more to make, its price begins at about $300 above the 230SL.

Note to 230SL owners: the 250SL is not calculated to shunt your car into obsolescence, planned or otherwise.

For one thing, it's impossible to *tell* a 230SL from a 250SL without standing about six inches from the nameplate and squinting at the lettering. For another, the 230SL will continue being sold for an indefinite period; the 250SL's higher price ensures a place for both cars in the showroom.

Quicker pickup

You will zip from a standstill to 60 mph in a shade less than ten seconds in the 250SL, and the actual top speed (where legal) stands at 119 mph. This represents no change from the 230SL. What *is* different is pickup

in the middle ranges. This bigger engine pumps out more torque, and it has been put where it will do the most good. You enjoy an extra surge of power for passing; the 250SL is more responsive in city driving, when rapid takeoff is often called for while you're stuck in a higher gear. In summary, the 250SL is more tigerish where tigerishness is actually useful.

Inside dope: Mercedes-Benz engineers quietly filched this engine from the 250SE sedan series instead of simply boring out the 230SL version.

Besides larger capacity, you get another advantage: a seven-main-bearing crankshaft for smoother, quieter running.

Are these brakes necessary?

Since the 230SL already holds *Road & Track* magazine's all-time

record for quick stopping times with its disc-and-drum brake system Mercedes-Benz engineers were hardly under pressure to make changes for the 250SL. They did anyway. The 250SL's four-wheel discs provide that much more confidence—and that much less susceptibility to fade.

What isn't new

The engineers refused to tamper with those virtues that have earned the 230SL such favor.

The 250SL still sits on a fully independent, rear swing-axle suspension that in turn sits on fat, 14-inch radial-ply tires separated by an almost six-foot track. Its unit body is welded tight. There's more forward legroom than in a certain Rolls-Royce, and the seats—designed in consultation with orthopedic physicians—even have reclining backrests.

Power-assisted brakes are standard equipment. Power-assisted steering is an extra-cost option. It works so unobtrusively that the only way you can be sure you actually have it may be to look under the hood.

Your next step

"This combination of absolute security, complete stability, and plain old hell-raising fun must be driven to be believed," once wrote the Editor of *Car and Driver* magazine of the 230SL. Being the same car only more so, the 250SL requires the same proof. Your authorized Mercedes-Benz dealer will be glad to supply it. See him soon.

230SL resembles the 250SL!

250SL Coupe/Roadster–$6,897, 230SL Coupe/Roadster–$6,587, p.o.e. New York, exclusive of transportation charges, options, state and local taxes **if any.**

190 SL AND 230/250/280   SL SPECIFICATIONS AND COMPARISON

Engine	190SL	230SL	250SL	280SL
Type & Induction	4 cyl.	6cyl.	6 cyl.	6cyl.
	2 Solex	Port F.I.	Port F.I.	Port F.I.
Displacement	1,897cc.	2,306cc.	2,496cc.	2778cc.
Bore & Stroke	3.34x3.30	3,23x2.87	3.23x3.1	3.41x3.1
Compression	8.5:1	9.3:1	9.3:1	9.41:x3.1
Bhp & rpm	125@5,700	170@5,600	170@5,600	180@5,700
Torque & rpm	107@2,800	159@4,500	174@4,500	193@4,500

Chassis	190SL	230SL	250SL	280SL
Length	166"	168.8"	168.8"	168.8"
Width	68.5"	69.2"	69.2"	69.2"
Height	52"	51.4"	51.4"	51.4"
Wheelbase	94.5"	94.5"	94.5"	94.5"
Track front &rear	56"/56"	58.5"/58.5"	58.5"/58.5"	50.5"/50.5"
Weight	2,800lbs.	2,855lbs.	2,860lbs.	2,950 lbs.
Weight per HP	22.4 lbs.@HP	16.8 lbs.@HP	16.8 lbs.@HP	16.34 lbs.@HP
Weight@Torque	26.2 lbs.@ HP	18 lbs. @ ft. lb.	16.4 lbs.@ ft. lb.	15.3 lbs.@ ft. lb.

Engine Performance	190SL	230SL	250SL	280SL
0-30	4.9 sec.	3.8 sec.	3.6 sec.	3.5 sec.
0-60	12.7 sec.	10.7 sec.	10 sec.	10 sec.
0-90	n/a	24.0 sec.	21.0 sec.	20 sec.
Standing 1/4 mile	20.1 sec.@75	17.5 sec.@80	17.0 sec@84	17.0 sec @ 84

Price Comparison	190SL	230SL	250SL	280SL
Original Price	$3,998 in '55	$6,543 in '63	$6,897 in '67	$6,897 in '68
Equivilant $	$20,829 in '92	$29,275 in '92	$28,383 in '92	$27,293 in '92

OVERVIEW:
190SL

"Despite frequent labeling as the 'little sister' to the 300SL, the 190SL found a strong following in America. The 25,881 190SLs built during 9 years exceeded all factory predictions.

That quantity is spectacular when we recall the MG TD, the car that many people identify with causing America's love affair with sports cars, built only 30,000 cars! And MG's price was roughly one-half, at $2,300."

First indications that a 190SL was in development leaked in 1952 and the first pictures appeared in January 1954. The car was officially introduced at the 1954 New York Auto Show which yours truly attended. A prototype, it had a "tentative" instrument arrangement on the dash, an air scoop on the hood, and eye brows only on the front fenders. Considerable drive-train & production details remained to be worked out. Initial deliveries did not take place for fifteen more months. The final version appeared at the March 1955 Geneva Show.

The 190SL was the first and long-awaited overhead cam four cylinder Mercedes. Its bore was identical to the 300 6-cylinder engine. It stands up-right, with two Solex dual carburetors and a conspicuous cast aluminum intake air "ram" to have filtered air at the ready instantaneously. Mercedes-Benz used this design in many engines, and was researching adjustable length air rams for the 300SLR when the factory racing program ended. The objective of changing ram length was to extend the peak-torque to a wider RPM range.

The 190SL has a welded body-chassis assembly. Engine, transmission, and front axle are combined in a removable subframe. Suspension is independent all around. The delayed production date permitted 190SLs to receive the low-pivot single joint differential also introduced in 1955 on the 300Sc (a different size). The 300SL did not get this change until 1957 when the Roadster arrived.

Base price in 1955 was $3,998 in New York. By 1961, base price has risen to $5,129 in New York. After adding a Becker radio, genuine leather, and both tops, the 1961 bill was $5,758 plus state and federal taxes.

190SL Production

Year	Non-USA	USA	Total
1955	897	830	1,727
1956	2,183	1,849	4,032
1957	1,526	1,806	3,332
1958	2,094	628	2,722
1959	2,299	1,650	3,949
1960	2,713	1,264	3,977
1961	2,283	1,509	3,792
1962	1,468	772	2,246
1963	50	54	104
Total:	15,513	10,368	25,881

Road & Track magazine did two road tests on the 190SL: In October 1955 and 1960. Both tests were also re-produced in their year books. The Ziff-Davis "1959 Sport Car Directory" also tested the car. Except for broadening the torque range downward through a carburetion change and a gear ratio change in third to make city driving more flexible, changes during 1955-1960 were minimal. A wrap-around rear window was added to the removable hardtop beginning in 1960. Early cars were delivered without chrome trim on the fender eye brows and rocker panels, and many European cars only had a sun-visor for the driver.

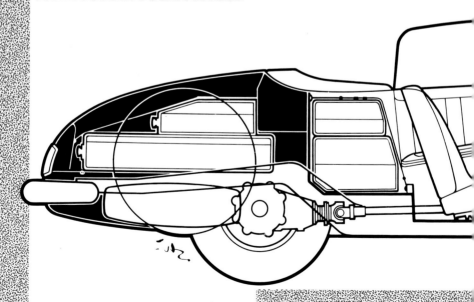

Acceleration and top speed remained at approximately thirteen seconds (0-60 mph) and 103 mph-106 mph respectively, throughout its production. Curb weight, grew slowly and gas mileage dropped. By the 1960s, the average was 18.5 mpg.

Interest and restoration activity on these cars is high today, and their value continued to grow during most of the latest recession. Each car must be examined closely for rust and wear as the price range doesn't yet reflect the costs of proper restoration, and the susceptibility of the body/frame unit to rust. Prospective purchasers need to examine underbody, rocker panels, and lower portions of all fenders closely, allowing sufficient funds for problems discovered.

190SLs will appreciate in value in the coming years, however with 25,881 built, the survivors present a severely mixed face to the public. This holds the average price down, and a justifiably wide range for prices. Unit body construction, while advanced in many respects, can add much work to restorations. As prices climb, show caliber ground-up restorations will become more justified. The hunt is still on for the remaining 190SLs that have never faced rust. They exist, but rarely below $25,000/$30,000. Remember the *SLML* "conventional wisdom" that show-winning cars should command at least double the overall average for a given category of car. If you "overpay" for a stunning, rust-free 190SL, you will probably look like a genius in five or ten years, and have a lot of fun driving and displaying it in the meantime.

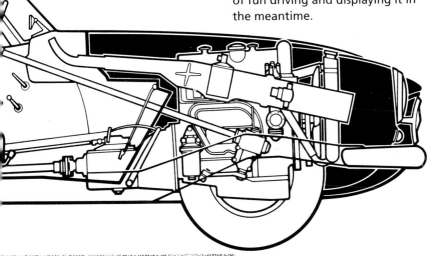

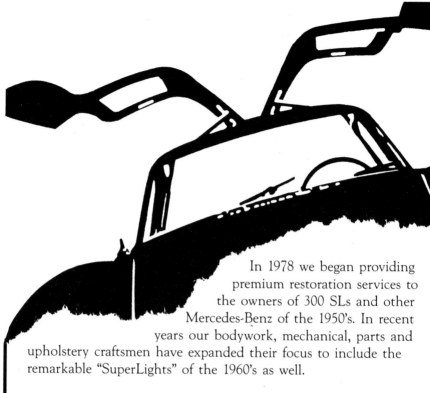

In 1978 we began providing premium restoration services to the owners of 300 SLs and other Mercedes-Benz of the 1950's. In recent years our bodywork, mechanical, parts and upholstery craftsmen have expanded their focus to include the remarkable "SuperLights" of the 1960's as well.

Sales and acquisition services grew from the requests of our clients that we bring our considerable restoration expertise to bear on the evaluation or marketing of their automobiles.

When considering the restoration, purchase or sale of a classic Mercedes-Benz SL please call or visit Paul Russell and Company in Essex, Massachusetts, a quaint New England shipbuilding village just north of Boston.

Paul Russell and Company

passionately dedicated to the art of building fine automobiles

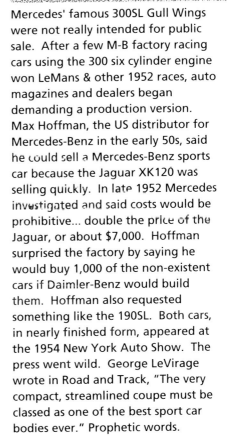

OVERVIEW:
300SL GULL WING

*"Perhaps the greatest indication
of the 300SL Gull Wing's
impact and significance in the
realm of collector cars
is the huge public awareness of the car,
despite only 1400 being built.
This car is probably on more
'dream collection' lists than
any other car in the world."*

Mercedes' famous 300SL Gull Wings were not really intended for public sale. After a few M-B factory racing cars using the 300 six cylinder engine won LeMans & other 1952 races, auto magazines and dealers began demanding a production version. Max Hoffman, the US distributor for Mercedes-Benz in the early 50s, said he could sell a Mercedes-Benz sports car because the Jaguar XK120 was selling quickly. In late 1952 Mercedes investigated and said costs would be prohibitive... double the price of the Jaguar, or about $7,000. Hoffman surprised the factory by saying he would buy 1,000 of the non-existent cars if Daimler-Benz would build them. Hoffman also requested something like the 190SL. Both cars, in nearly finished form, appeared at the 1954 New York Auto Show. The press went wild. George LeVirage wrote in Road and Track, "The very compact, streamlined coupe must be classed as one of the best sport car bodies ever." Prophetic words.

A substantial metamorphosis had occurred to make the '52 race car downright handsome. Other major changes improved engine cooling and incorporation of the world's first gasoline injection system for automobiles. Robert Bosch Corporation had experimented with injection for airplanes as far back as 1930, and for Mercedes-Benz Grand Prix race cars for 1940 (a season that never happened). A few airplanes of both the USA and Germany used fuel injection during WWII, but auto applications

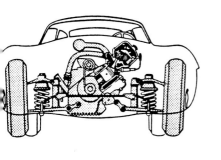

eluded necessary completion until the production 300SL. Interiors of the cars also received appointments befitting a senior Mercedes. There was a double-bottom ash tray, horn button for the passenger, windshield washers, non-glare rear-view mirror, two heaters, ...things never before found in sports cars. The cars were an immediate hit with the small group well enough heeled to buy them. In those days of less concern for privacy the factory proudly released names of purchasers, a virtual who's-who of the world's car aficionados. Original owners even included rivals, American Ferrari racer **Luigi Chinetti**, Aston Martin's early owner **David Brown**, **Ed Gaylord**, who attempted to build the Gaylord car. **Richard Teague**, Chief of Styling for Packard & American Motors owned one. **King Hussein of Jordan** actually raced his 300SL, which prompted the **Shah of Iran**, **King Faouk**, **The Aga Kahn** and a half dozen other kings to buy them. **Aly Kahn** of France and **Montague** of England lead the list of Princes, Counts, Lords and Sirs. Famous race driver/owners include **Augie Pabst, Jacky Icky, Oliver Gendebein** and **Lothar Motschenbacher** . Hollywood's sub-culture further added to the car's visibility. Some were titled to large corporations or their chairmen and families: **Thomas Watson, Jr., Huntington Hartford, Knight Kiplinger, William Lear, James Leake, Peter Sachs, Jack Lehman III**. **Bruno Sacco**, M-B's current Chief of Designing just had **Paul Russell & Company** do a body-off restoration of his Gullwing. The list of museums displaying Gullwings today is the frosting on the cake.

Daimler-Benz never geared the program to a large market, allocating only enough space and staff to build forty to sixty cars per month. First deliveries began in mid-1954. Because of Hoffman's order between 1,050 and 1,150 coupes were equipped for US roads, and USA lighting & bumper requirements. Approximately 50% of these cars went to California purchasers, and 1/3 of them remain there today.

GULL WING PRODUCTION BY YEAR:

Prototypes:	2
1954	146
1955	867
1956	311
1957	76
Total	1,402

Data gathered by the *SL Market Letter* suggests the following geographic distribution and survival numbers: Of the 1402 300SL coupes, 330 (approx.) are presumed destroyed, roughly 300 were sold originally outside the USA into south and Central America, Canada, the Middle East, Australia, Asia, and of course, Europe. Another 350 have left the U.S. during the 1980s.

Of the remaining 420 in the USA there are roughly 250 in average to concours-winning condition, 85 more in average to poor but licensed and running condition, and another 85 not running, unlicensed, but still intact vehicles. Privacy prevents closer guesswork than this estimate.

The growing value of 300SLs is turning them into historic treasures... virtual retirement investments for their owners. Their appreciation has enabled owners to do copious part-by-part restorations that stop the clock at their original year of manufacture. Parts availability for repair and restoration is way above average because of selected remanufacturing by GWG and its members, availability

of some parts cars, and a surprisingly good supply of new parts still available through Mercedes-Benz dealers (on special order basis). On a limited basis, out of stock parts are remanufactured by M-B every year. Bosch & VDO have also been very helpful.

Mercedes-Benz racing success in the 1950s, plus the 300SL's photogenic popularity, has made the "Gull Wing" a powerful symbol of Mercedes-Benz which they naturally keep alive. **The picture (above) of three 300SLs at a Hershey, PA Concours shows typical reaction.** Now, thirty(+) years later, public awareness of the 300SL remains clearer than it is for some new cars.

EARLY 300SL PROTOTYPES

As if the 300SL weren't rare enough, some enthusiasts have sought out specific chassis' with special histories. A man in Texas, for example, now has the chassis that won that Le Mans race in 1952. He is gathering up original carburetor engine parts used in 1952, and will have a body hand fabricated from 1952 factory drawings by Paul Russell & Company, in Massachusetts. The factory's first prototype 300SL Roadster (with chassis no. **8427 198 118/1**) has also been located and restored recently by Scott Restorations in California. Recreating these cars sometimes gets controversial, even when the factory is involved. Below is a car prepared in Mercedes-Benz own restoration shop for exhibit in their museum, and the liberties taken on it rival things done in the USA.

300SL side-vents are a story in themselves. Mercedes-Benz engineers using air tunnel testing of models in 1952 determined air entering the front of the car for cooling was better directed out the sides than going out underneath as normally done. Air buffeting underneath saps top speed and horsepower. For the same reason full belly pans were standard. Fender vents first appeared in different form on a 1953 prototype, and then the 1954 production model. The vents also reduced passenger compartment temperatures.

*At the Mercedes-Benz Museum near Stuttgart, a 1952 300SL racer sports
LaCarrera Panamericana signage and "buzzard bars"
which were unique to the car that Karl Kling drove to victory in Mexico in 1952.
Closer investigation shows it is not prepared as the actual car Karl Kling drove,
as none of the 1952 300SLs had air vents behind the front wheels.*

Walter Gotschke's unique style earned him 15 years of unquestioned leadership
as an automotive illustrator. His attention to detail such as included **Alfred Neubauer,** M-B's
Racing Team Director (left in dark suit). His signature can be found in sales brochures of
1950's & 1960's Mercedes, Volkswagen, Tanus and
non-commercial features for Road and Track.

PAST AND PRESENT: The famous 300 SL gullwing coupe and its improved replacement, the fabulous 300 SL Roadster.

GREATGETAWAY CAR: **MERCEDES-BENZ**

Escape to the great green world of spring and summer. Motor to the mountains, drive down to the sea. Slip the surly tethers of the working day and learn that <u>how</u> you go can often bring more satisfaction than where. Point the long potent snout of your Mercedes-Benz sports car down the highway and, as distance dissolves, thrill pridefully to the incomparable control you exercise over the machine. Shift down…fast. Corner! Watch the tach plummet then climb as you surge forward. Sense the superiority of this automobile as you become more and more a part of it, sensitive to the perfection of its moves and its indescribable subtlety. For this is the greatest motoring experience on earth…driving your own Mercedes-Benz. Can you think of a better means of getting away from it all?

Mercedes-Benz Sales. Inc. (A Subsidiary of Studebaker-Packard Corporation)

Sedans, convertibles, sports cars … prices range from about $3,300 to $13,000. *European delivery can be arranged.*

OVERVIEW:
300SL ROADSTER

*"If you have ever quizzed
300SL Roadster owners,
they seem well-versed on their model's
superiority over the earlier
Gull Wing. Improved handling,
more trunk space,
easier entry, more civilized.
But is it faster?
Not really. More exciting?
Not really.
More Collectible? No."*

*"The cars are very similar
and very different."*

Gull Wing Coupes are a step closer to a racing machine, like the Ferrari Daytona compared to its less "earthy" sister the 365 GTC/4. Both the Gull Wing and the Roadster received glowing press and test reviews, though M-B expected the conventional doors and more practical space usage would increase Roadster sales. On a year's produced basis this did not happen. The Gull Wing was built for roughly three years: 1402 cars divided by three years = 467 per year. The Roadster's average: 309 per year.

Roadsters and Gull Wings are both ultra-rare by any standards. The Roadsters introduced a lower, single pivot differential, a normal trunk, and conventional doors - all major changes. The factory reported the Roadster's first total weight to be only 176 pounds more than the Gull Wing. Shortly after introduction, a removable hardtop was offered, though these were hand-fitted and not always interchangeable between cars. The gas tank was reduced from 34 to 26 gallons, making room to lower the spare tire into the floor. Disc brakes were introduced in 1961, and the engine block became aluminum in '62, dropping 50 pounds. These 1961 through 1963 models do command perhaps 10% higher prices, but percentage wise, they haven't been appreciating faster than earlier drum brake variants. Some 1961 through '63 spare parts are harder to get, too.

Five rear axle ratio choices dramatically change top speed, acceleration, and gas mileage. The most common Roadster ratio for Europe is 3.64:1, and for the USA, 3.89:1. Vintage racing buffs like the 4.11:1 ratio because most short tracks have so many curves that low and mid-speed acceleration is more important than exceeding 130 mph. The 3.25:1 ratio, actually quite uncommon, delivers 155 mph, and miraculously high gas mileage. Good gas mileage is a unique characteristic of all 300SLs, averaging 18 to 21 mpg. It is a rare Ferrari, Jaguar, Aston-Martin, Maserati or Corvette that gets over 13 mpg.

Features unheard of on 1950s sport cars were common on many 300SLs: fitted luggage, multiple speaker signal seeking radio with power antenna, clock, back-up lights, nonglare rear view mirror, dual heaters, soft and/or hardtops and even a self emptying ash tray. The Roadster's standard direct block fuel injection engine produces 250hp from a mere 183 cubic inches. 1,858 300SL Roadsters were built plus one or two prototypes and two racers. Approximately 1,400 came to the USA. No one knows how many have survived. Original price of 300SL Roadsters in 1957 was a hefty $10,970 (USA), plus options.

300SL ROADSTER PRODUCTION BY YEAR*

Year	Production
1957	618
1958	267
1959	200
1960	241
1961	256
1962	182
1963	91
1964	3
Total:	1,858

*The assembly area in the factory used for both 300SL and 190SL was reassigned to other cars in March, 1963, however three cars, #3207, #3230 and #3257 were not released until 1964. Also, at least one prototype was built during 1955/56 and the two cars built for Paul O'Shea are not counted here.

All 300SLs have power brakes and fully synchronized four-speed transmissions (Jaguar did not get around to synchronizing low gear until 1963). All 300SLs have a fourteen-quart "dry-sump" oil system so effective that most owners have problems getting their engines warm enough while the rest of the world's sports car owners struggle with the perils of overheating. "Overbuilt" traits abound, from the large diameter steering wheel to the thick gauge bumpers, thick leather, truck-sized starter, generator and suspension parts and huge 3" wide brake shoes. It is built for a long haul, whether it be a grueling five-day Panamerican Road Race (1,900

Harold Cleworth's photo-like paintings are legend.
This fire engine red
300SL Roadster, with black interior, is available
in a limited series of 50 lithograph
artist's proofs, for $300 each.
Sales direct from artist: (213) 851-5558

miles), or the decades of service they have given their long-term owners.

With the top up the Roadster has basically the same ventilation system as the Coupe, earning both cars a reputation for being too hot in summer weather. True or not, it has not prevented over 1/3 of all 300SLs from having California, Texas, and warm-climate residences. There are a number of tricks that reduce interior heat: removing one or both of the heater radiators and fans from the in-air ducts (faithfully storing them for posterity) doubles the air flow from the grille area. Restoration centers allow the sacrilege of installing air conditioning with

discreet ducts that even concourse judges miss. We can't say we've have ever been bothered by too much interior heat; the sheer excitement of driving keeps one's attention.

The extremely rigid "bird cage" frame does not creak or twist, even on 30-year-old examples. The driver's view over the massive hood and sculptured fenders, its unique engine sounds, and a cradled feeling as the rear suspension does its work (never bottoming or bouncing) allow Roadsters to convey a driving experience unlike anything else, except the Gull Wing. Unidentical twins!

Early version by the Sports Department
w/ fiberglass tonneau

"USA Version" temporarily fitted
with a low two-person windscreen

Two USA Versions
were sent to America for O'Shea/Tilp Team

300SLS AND 300SLR
SPECIAL ROADSTERS

"How many SLs were actually built or modified for owners by the Sports Department has not been determined."

"The most famous of the special Roadsters were two supplied to the American O'Shea/Tilp Team that campaigned successfully in 1957."

While developing the 300SL Roadsters in 1956, Mercedes management discussed calling the new open version "300SLS." This did not happen, but when news of the new Roadsters broke in a dramatic six-page color spread in Colliers Magazine, October 12, 1956, it was titled "The Secret SLS," leaving the incorrect impression that all new Roadsters would be identified "SLS." Separately, two modified 300SL Roadsters built for **Paul O'Shea's** 1957 USA racing season have been called 300SLS, though not by O'Shea or the American press in 1957. Work Shop Manuals and other M-B publications refer to all roadsters as 300SL Ro. Even this final designation was conveniently confused by people claiming they had seen or now owned a "300SLR," which was yet a third model (with 8 cylinders) reserved only for racing and never sold to the public.

At the end of 1955 when Mercedes-Benz officially stopped racing, **Alfred Nuebauer's** Sport Department remained in existence to take care of customer's special requests, assisting private 300SL owners wishing to enter their cars in 1956 and later races and rally events. As the new 300SL Roadster took shape, the Sports Department was assigned to build one or several roadster prototypes, and one or both of Paul O'Shea's light weight racers. How many other cars were actually built or modified by the Sports Department has not been determined. Two recent German books about 300SLs document three different windscreen variations.

THE O'SHEA/TILP TEAM CARS

The rarest 300SL Roadsters were two supplied to the American O'Shea/Tilp Team that campaigned successfully in 1957. Paul O'Shea, already SCCA's National Driving Champion for 1955 and 1956 (driving a Gull Wing) was provided with two light-weight Roadsters and two factory mechanics for the '57 season. The cars raced in SCCA's modified Class D. Just how "special" the Paul O'Shea cars were has been the source of conflicting stories. O'Shea remembered both cars as having aluminum bodies, but several sources contradict him. **Karl Ludvigsen's** 1978 book *The Mercedes-Benz Racing Cars*, suggests that a non-aluminum car was one of the two cars prepared for O'Shea.

Ludvigsen described O'Shea's cars as "constructed as lightly as possible" and having a unique air inlet to the engine and air governor. The transformation of car #2 was extensive, including lighter racing seats, no rear fender skirt or chrome behind the rear wheels, fake headlights with simplified wiring, no side windows, a small thick plastic driver's windshield with racing cowl and matching caps for the door tops. It sports a fiberglass racing cowl reaching from the instrument cluster over to passenger compartment and back behind the drivers seat. In our picture is a standard steering wheel with horn ring, though removable steering wheels were mounted on both O'Shea's cars.

Thirty years later, while researching his outstanding 300SL book, **Jorgen Lewandowski** was allowed to read old company 300SL files of **Rudolf Uhlenhaut**. He found several inter-office memos about O'Shea's cars (see chart, p 69). This report substantiates Paul O'Shea's conviction that his cars had aluminum bodies, but not his recollections that the cars weighed only 1,600 pounds. While O'Shea remembers his two cars to be identical, Lewandowski's search indicates the second car was specially ordered with different components from the Advanced Testing Department. An order was found for five specially built engines with aluminum housings. Orders for two sizes of aluminum fuel tanks were also found.

It is remarkable that not even one O'Shea Roadster, i.e. aluminum body, aluminum engine housing, and/or aluminum frame, has been located by someone in thirty years. O'Shea, who died in 1990, told us he would get at least one phone call a year describing a car thought to be one of his racers. None were correct.

The mystery thickened when DBAG Museum Director Max vonPein wrote to the *SL Market Letter* in April 1989 saying that veteran employees of the Sports Department now working in

the Restoration Shop do not think
the cars they sent to O'Shea pos-
sessed aluminum bodies.

Keep your magnets handy. Maybe
you will find the rarest 300SL of them
all!

	In Road Trim*	Dry Weight	Engine Weight
Std. 300SL Rdsr (no bumpers or heater	3,036 lbs.	2,728 .lbs	542 lbs
300SL Rdstr prior to O-Shea Cnvsn.	2,688 lbs.	2,359 lbs.**	459 lbs
300SLS Rdstr USA Version (O-Shea)	2,292 lbs.	1,985 lbs.***	408 lbs

*In Road Trim meant full of gas (26 gal.), oil, water, tools, and spare wheel, but without driver
**Alloy engine & chassis, no heater, or bumpers.
***Alloy body, removed headlights, windshield,
side windows, soft top, generator or fan, simplified wiring.

*O'Shea's 1957 Driver's Championship
with SCCA was not as easy as
'55 and '56 for two reasons:*

a) the new Roadsters were not in
production soon enough to prove
they were eligible for SCCA's production car classification; knowing
they'd be placed with Class D
modified cars, the light weight
versions roadsters were prepared,

b) by 1957 competitive designs had
caught up with the 300SL's original
advantages, except, apparently its
indestructible perseverance. Paul's
strategy was to appear at as many
races as possible. He didn't always

win, but his consistency among the top few places earned him a third Championship.

Some other private 300SL victories were Schock/Moll's 1956 *European Touring Car Championship*, *Mairesse/ Genin's 1956 Liege-Rome-Liege Rally*, 1957's *Round Spain Rally*, a Caracus-Cumana-Caracus event, and 1958s *Neige et Glace Rally*.

In October 1957, **Alfred Neubauer** sent a letter to American M-B Sales Director **Heinz Hoppe** saying, "I am against any further participation in U.S. racing events. Considering that we won virtually all champion-ships a few years ago, people naturally expect us to score overall wins." Consequently O'Shea's services were terminated and the two O'Shea cars were offered for sale in late 1957 to "enthusiasts of our marque who will not use the cars for racing." One was priced at $5,000, the other $6,000.

The two mechanics assigned to the O'Shea/Tilp Team returned to Germany. A recent MBNA employee thinks one of these cars was returned to the factory, though both are un-accounted for as of 1992. Their chassis numbers were **8467 198 106/2** and **8742 620 070/1**.

After the factory's withdrawal from racing at the end of 1955, **Alfred Neubauer** became head of the Museum, and **Karl Kling** took over the Sports Department. Daimler-Benz' spectacular role in the 1950s racing shifted to support of long-distance rally contests, first with the 300SL, and increasingly with sedans. Mercedes victories in international rallies continued throughout the 1960s and 1970s.

Wooden four-spoke pop-off wheel,
special seats and various wind cowls
will fit on any 300SL Roadster.

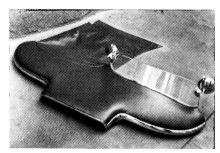

Front air scoop was functional.
Cowls were covered with leather.
There was even a clock.
300SLs were nick-named "boudoir racers"
because they were so well equipped.

S C O T T
RESTORATIONS, INC.

Masters from blueprint designs through immaculately restored automobiles. All work done on the premises.

SALES, PARTS, RESTORATION, SERVICE AND STORAGE OF FINE AUTOMOBILES

SCOTT RESTORATIONS, INC.
14661 Lanark Street, Panorama City, CA 91402
Fax: 818/787-3291
Phone: 818/787-2881

Photo: Natalie Boehm

Most great works
of art follow
classical form.
And a rare
few create it.

ENGINEERED LIKE NO OTHER
CAR IN THE WORLD

THE 1990s SL:
300/500/600SL

Each time a new SL is created there are two big questions. What is it, and how will it affect the value of previous models? Typically a certain number of owners rally around the previous model immediately after a new version is announced. The new 300/500/600SL (Body code 129) was no exception. Styling changes of each new SL would have to be called more than evolutionary. Big changes inevitably cause some retreat to the past by those who dislike a new model. This time a 30 to 50%+ price jump on the new model's V-8 ($83,000+ in 1990, and $98,500 for 1993, plus gas & luxury taxes) gave more people reason to look back. Never-the-less, Mercedes had done their homework and knew there were sufficient households able to afford the newer models, thus creating a new step into the heavens. Finally the 600SL has created a second new step at the top.

Since Mercedes has a habit of building new SLs every year, the price of 1980s and 1970s SLs pushes downward toward a "floor" of about $12,000 for the oldest 450SLs. We envision 1970s and 1980s #107 bodied SLs compressing to their own "pecking order" between $12,000 and $40,000. Condition, engine size, and authentic options will grow more important than specific model year. A separate pricing "zone" will emerge from $30,000 to $65,000+ for used 1990s 300SL and 500SLs. There is a good chance used 600SLs will have their own price category, never dropping below $60,000, unless tainted by accidents, assassinations, or high mileage. We say high mileage not because they won't take high usage, but because collectors in the next century will favor the most original examples they can find. Original paint. Original interiors & tops... even original decals in the engine bay. And low mileage. They'll be found too.

The higher prices of each SL series are not merely a consequence 500%+

inflation since the mid-1950s. The latest SL is substantially more complex, with literally three times as many parts as SLs of the 50's and 60s. As advanced as 300SL Gullwings were, none of EPA or DOT's regulations had been created, and no ABS brakes, airbags, ADS, or even central-locking existed. Each generation of SLs is obliged to take on the latest technology in addition to inflation. After eliminating inflation, the result suggests state-of-the art technology of 1990 SLs has increased SL prices by a multiple of 3 since 1954.

Criteria	1954 300SL	1993 300SL-24	1993 500SL	1993 600SL
Length	177.5"	176.0"	176.0"	178.0"
Width	70.5"	71.3"	71.3"	71.3"
Height	51.2"	5013"	51.3"	52.0"
Wheelbase	94.5"	99.0"	99.0"	99.0"
Turning Circle	37.8 ft.	35.3 ft.	35.3 ft.	35.3 ft.
Weight	2,855 lbs.	4,035 lbs.	4,165 lbs.	4,455 lbs.
Tire Size	6.50V-15	255/55ZR x 16	255/55ZR x 16	255/55ZR x 16
Head Room	36.6"	37.1"	37.1"	37.1"
Leg Room	38.2"	42.4"	42.4"	42.4"
Engine & Size.	6 cyl, 182.8 cu. in	6 cyl, 180.6 cu. in.	V8, 303.5 cu. in.	V-12, 367 cu. in.
Hrspwr	240 HP @ 6,100 rpm	228HP@6,300rpm	315HP@ 5,600rpm	389 HP @ 5,200rpm
Trqe	217 ft.lbs.@ 4,800 rpm	201 ft lbs.@ 4,600rpm	347 ft lbs.@ 3,900rpm	420 ft.lbs.@3,800rpm
Trans.	4 spd, fully synchrnzd	4 spd. automatic	4 spd.. automatic	4 spd. automatic
Weight per HP	11.9 lbs/HP	17.7 lbs./HP	13.2 lbs./HP	11.45 lbs /HP
Weight @1ft.lb.trq	13.15 lbs./ft. lb.	20.1 lbs. /HP	12.0 lbs./HP	10.6 lbs. /ft. lb.
Axle Ratio(s)	3.25:1 = 161.5 mph	3.69:1 = 140 mph	2.65:1 = 155 mph	2.65:1 = 155 mph
w/ max. speed	3.64:1 = 146.0 mph 4.11:1 = 129.0 mph	3.69:1 = 140 mph	(electronically limited)	(electronically limited)
0-60 Acceleration	3.25:1 = 8.4 seconds	3.69:1 = 8.3 seconds	2.65:1 = 6.4 seconds	2.65:1 = 5.9 seconds
per axle ratio	3.64:1 = 7.4 seconds 4.11:1 = 6.7 seconds			
Original Price	$7,255 (w/dlvry)	$92,400(w/fed. tax)	$110,500(w/fed. tax)	$132,000(w/fed. tax)
Eqvlnt $ =1:5.21	$38,500 in 1992 $	$17,735 in 1954 $	$21,204 in 1954 $	$25,328 in 1954 $

This chart shows how the three most popular models compare to the first famous SL. The 300SL 12 valve version, (not in chart), is not offered at all in some markets, such as the USA. Engines are the primary differences in the cars. All but one option, ortho seat adjustments, are standard on the 600SL. The 600SL's Adaptive Damping System (ADS) a self leveling, automatically adjustable suspension, is a desirable option for the 500SL and 300SL.

FEATURES

The famous automatically rising roll bar is standard on all three cars. This bar, which normally forms part of the rear compartment surround structure, pops up and locks in place in a third of a second if sensors detect an impending rollover. These conditions also lock the seatbelts and unlock, but not open, the doors (if they are

steering wheel, shoulder belt height and all three mirrors. Rear view mirrors are now adjustable by a single, console-mounted joystick control. 1950s SLs were praised for bringing the first non-glare rear view mirrors to sportscars. 600SL rear mirrors automatically adjust reflectiveness to reduce the glare of following traffic. The 600SL's center console has a rolled wood cover and a hands free cellular telephone.

Another distinctive feature is the first fully automatic soft top in the auto industry. Pressing a single switch on the console unlatches the top from

locked). The padded, leather covered bar can also be raised and lowered by a switch on the console. Air conditioning now incorporates an electrostatic air filter which removes pollen and dust from incoming air. Ten way power seats include a three-setting memory system which positions the headrest, tilt-telescopic

the windshield and begins its decent, simultaneously lowering side windows, retracting the roll bar, and opening the rear deck storage compartment lid. The top folds into the compartment and the deck lid closes and latches, while the windows and roll bar return to their original position.

BRAKES

Beginning on 1993 models is a lateral-acceleration G-force sensing brake proportioner, which reduces the brake pressure wherever the weight is lightest... for example when the front goes down in braking rear weight momentarily shifts forward, making the rear nearly weightless. Rather than permanently smaller rear brakes, the solution of the past, the SL varies pressure to conditions.

scoot around town and country daily as always, consuming 12 to 20,000+ miles of wear & tear annually, the case for both 300SL and 500SL increases; They are thoroughly comfortable, handsome, and safe SLs to "consume" ...though you'll have to work hard for several decades to wear one out! Genuine consumers are still having trouble extinguishing their 450SLs, now reaching their third decade!

CHOICES

As in past models, every 1990s SL model will be preserved by collectors, but we expect the 600SL to be the favorite. With less than 30 built per day for all markets, the 600SL is as rarefied as SLs are going to get in this decade. The C112, if ever marketed, would require over $300,000 each and would not be feasible to drive around much.

If you are debating purchase of a 500SL versus the 600SL, we'd ask how you'll use the car. If you intend to

If your objective is more idyllic; a reward to you of state-of-the-art technology that will exemplify the last decade of this century forever... the 600SL is a safe ticket. The world has always been in awe of Mercedes-Benz, and it has always loved top-of-the-line convertibles. A mean combination. Adding to this, when car historians look back on this century, the footprint cast by Mercedes-Benz will be mighty and long. Mercedes will often be mentioned before Ford, and the 600SL V-12 will be a fine cornerstone for this end of the century.

The 600SL's main attraction is the engine itself. Its most apparent benefit is greater torque in the 2,000 to 5,000 rpm range, and less engine effort at all speeds ...less shifting than ever. More quiet power. Exactly how the grandest 1990s sports tourer should behave.

SLs have always been heavier than their competition, as the chart shows, even six cylinder models now weigh over 4,000 lbs. Width, track, and wheelbase, and tire size are the same, and suspension tuning makes the 500's & 600's weight gain almost indiscernible. 600SLs sit .7" higher to allow slightly greater suspension travel, though ADS automatically lowers the entire car at highway speeds. Steering & handling quickness totally belies the weight. The V-12 fits into the engine bay with only minor changes. Oil sump, air filter, intake & exhaust manifolds were altered, as were fuel, coolant, and wiring routes. ABS, ASR & the hydraulic systems were also repositioned.

Internally the V-12 is the same motor found in the 600SEL & new 600SEC. Zero to 60mph is slightly faster than the 500E and other S-Class models. All 500 and 600 powered Mercedes-Benz have an electronically limited top speed of 155 m.p.h. The 600SL may be the ultimate autobahn cruiser with 23% more horsepower and a heavier engine; no risk of front-end "float" above 125 mph. which is the nemesis of many famous sportscars.

THE BEST OR NOTHING
As a leader in new technology Mercedes has lived for decades with criticism that they insulate the driver from the sensations of the road. Owner's manuals for the 1957 300SL warned: "On account of its outstanding roadholding ability and springing, it is only too easy for you to not realize how fast you are really traveling." As automatic shifting & power steering came to SLs in the 1960s, and decibel counts inside cars dropped during the 1970s & 80s, the old definition of sportscars gave way, but not without annual chants that driving fun was being destroyed. To the contrary, what impresses us about all new S-Class models is their ability to anticipate our wishes faster than we would have implemented them manually. Almost spooky at times, M-B's computer interceding power, braking, suspension & climate are logical extensions of existing technology. They're just new to automobiles. Extracting more results with less friction & fuel, faster braking in straighter lines, less human damage in accidents, and wherever else research bequeaths, is what building "the best or nothing" is all about. Are detractors asking the future to behave like the past? That's not how it works. For 1990s state-of-the-art "greatness" we think the 600SL will wear just fine.

190SL
Model years 1959 - 1963 (14,068 built)

Jan/Jun	High-Avg.	Avg.	Low-Avg.
1986	$19,360	$14,100	$10,800
1987	$21,290	$15,365	$10,800
1988	$23,680	$16,180	$12,190
1989	$26,694	$18,600	$12,145
1990	$31,305	$23,244	$15,580
1991	$36,603	$26,014	$18,921
1992	$32,418	$24,832	$18,236
5 Yr % Gain:	+52.3%	+61.6%	+68.9%

3.
Purchases and Restorations

MONITORING
PRICE
TRENDS

300SL Roadster

Year	15% Compound Yearly Projection	Typical Yearly Price
1970	$9,400	$94,00
1971	10,810	11,100
1972	12,432	12,700
1973	14,296	13,400
1974	16,441	15,700
1975	18,907	17,500
1976	21,743	19,150
1977	25,004	22,800
1978	28,755	24,750
1979	33,068	27,500
1980	38,028	32,000
1981	43,732	39,000
1982	50,292	43,300
1983	57,836	43,870
1984	66,512	40,880
1985	76,488	47,270
1986	87,962	54,550
1987	101,156	75,170
1988	116,329	136,900
1989	133,779	247,500
1990	153,845	262,750
1991	176,922	239,635
1992	203,461	$204,217
1993	233,980	
1994	269,077	
1995	309,438	
1996	355,854	
1997	409,232	
1998	470,617	
1999	541,209	
2000	622,391	
2001	715,749	
2002	823,112	
2003	946,578	
2004	$1,088,565	

Stating values of anything in books almost guarantees prompt obsolescence. We've looked at historic trends in Chapter 1, and prognosticated in Chapter 2 about the 1971-1989 SL's future value. The multi-decade reappreciation pattern of SLs has survived all past recessions and also convinced us monitoring price fluctuations monthly or from one over publicized auction to the next, is altogether near sighted. A basic feature of the *SL Market Letter* (*SLML*) since 1982 has been reports of...

1. **High-Average**,
2. **Average**, and
3. **Low-Average** prices...

on each SL model every six months (see example). *SLML* collates thousands of offerings of SLs and other rare models annually. After appearing in the *SLML* this data remains on computer to be pooled with actual sales *SLML* learns about from many sources. Prices were reported quarterly in the early 1980s, but it soon became apparent that totalling the data twice a year was quite sufficient... especially as cars get older. Larger half-year data bases are also less prone to errant deviations. We've also examined data regionally but never felt it consistently enough different to report. Fluctuations in regional economies (up and down) do of course affect supply and demand, but for every example caused by that, we see as

300SL Gullwing

Year	15% Compound Yearly Projection	Typical Yearly Price
1970	$13,800	$13,800
1971	15,870	15,300
1972	18,251	17,100
1973	20,988	19,500
1974	24,136	23,800
1975	27,757	27,000
1976	31,920	31,000
1977	36,707	36,500
1978	42,215	41,000
1979	48,547	48,000
1980	55,829	56,700
1981	64,203	66,000
1982	73,833	77,700
1983	84,908	78,270
1984	97,645	80,000
1985	112,291	82,830
1986	129,135	88,720
1987	148,505	125,640
1988	170,781	220,900
1989	196,398	343,580
1990	225,858	350,200
1991	259,737	335,200
1992	298,697	$290,200
1993	343,502	
1994	395,027	
1995	454,282	
1996	522,424	
1997	600,787	
1998	690,905	
1999	794,541	
2000	913,722	
2001	$1,050,781	

many parallel cases elsewhere that high or low price is attributable to things other than location.

One of *SLML*'s long term studies on the 1950's 300SLs shows how they've fluctuated, plateaued and appreciated since 1970, through good times and several recessions. During each recession short-term experts use the latest expressions to declare "the bubble has burst," or "they've hit the wall,"or "investment delusions" as Forbes did in Nov.,1992. However, through 23+ years 300SLs have hovered near or returned to 15% compound average annual appreciation. Whenever they've dropped below that curve, buyers have come out of the wood-work, world-wide.

During 1990-92 the 190SL market has seemed oblivious to the recession. Same thing for 6.3, 600, and 6.9 SEL sedans. At the same time, '50s 300SLs took one of their rare drops in value. Most car enthusiasts admire Mercedes-Benz cars, but gains still occur at different times for different models. Many *SL Market Letter* readers get their first subscription for 6 months to help on a specific buying or selling decision, yet fully a third of them renew for two years when the time comes, to keep updated on prices and other news.

Cautions
When Buying

One of the big auto leasing companies has a slogan, "If it depreciates lease it, if it appreciates buy it." Nice of them to promote our area of interest!

We've all bought plenty of cars, though selecting an older car that one dares think is a permanent asset or investment is another scene altogether. "Permanent" cars are out there, it's a matter of doing your homework and some intelligent pre-purchase inspections. After reading this book and listening to six or eight owners and/or sellers of your favorite model, you will discover you're beginning to know as much about one specific model as most of the people to whom you are talking! That doesn't mean you're an expert (yet), but its a good start.

Take stock of which activities you enjoy as well as taking stock of your pocketbook. If this activity is going to remain fun (that is one of the goals) you need to recognize what parts of this hobby you most enjoy. Some people are basically closet mechanics. They really enjoy restoring or supervising the restoration of their dream car(s). Others hate the details of a restoration but like driving a distinctive car or bringing it to events and the resulting friendships. Decide which person you are (now), and buy a car that fits. [We've found ourselves enjoying different aspects of the hobby in different decades.]

Whether you are getting into your first or fifth "collectible" car don't hesitate to get some help. Pay an expert to help selecting the car. And decide early on if you will really trust any restoration you have not commissioned. It's tough finding original old cars and restored cars that we can be positive were done right. Most buyers can't rest until they've personally inspected every panel and cranny to be sure their new treasure is solid. To avoid the disappointment and cost of buying a bad car, it is often best to go straight to a good restoration company and invite them help you find or evaluate your dream car. They'll outline the costs of sprucing up an average example versus picking a lower priced, weathered car which they restore to your requirements.

We would also suggest not limiting your search for or sale of a car (or a restoration company) to your own city. When a rare car comes on the market it usually doesn't have much competition locally, which makes it appear necessary to swallow a higher price or weaknesses in the car ...but 500 miles down the road another one may exist, multiplying your options. Ditto for sellers... advertising beyond your community makes you less apt to suffer with only a wholesale purchase offer. When your interest is rare cars, your colleagues are rare too, but they're out there!

For out-of-town inspections, it is fairly easy to hire an expert to look at a car for you in other parts of the country. Diagnostic centers, appraisers, restoration centers (some listed in this book), and authorized Mercedes-Benz dealers, are usually happy to rake a used car over the coals for you for $75 to $125+ depending on time & travel involved. When you're considering a $20,000 to $200,000+ purchase, this step is helpful even if you are a knowledgeable enthusiast. And it is a lot more efficient use of time & airfare to get help inspecting few cars to reduce surprises when you do get on the plane yourself, hopeful to conclude a purchase and drive it home. One caution; evaluators are sometime so conscientious about their job that they describe or accentuate a car's shortcomings beyond their significance.

If you skew priorities in any direction it should be to finding rust-free cars. The "success-rate" in fixing mechanical weaknesses is much higher than permanently removing rust. This is because [in our opinion] 19 out of 20 body shops aren't oriented to viewing cars as permanent assets. Body shop managers and owners all talk a good line; They all say what you want to hear, but few of them have employees genuinely trained for your goals. Shops that are dedicated to your objectives are rarer than the cars, especially those specializing in Mercedes-Benz! Also, most body shops are blind to guarding a car's other components...

suspension parts, engine bays and interiors get unimaginably dirty and frequently oversprayed with primers or body colors. Some shops even have the right facilities, but in the pressure of daily goals paint flies.

There really are a lot of design and construction differences between a Mercedes-Benz and other cars, so there is a lot to be said for companies genuinely specializing in older Mercedes-Benz. As distinguished from "body shops" the best restoration companies understand your whole car. Most of them have specialists on premises to "remanufacture" any part of your car, and most have done your model a dozen or four dozen times. We've invited North America's best restoration centers to advertise in this book.* Visit one or several of them. Most are happy to give tours by appointment. Some of you will be amazed.

On your own or using an expert, its good to make similar inspections of every car. Expect sellers to be up-front with invoices they have on their car (during their ownership and previously), including names of mechanics. Sellers who "never keep the receipts" hurt themselves at selling time. Absence of this proof of history makes a car much less valuable.

Feel free to make copies of the Check List on pages 84 and 85.

Also important:

Paint finish
can be most misleading. A shiny finish may fool your senses as much a dull finish. Neither is especially predictive of the rest of the car. Undercarriage inspections on a hoist are essential. Recent undercoating jobs are suspect. Open up any strange lumps or peeling coating to see if trapped moisture has been too busy.

Repair costs
typically are double our personal estimates.

Restoration Centers can sometimes be powerful negotiators for you, as sellers are less likely to argue with their evaluations.

Fake Convertibles
As the stakes in car collecting grow higher, so does the temptation to a) make phony specials, b) steal real ones. One type of "fake" is the modification of other models to simulate prominent types. Converting 280SE 3.5 coupes into convertibles is an example. If clearly identified as a conversion, no one is harmed, but beware when paying for the real thing. Some fakes travel in good company. R. Straman Co. has been making roadsters (Spiders) out of Ferrari Daytona Coupes for years. Such conversion of Ferraris and Mercedes-Benz are well enough

See advertisements on pages 14, 32, 56, 71, and 94.

CAR CONDITION AND REPAIRS EVALUATION

Apply similar standards/judgements to each car considered, strengths/weaknesses at this point in time, cost to correct, and options included.

Exact Model & Engine _____ **Year** _____

Complete VIN # _____

List all options and special features on back of this page.
Include type of seat material, type floor & trunk coverings,
type of wheels, 1 or 2 tops, etc.

Owner _____

Owner's Adrs _____

Owner's City/State _____

Owner's Phone(s) _____

Color(s) _____

	Out-standing	Good	Pass-able	Needs Work	Needs Change	Cost or Hours to correct?

BODY CONDITION

1. If paint is original, can it be saved? If repaint use a wrapped magnet to detect excessive plastic filler. Was all trim and rubber removed for painting, or is tell-tale overspray?
2. Chrome & Rubber: - consdider size of bad pieces. Are emplems deteriorating?
3. Glass - Look for fogging & stone flaws. Are tail light lens unevenly faded? If so, why? Top(s) - do they latch fully? Is fabric correct, and/or noticably worn?
4. Top(s) - do they fit, do they latch fully? Is fabric correct, and/or noticably worn?
5. Body- Look down sides, frt. to back, for unevenness, spots in panels, paint & door gaps, general cleanliness.

UNDERCARRIAGE

1. Judge general cleanliness, locate source of oil & grease leaks.
2. Any rust or bare metal ndg repair; esp. on a hoist: chk wheels, rocker & fender panels.

84

ENGINE & TRUNK COMPARTMENTS

1. History & miles since major engine over-haul, & age of starter, water pmp, battery, etc. Ask for proof (invoices) of repairs. If strong documentation missing, an engine diagnostic is called for, incldg. cmprsn. test.
2. Scratches & cleanliness on metal surfaces, i.e. frqnt careless repairs.
3. Electrical wiring safety and neatness.
4. Age of radiator, hoses, and belts. Trunk cleanliness, condition of mat, spare, jack and tools. Check floor under mat.

INTERIOR

1. Door panels, hareware, door seals.
2. Look & "life" of seats, armrests, and carpets.
3. Cracks or fade on dash, dials, buttons, pedals, steering wheel.
4. Operation of wipers, horn, brake lights, turn signals, hand brake, radio, heater, air conditioner (not just fans), all power equipment.

GENERAL DRIVING

1. Note engine idle & muffler noises or smoke.
2. Pmp brakes & hold dwn, to see if pressure holds.
3. Sense handling, body & engine sounds; chk on bumpy road & highway 10 mph faster than you normally drive. Price all irregularities.
4. Does exhaust emit new color upon hard acceleration or deceleration? Does oil pressure drop on sudden acceleration? Both are negatives to be priced.

CONCLUSION:

Add all correction costs to asking price, or use to negotiate lower price. Add your time & time-cost of an unusable investment during repairs.

NOTES:

TOTAL
HOURS
OR COSTS

85

regarded to bring more than the coupe untouched, but rarely enough to cover the $15K to $20K+ necessary to do it right.

Nonmatching Numbers

Subscribers call the *SL MARKET LETTER* regularly asking why their engine numbers differ from their chassis numbers. "Is my engine authentic? Do I have something that has been stolen? Is my car worth less because of mixed numbers?"

Mercedes engines are assembled and bench tested independent of their bodies and/or chassis. Matching component numbers rarely were finished together, even on the very low production models. We owned 300Sc Roadster body #0001 for eleven years; it was built with chassis #0005 and engine #0003 ...they couldn't even get it synchronized on the first body! Of course they weren't trying.

Learn Your Car's Language

Cars can talk pretty well, in fact they'll talk to anyone that will listen... not just their owners. They actually try hard to let us know how they've been treated:

BUZZ: in or near the dash, is often a speedometer cable.

HOWL or GROWL: when engine is running could be transmission bearing, clutch, or drive shaft.

KNOCK: in the engine may be main bearings, connecting rods, or piston pins. Ditto for a chattering oil pressure gauge.
HUM at the rear as car gains speed is usually a drive shaft or rear axle bearing, or a gear.

HISSING: around the engine could be air escaping from a vacuum hose, a loose spark plug or a faulty heat-riser tube.

RATTLES: are usually metal hitting metal- a muffler hitting the frame, a loose bolt on a shock absorber, a fan blade or a window lift mechanism.

SQUEALS: typically slipping fan belts, worn or miss-adjusted, a water pump, or bad generator brushes. Brakes & tires can also squeal.

SNIPPETY-SNAP: from the engine may be a cracked distributor cap, broken or bare spark plug wires, or other loose connections.

Learning your car's language can save embarrassment and thousands of dollars via less expensive, early repairs ...or a lower vehicle purchase price.

Same "program" for other models.

The conclusions of **Gerald Roush's** April 19, 1986 *Ferrari Market Letter* deserve repeating. Most of his answer fits for Mercedes-Benz as well as Ferrari:

"*It is a common misconception that each engine was built for a specific chassis. In actuality the engines for production Ferraris were assembled independently and only after passing all inspections and a dynamometer test were they assigned to a chassis.*" Same situation as with Mercedes.

On engine switching

Roush continued, "*More than one well-known concours-winning older Ferrari would be found to have a non-original engine if the internal number on the block were checked, and not just the chassis number stamped on the block. It seems to me that this insistence on "matching" numbers unfairly penalizes the restorer and would-be preserver of older Ferraris, or encourages them to practice deceit.

"The emphasis on matching numbers becomes even more ludicrous when competition cars are being considered. Replacing a sick engine in the interest of winning a race was obviously of greater importance than preserving the car's virginity in the interest of its future collectible status. Having the right TYPE of engine is important in preserving the original character of the car; having the right engine number is not."
Also, the Mercedes-Benz repair policy has for decades been to encourage replacement blocks for badly worn iron or alloy block engines. As Roush says, installing the correct TYPE of engine is the critical point.

Provenance

There is of course a limit to acceptable component changing, i.e. "this is the same hatchet with a new head and a new handle." Logic dictates that for any car to claim a particular moment of origin, it must with certainty retain over 50% of it's original primary components, presumably the following:

1) original chassis (frame) & body
   (w/ correct replacement engine),
2) original chassis and engine
   (w/ correct replacement body), or
3) original body and engine
   (w/ correct replacement chassis
   & documented demise of 1st
   frame)

This third alternative is not always feasible or comfortable. In the case of unitized body cars the body and

1955 300Sc Roadster with body no. 0001.
Olson drove this car
92,000 miles over 11 years.

chassis are one, and secondly, many states only record chassis numbers. While an owner could arbitrarily switch chassis numbers to another chassis, it behooves everyone to publicly document the demise of the removed chassis (frame), least it reappears one day!

This standard is just as important regardless who makes the changes. The Mercedes-Benz factory and their restoration shop have shown no reluctance to swap bodies, engines, chassis', rear axles, and even install disc brakes and alloy engines (300SL Roadster components) in dozens of Gullwings.

If your receipts prove it was the Daimler-Benz factory shop that replaced a major component with a non-original part, that is one thing, but if you have a chance at your neighborhood restoration center to put a 280SL engine or rear disc brakes into a 230SL - don't. Those parts are more valuable retained for correct placement in a 280SL body, even if you don't happen to own a 280SL.

Eleven 300SL racers were built by DBAG during 1952. As previously mentioned a few of these racers were rebodied with near-standard 1954 Gull Wing bodies & engines & sold to employees or friends of the company. Photo-journalist **Jesse Alexander** bought one direct from Daimler-Benz for only $2,500 in the late 50s. The car was later determined to have the actual chassis that won LeMans in 1952, but after it's racing days it was severely altered as a factory test vehicle. Before it was sold the factory had installed a standard production 300SL fuel injection engine and a standard Gullwing body. It also received a single low-pivot differential which involves frame alterations. Applying our provenance criteria, less than 50% of the original 1952 LeMans winner remains present here. In these cases the factory has ironically dismantled several of its most famous 1952 racers.

RECORD KEEPING AND INSURANCE

Just as you hope for good car records before purchase, you too have some "stewardship" duties. Regardless how you "package" service invoices and records we'd recommend that you keep everything... and group it in the following categories below.*

- **Annual Check List of Recurring Maintenance**
Keep a simple check-off spread sheet, so you can mark the date when you last purged the brake fluid, and changed transmission and rear-end oil, and so on. Refer to your model's original frequency of maintenance list or booklet to be sure you're doing everything. We keep our perennial list of one time TO DO projects here too, and recording when they are done.

- **Vendor Reference List**
Build an address list of everyone you utilize caring for this car. Ideally also gather names of previous mechanics, in case they ever need to be called.

- **Invoices**
or a signed, dated statement of work done, separated by subject such as:
Body and Paint
Trim & Accessories
Interior Engine
Electrical Systems
Ignition System
Oil Systems
Fuel System
Cooling System
Drive Train
(Transmission & Differential)
Brake System
Suspension & Undercarriage

* *During 1993 the SL Market Letter will publish an attractive, three inch thick, three-ring binder with labeled dividers and advice for keeping all records on your Mercedes-Benz. Check with SLML 612-377-0155 for the exact publication date*

Past History

We always write to the Mercedes-Benz, Museum Archives, Stuttgart, Germany, for a copy of each car's build record, which shows exactly how the car was equipped when new, confirming color, interior materials, etc. This information seems self-evident, but the factory's reply, along with any correspondence and pictures you are able to gather from past owners, authenticates a car's provenance. When you buy a car try to arrange a picture of yourself and the previous owner, with the car. Include any past owner trip photos, and notes of their recollections about the car. It is fun to determine as much about the car's life as possible. Significant trips, dormant periods, accidents. Everything.

Current History

Same as previous section, but your history with the car... from the moment of your purchase. Chronological description of major trips, events (good and bad) & car show appearances. Narrative summary of bills founds elsewhere.

Insurance

Retain sampling of premiums paid, claims, and the current policy.

INSURANCE "MUMBO-JUMBO"

As cars become collectible they also become eligible for (or pushed into) special policies and also specialized insurance companies. This has caused many misunderstandings for owners and more than a few insurance agents. Most of the trouble is in policy labels so misleading that even agents get confused and make inaccurate assurances. Briefly there are two type of coverage:

1. *Indemnity Insurance* is the most common automotive coverage wherein the insurer agrees to return the insured to the same financial condition as before a loss, while they both agree the insured should not be permitted to profit from the loss. Coverage is accomplished by one of the following. An *Actual Cash Value* (ACV) Policy, limited to what a car is worth at the time of loss, not exceeding cost new, or by a Stated Amount Rider, wherein the premium is based on a stated upper limit of coverage, though ACV at time of loss still determines the amount to be paid.

2. A *Stated Value Policy* can be written. Technically, this is not indemnity insurance when the term is used correctly, in that value is agreed at the time the contract begins, not at time of loss.

The stated or agreed-in-advance value is what everybody thinks they're buying, but many aren't. Many insurance companies ask for an advance appraisal and/or photographs, and attach a "value" declaration to their ACV policy, which creates an illusion of an agreed amount when in fact the value will be re-established at "the time of loss." Policy holders usually pay a higher premium than regular coverage would cost for the same car & received ACV coverage... up to a stated ceiling. Some companies insist that a stated amount rider be added to their regular indemnity insurance after a car reaches a certain age or value, because a premise in pricing their standard car insurance is that the asset will depreciate over time. Some policies have "Original Cost New" (OCN) maximum liability clauses to protect themselves against reappreciation. Stated amount and stated value riders allow this "cap" to rise to a new ceiling mutually agreed with the client. What clients don't realize is that agreeing to this personalized ceiling, and higher premium, rarely eliminates the "at time of loss" settlement clauses.

Some owners of older, reappreciating cars manage to keep old cars on standard policies used on their modern cars, figuring good restoration records & clippings of prices for similar cars will give them a strong, "at time of loss" claim if the worst happened. Maybe. If your premiums have been based on the obsolete premise that the car is just plain old, be sure what your policy says about its maximum coverage. An "original cost new" ceiling would be unfortunate if you found out your car's value was worth twice that much... or more.

Mixing "actual cash value" with "stated value" or "agreed value" riders is not illegal; but the misunderstandings it is causing are wide-spread. One of the loudest critics of the situation is **J. Bradley Flippen**, of Virginia, (703)-631-6078. He became so incensed after being offered 30% of his stated amount policy in 1989, that he's written a copyrighted 12 page "white paper" on the subject. In it he describes surveying 21 agents representing many insurance companies & found of those offering collector car policies, half said their policy would pay the full amount in event of total loss. The other half did not know but would find out. "Only one agent in the 21 contacted actually knew their policy did not offer valued or agreed amount coverage. He noted it was a stated amount policy, only paid the ACV at time of loss, not to exceed the stated amount, and was not any better than their standard ACV policy."

Even the most famous antique car insurers use ACV policies despite "agreed amount" riders. Chubb & Son's "Collector Vehicle Program" uses their standard car policy with an

endorsement attachment deleting the standard limits of liability with such obtuse statements as: a) "we will pay the amount in the declarations if there is a total loss..." on the same page with "if there is a partial loss...we shall have the right to change the amount shown in the declarations." Within the policy a section called Condition applicable to all parts: #10 "If insured & company fail to agree as to amount of loss, either may demand an appraisal of loss."

"In such event each party shall select a competent appraiser... appraisers shall select an umpire... appraisers shall separately state the actual cash value..." Sad, but who's going to win an argument with these folks? Allstate's program is basically the same. To add insult, these companies usually also expect you to move all your cars and home under their "protection".

We finally tracked down a genuine Stated Value Policy at Sneed, Robinson & Gerber, Inc. (901)372-4712, without depreciation or mileage limitations! They are not prepared to take on cars worth much over $30,000, but that still includes many Mercedes models. It is an all risk physical property damage policy for fire, theft, vandalism, windstorm, hail, collision, etc. To soften their $3 per $1,000 annual rate, they suggest liability coverage be kept with your standard carrier, as multiple car clients usually only have to pay this

on one or two of their cars on the premise that they won't all be driven simultaneously. Your standard insurance carrier shouldn't object to granting that kind of coverage even on a 600 Pullman.

Recommendations

We had hoped to build a chart comparing types of policies & carriers, with rates, but there are too many variables, regional & driver factors. We can say the following:

1. Know exactly how your policy's maximum coverage works, and when your vehicle value is measured. To be sure you haven't missed anything, ask a claims agent to write you a letter listing the parts of the policy that speak to the subject. There are usually several spots (example above).

2. On cars which have not yet climbed above the policy's maximum vehicle coverage, check if standard insurance is higher or low priced than the amount you'd expect for a total loss. *Example: cost new of the 6.9 SEL went as high as $50,000; if your regular insurance uses OCN plus an annual depreciation formula, ask yourself the stated amount you'd expect in a total loss. Maybe it is $25,000 or less. You may get a lower premium rate with a stated value policy. If driving restrictions are not too much for you, consider changing. Of course, re-view the stated value annually.*

3. When your car clearly exceeds the maximum value coverage of a standard policy, a change seems to us essential. Despite the easy confusion described here, a plan mixing ACV w/ Stated Value can be an interim choice, if you dare to trust the goodwill of your carrier to treat you fairly in a crisis. If this carrier permits you to switch down to a storage rate during the winter, averaging the winter & summer premium together is quite competitive, and it allows unrestricted driving in the summer months. The rates to select a pure *Agreed Value Property Policy*, coupled with your regular carrier's liability policy, will in most cases be more expensive... but the chance for unpleasant surprises should be gone.

The principle of "reasonable expectations" is obviously being stretched by the way ACV is mixed with stated value riders. If you feel mislead by a policy or rider, check with your lawyer, and give Mr. Flippen a phone call.

THE RESTORATION PROCESS:
A CUSTOMER PERSPECTIVE

by Bruce L. Adams

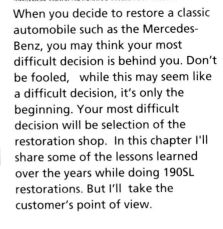

When you decide to restore a classic automobile such as the Mercedes-Benz, you may think your most difficult decision is behind you. Don't be fooled, while this may seem like a difficult decision, it's only the beginning. Your most difficult decision will be selection of the restoration shop. In this chapter I'll share some of the lessons learned over the years while doing 190SL restorations. But I'll take the customer's point of view.

An investment grade restoration should be viewed as a cooperative management task between the customer and the restoration shop. It's a complex project. For example, a "frame up" restoration on a 190SL will require 12 to 18 months to complete, may cost between $50,000 to $120,000; but more than time and money, it will require careful planning.

In my experience, a successful project plan for your 190 should focus on three areas: 1) a written workstatement, 2) a comprehensive billing system, and 3) an audit trail mechanism. In my view, a shop that can't supply a detailed description of the project, or that doesn't make this investment in planning your restoration, should not be considered for the job.

The remainder of this article will center on these three project areas. Other shops may use different terminology, but in general, a restoration project can be broken down into: the plan, the bill, and the audit. Regardless of the terminology they use, all three aspects should be addressed by your shop's plan. Keep in mind that the professionalism and completeness of the initial plan that's produced by your restorer are probable a good indication of that restorer's concept of management. A sloppy or incomplete plan will not produce a precise investment quality restoration, or a reasonable time schedule.

The Workstatement

Simply put, the workstatement is a written document that describes the detail of your restoration project. In my opinion, the workstatement is clearly the most important aspect of any restoration. It doesn't matter if you're talking about a "frame up" concours level effort, or a "driver," the plan must be in place well before the actual restoration work begins.

The workstatement will be written by the restorer, but the customer should have strong input and final details will undoubtedly be negotiated. At Sports Leicht, we always start the project with the customer by presenting a workstatement template that contains the general detail of any restoration. Then, working with the customer, the details of their particular project are addressed. I don't want to give the wrong impression of the workstatement. It's not chiseled in concrete. Rather, it's a living docu-

ment which will change via agreed amendments as decisions are made over the course of the project.

One of the first questions you must face is: What type of restoration are you having done? Does "show class" mean the same to you as the restorer? What's a "driver"? The following list of five classes of restorations has proved helpful in explaining the various types of restorations. I use it as a baseline of understanding with my clients. Your restoration should fit into one of the classes listed below, and its definition should be included in the workstatement.

Class One would be considered a top show car capable of winning a national meet. The car is not driven, it has been restored to the top professional standards with expense being a secondary consideration. If the car loses points at the Concours, which all cars will, it is more than likely that the reason is dirt. To be more explicit DUST, or streaks due to not cleaning the windows properly. Possibly too much grease on a door hinge. But there is seldom found something done incorrectly. All parts are New Original Specification (NOS), if available.

Class Two would be what most hobbyists consider to be condition one. The car may have minor flaws on parts that were restored but did not come out as if NOS. A class two car is garaged, driven occasionally, (averaging 1500 miles per year), but only in good weather. All of the accessories work as intended. The engine compartment has been detailed, the engine rebuilt to factory specifications, new leather interior installed, body completely removed of all rust, and a show quality, category 1, paint finish provided. Not all parts are NOS, but rather reproduction or reconditioned NOS. An example of this is NOS Solex carburetor are currently selling for

$2600.00 a set. Mikuni and Weber are available for $500.00 and perform better. Category one would install Solex's since it is not driven and requires NOS parts for concours. Category two would use a new Mikuni or Weber, or a reconditioned Solex. This type of car would win top place in sectional meets.

Class Three cars are also garaged, pampered and driven regularly in good weather. They may have the fine polished edge worn off of a few items but the car is generally very presentable and would be considered a very good used car. In appearance, it would be similar to a used car bought from a reputable dealer, in that the car had been gone through, thoroughly cleaned and waxed and put on the front line to attract customers in.

Class Four would be a well-used car needing no major work to be functional as a driver. This is what I would consider most of the 190SL's driven that I have seen to fit into this category. Some of the accessories may be missing, modified (such as transistorized ignition and radio, electric fuel pumps, etc.) or replaced with non-original equipment. The paint needs to be redone either due to old paint or a quickie paint job that shows up on rubber and chrome parts.

Class Five would be a motorcar that needs total restoration. Not total restoration to drive, but to be a number 2, everything on the car would have to be restored. The engine may or may not run, and if it does the car may or may not move on its own power. But a prudent person would be leery of driving it in that condition for any distance. The brake system needs to be completely restored due to lack of maintenance. Very few pieces of the chrome do not need to be restored to look new. There is a lot of rust that must be cut out and replaced with new parts. This is the area that must be ad-dressed honestly by the owner and is best left to a professional as to the cost of restoration unless the owner is qualified to do this type of work himself.

A good workstatement will also cover the terms and conditions of the project in detail. Some questions you should consider within the terms and conditions of the workstatement are:

How *much of a deposit is required?*

Who *makes the buying decisions for parts and materials?*

How *are third party relationships (subcontractors) handled?*

How *are significant differences from the estimated costs handled?*

What *happens if after starting the project, you are unable to complete the job?*

How *long would the shop store the car?*

What *is the charge?*

How *long will the work be warranted?*

What *conditions would void the warranty?*

Who *maintains liability, theft, fire, collision, or other insurance on the car while at the restorer's shop?*

While it's detail you're after in the workstatement, some areas will have to be estimated. This is especially true of the delivered cost. Be wary of any restorer who promises a fixed price for the job. There is absolutely no way to give a fixed price without examining and testing every component. Clearly this cannot be done. However, you should expect a restorer to be able to give you examples of his track record regarding estimates versus actuals on past restorations. Keep in mind that a fixed price shop will make tradeoffs in favor of meeting their price; whereas, if your goals are authenticity and safety, then different tradeoffs should be made.

Earlier, I divided conditon into five different classes. Regardless of the class of restoration, each project can be broken down into its component categories. This is done to pinpoint spending actuals against the estimated budget (more on this in the billing section). At Sports Leicht, we use the following category list to estimate the total project plan.

PROJECT PLAN:
(CONCOURS BUDGET)

1)	Parting Out Car & Dry Blast	00.00
2)	Welding	00.00
3)	Body Prep & Paint	00.00
4)	Fuel System & Carburetor	00.00
5)	Engine & Transmission Rebuild	00.00
6)	Engine Bay Detailing	00.00
7)	Front End Rebuild	00.00
8)	Rear End Rebuild	00.00
9)	Drive Shaft Rebuild	00.00
10)	Interior	00.00
11)	Chroming & Plating	00.00
12)	Brake System	00.00
13)	Electrical	00.00
14)	Heating System	00.00
15)	Rubber	00.00
16)	Exhaust System	00.00
17)	Final Assembly & Prep for Delivery	00.00
18)	Misc.	00.00

Estimated Project Cost:	**$ 00,000.00**

Of course, each of these categories in an actual workstatement would have complete detail based on the condition of the car to be restored. Remember, detail requires details! On your workstatement, you don't want to see an item such as :

Generator Rebuild

.... **$150.00**

rather, look for the restorer who can give you the following:

Generator Rebuild

.... **$150.00**
LJ/GEG160/12-2500RA: replace armature, brushes, 2 bearings, wrap field coils, labor and test 211550835 generator bracket

If you can imagine a complete workstatement with detail for each of the eighteen categories listed above, it is easy to see you're going to have a workstatement that runs into many pages. A complete detailed workstatement is your best insurance for a complete and thorough restoration - a restoration without surprises!

The Billing System
The billing system must be more than a typical "work performed / money owed" statement. It should be tied back to the workstatement catego-ries. It must not only answer the question, "How much do I owe this month?", but should be able to tell you where the money and efforts were spent this month as well as how the total monies expended to-date

Before: California Diamond in the Rough   *Body-off began after our*

match the workstatement estimates.

For example, if the engine restoration was estimated in the workstatement at $5,000, you should expect to see detail billing entries that show the progress being made - not just a hand-written one-line entry on a bill saying, "Engine - $5,000." When was the engine removed? Who did the work? What parts were needed, and how much were you charged for each part? Were the parts NOS. used, or reproductions? The detail on an engine-rebuild may exceed two and one-half pages. Just consider the materials, parts, and labor!

At *Sports Leicht*, we use a billing system that includes both a summary statement and a detail statement.

The summary statement tracks the original estimates from the work-statement by the eighteen categories. Side-by-side with the category estimates, a running total of project-to-date actual amounts is given. Both columns on the summary bill are totaled so that the customer knows month by month, what the estimate was, and what actual expenditures have been to-date. Finally, the summary page of the bill lists total payments made to-date by the customer as well as the amount currently due.

The detail section of the monthly bill does exactly what you'd expect. It provides detail! Every part used, every hour of labor, every outsourced sub-job are clearly listed by date, part number and type (NOS, used, repro-

2,000 mi. drive home.   *3,000 hours later: a new car, ready to go ...and show.*

duction), and dollar amount. Chroming and coach work are two areas that most restorers don't do themselves. They out source these jobs to their sub-contractors. Each line of the detail bill also has a category entry that refers back to the original workstatement. Again, the category entry is used to summarize the detail.

A good billing system will provide you with a month by month progress on your car. Remember, a 190SL restoration project can take 12 to 18 months. You don't want any surprises, and it's the billing system that can give you assurance that everything is on target.

The Audit Trail

If you have a detailed workstatement by category that clearly states what work that is to be done, and you have a monthly billing system that relates all work performed by category back to the workstatement, what can possibly go wrong? A lot - and a formal audit trail will go a long way towards solving problems before they occur. For example, go to a coach trimming shop and ask to see the "green" leather. The variations on "green" as a color are innumerable. Is the "green" you're looking at the correct one for the year and model of your 190SL?

Since the total project can span many months, its a good idea to have an audit trail mechanism that goes beyond the workstatement and billing system that I described. At

Sports Leicht, we use three: a 35mm picture portfolio, a video, and customer visits.

The picture portfolio is created month by month along with the billing detail. Each month, before and after pictures are taken of the work being done. Two sets of pictures are created. One goes to the customer with the bill, the other is put into a shop portfolio for the 190SL.

As the cost of video technology has decreased, we at Sports Leicht have started to take advantage of video to let our customers experience the progress of their car's restoration. The video camera comes out whenever we reach a milestone: the original parting out of the 190, return from the stripper, after the primer coat, the return of the major components (engine, transmission, rear end), the final paint, etc.

The final area of the audit trail comes from you! If at all possible, visit the shop. Not every week, but certainly at the critical stages. You may even consider visiting any of the sub-contract shops that your restorer is using. If you do this, you should involve the restorer in the process. After all, its the restorer who is ultimately responsible. Don't forget that along with the responsibility, your restorer should have authority to insure that you get the very best in materials and skilled labor that's available.

Some examples of critical stages include:

The **coach trimming**. Get samples of the leather and carpet being used. The leather should be split and scived (trimmed in thickness to fit contours and prevent blunt edges). You should expect to be shown examples of the coach trimmer's work.

You should have the opportunity to view the major **mechanical components** when complete, but before installation. This is especially important if you're doing a Concours level restoration. Little details that won't be noticed by you after the components are installed will be seen by judges during competitions (Speaking of competitions, does your prospective restorer compete in national and regional events? Has his shop won any *awards*? How do his customers do in competitions?).

One final point on visits. Plan to visit *before* the delivery date. Drive the car for two or three days and create a "punch list" to be worked before you take final delivery. Don't be shy when creating your list. Both you and your restorer should be looking for perfection.

Of these three audit mechanisms, I would insist on two. I would insist that **35mm pictures** be provided. Furthermore, I wouldn't do business with someone who didn't want me visiting during the critical stages. The video, while its a nice 'extra', is something that I wouldn't insist upon.

Besides preventing problems between the customer and the restorer, a good audit trail system will protect the investment that you're making in your automobile. Imagine the impact on a potential buyer if you can provide a complete history of the restoration. The reputation of the restorer can also have an effect on the potential value of your restored automobile.

SUMMARY
In this article I've taken a customer view of the restoration process. I've used my own practices as the example of what I believe customers should look for in a restoration shop. My systems - Workstatement, Billing System, and Audit Trail - are not the only way to ensure good customer relations. Other shops have other practices; however, in doing any restoration project, I'd recommend that you look for the same intent; a restoration with no surprises —regardless of the terminology used by the restorer.

Bruce Adams is the owner of Sports Leicht Restorations, (508)779-6513, a 190SL Restoration & Service Company in

DESIRABLE MERCEDES-BENZ OPTIONS

KEY (1): Most desirable options and often most difficult to add or replace. (2): Desirable (3): Popular (4): Less desirable but still more so than the large number not listed at all. AMG performance options refer only to power train & suspension components, not AMG cosmetics.

Some items listed as options for the 107 Bodies were in fact standard on North American cars.

Items	198 300SL Cp.	198 300SL Rdstr.	121 190SL	113 230-280	107 * 280-560
ABS Brakes	na	na	na	na	(1)
SRS Airbags	na	na	na	na	(1)
Air Conditioning	na	(4)	(4)	(2)	(1)
Automatic Antenna	(3)	(3)	(3)	(2)	(1)
Automatic Transmission (280/300/350SL)	na	na	na	(4)	(3)
Becker Radio (Mexico/Grand Prix)	(2)	(2)	(2)	(2)	(1)
Bumper Guards	(3)	std.	(3) rr std '57	(4)	(4)
Country Horns	(4)	(4)	(4)	(4)	(4)
Custom Paint (see text)	(1)	(1)	(1)	(1)	(2)
Five Speed Transmission	na	na	na	(1) frm '66	(2) 280SL
Fog Lights	(4)	na	(3)	(4)	std
Hardtop	na	(2)	(2)	(2)	std
Soft top	na	(1)	(1)	(1)	std
Heated or Orthopedic Seats	na	na	na	na	(4)
Heated Rear Window	na	na	na	(3)	std
Jump Seat in Rear	na	na	(2)	(3)	(4) Europe
Leather (seats only)	na	na	na	(4)	(2)
Leather (full, including dash, visors, all sides)	(1)	std	(1) std. on Cpe	(1)	(na)
Light Alloy Wheels	std magnsm	std mgnsm	na	(2) from "70	(3) pre '76
Luggage Set	(1)	(1)	(1)	(3)	(4) pre '75
Performance Options	(1)	(1)	(1)	(3) AMG	(1) AMG
Power Steering	na	na	na	(2)	std
Rudge Knock-Off Wheels	(1)	(1) pre '61	na	na	na
Show Car Detailing	(2)	(2)	(2)	(2)	na
Chromed Wheels	(2)	(2)	na	na	na
Tinted Glass	na	na	na	(3) from '66	std
Belly Pans/a, Undershields/b	a/std	a/std	b/(3)	b/(4)	b/(4) '67-'80

Rare Accessories:
The Frosting
On the Cake

by Robert Platz

If a scholarly effort was rendered on all Mercedes-Benz SL options it would fill a book by itself. There are over 100 options and most of them change for each SL, plus groups of suboptions. For example, suboptions of Becker radios would involve Europa, Grand Prix and Mexico models, in mono and stereo, which in turn had multiple model changes. Our goal here is to limit the option list to those items that have a significant impact in the collector car market place. 27 options are included in the chart at the left with a "rating" number by each one; 1 = most desirable, to 4 = less important but still more desirable than the large number not listed at all. Their desirability is not necessarily a function of cost but it is certainly true that, all else being equal, the larger the number of authentic accessories your car has, the more desirable it becomes. Some accessories are easy to add, while others like ABS brakes, airbags, or a 5 speed transmission are formidable conversions. This chart is my subjective assessment, based on 25 years of involvement with SLs. Hopefully it will contribute to the decision-making process when purchasing a collector SL, or when up-grading an existing one.

Anti-Block System (ABS)
Thought by Americans to be a mid-1980s innovation, ABS first appeared on Mercedes-Benz trucks in 1971, and the earliest sightings on Mercedes-Benz passenger cars is

Mercedes-Benz passenger cars is 1977, in Europe. So you will occasionally find a late 1970's European 350/450SL with ABS. Many of the "grey market" SL V8s from 1980 on have ABS. It was initially an unpopular option because few people understood it, or how it could be worth the $1,100 extra cost. It became standard on USA SLs in 1985.

Air Conditioning
Factory authorized, dealer installed A/C was offered in the late 1950s. The 190SL unit was entirely front mounted, and a rear mounted unit was prepared for the 300 series

decade.

Country Horns
Mercedes has always offered a country horns option, which entails two additional louder horns. They were absurdly heavy in the '50s & '60s. An on/off switch is mounted under the dash.

Radios
Mercedes cars were delivered without radios more frequently than American cars, but they are interesting examples of period technology that collectors like to have in working order. Becker has been the dominant radio supplier

Norbert Lamp, Bob Platz, and Howard Byron examining an engine bay. Is any car ready for this?

(including one for the 300SL Roadster). Both were built by an American Company, Arctic Air. 230/250/280SLs received an underdash design by the same company with the label "FrigiKing." It became an increasingly essential option with each

since the 1950s, though factory price lists in Europe also included Blaupunkt models. Non-German components are unauthentic until the 1990s, when we see Bose speakers for example.

Antennas

Naturally your radio must have a proper German antenna... manual or automatic, usually made by Hirschmann (some early Gullwing units were made by Wisi). The exact fender mounting hardware varies with every half decade, and model, too. Viva la details.

Bumper Guards

Whether rubber faced or solid chrome they have had no functional value (until 1974's 5 mph bumpers) and most SLs look well without them. Some people make sure they have the correct guards, but don't mount them.

Custom Paint

Personal paint requests beyond the factory's offerings were accommodated intermittently during the 1950s and 1960s, for decidedly premium fees. As production became computerized, special requests became hard to manage, and by the mid-1970s personalized passenger car paint requests were declined, unless you also were the Minister of Transportation ordering 100 Mercedes-Benz buses for the Kingdom of Tumalli. For a given year and SL model, there were a standard group of colors for selection and at extra cost, a greater group of colors was made available. Metallics tended to be in the latter category.

Color Changes

The crucial point here is that paint color is an option. The controversy comes about whether or not a color was original on the car. If the repaint is of equal or better than factory quality, and the paint color is a correct option for that year, then the changeover is acceptable. But typically, for the repaint that is less than factory quality, a color change will not be acceptable. A documented custom paint color, a rare standard color or a legitimate color at extra cost are all fair game to make a distinctive restoration.

5 Speed Transmissions

The 1960's ZF 5 speed gearbox is very rare. Offered from 1965 through 1969 (USA), and through '71 (Europe) it is found in two forms, a) fifth gear as .85 overdrive, or b) for mountain driving with closer ratios and a 1:1 fifth gear. When the twin-cam 280SL arrived in 1974 a Getrag 5 speed manual shift was offered in non-American markets. Since V-8 engines were trending to ever lower rpm ranges (quieter and easier to meet EPA rules) the 450/500/560SLs were only delivered with an automatic, geared to the growing regulations. It might surprise you but a properly tuned 1969 280SL five speed, with 9.6 compression and a 4.08 rear will out accelerate a USA delivered 1979 450SL with automatic. It'll pass the 450SL on the autobahn too, albeit more pollution, more too, albeit more pollution, more noise and less safety features. Pick your medicine.

Fog Lights
Now we come to those stylish fog lights. The horizontal Hella lights of the 1950s are often confused with the 356 Porsche but are in fact a slightly larger dimension. The 190SL light was distinguished by an over-hanging lip or hood on the lens frame. No other Hella or Bosch units have such a hood. The Gullwing used the same housing, but with a plain frame (no hood). The 300SL Roadster has its fog lights built into the tall headlight assemblies so no option was needed. The 113 cars of the '60s had circular lights. The #107's had horizontal lights mounted beneath the bumper as standard equipment.

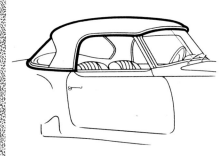

Hardtops
This is one of those options everyone wants but few use, as older SLs are sheltered more from foul or cold weather. Some 300SL owners have even retained the handsome wooden container their removal hardtop was

shipped in when new. Heated rear windows began in 1969, a sensible addition you'd expect from Mercedes-Benz... but you'll have to put your hardtop on to take advantage of it!

Soft tops
It is hard to think of a soft top as an option, but until the #107 came along, one could buy any SL as a roadster only, a hardtop only, or coupe/roadster (two tops). Hardtop only cars were bought by people who liked SLs but disliked convertibles. A variation of the 230/250/280SL "coupes" with a rear bench seat was unofficially nick-named "Californian." Today's collectors of SLs generally will add the soft-top, though it is not a simple addition, and parts are scarce.

Jumpseats
Driving an SL on a double date in college was feasible because of the jumpseat option. In the 190SL you drove the car; the two girls were in front, and the other guy was in back. A cushion between the two seats with no parcel box (a la #113) made this possible --lots of fun too. In a #113 or #107 on a blind date you would drive the car, the guy is in the passenger seat with his date in his lap, and your date is in back. Of course on a regular date, you get the other guy to drive, you and your girl take the passenger seat with the driver's date in the back. And with the 300SLs, forget it.

Leather

Most collectors view leather trim with suspension. At best it is an understandable cost cutting measure. Complete leather upholstery is what most everyone wants initially or at restoration time. Be cautious of reupholstered SLs as few upholsterers acquire the materials and apply the skills necessary to recreate an authentic looking interior.

Light Alloy Wheels

First offered as an option in the fall of 1969, they became standard beginning in 1976 (in the USA). Hence '70 and '71 280SLs could have this wheel option with part number 108 400 09 02 stamped on the inside of the rim. This number is supplied as the 350/450SL alloy wheels were different, and there are a lot of "fake" aftermarket variants. These early alloys were painted silver without clear coat. Americans call them the unknown option since no USA sales catalogues for 1970 or 1971 can be found to indicate their availability. An order in the spring of 1970 resulted in delivery of nine wheels. The car was built with standard steel wheels and four alloys came along as an extra, until July of 1970 when the factory got around to installing a compatible spare tire holder for an alloy wheel.

Fitted Luggage

Attractively upholstered wooden boxes conforming to the storage areas of the 1950s SLs were manufactured by Baisch and offered as luggage sets by Mercedes-Benz. These original suitcases in excellent condition are highly prized today. Some were covered in vinyl with pig skin leather corners, and others were 100% leather. In 1959, Mercedes phased out these individual sets with a single line of lighter, soft shell cases

made by Hepco. They were distinguished by large leather reinforced corners, and since the Hepco line comprised six cases, there was enough variety to outfit the 190SL. From 1959 300SL Roadster sets continued to be offered with hard shells, then made by Hepco. It is hard to beat the elegant appearance of a show quality SL with correct, fitted luggage. In 1963 Mercedes took over the luggage business themselves, using the same dimensions as Hepco, and producing an all vinyl luggage line for the 1960s and 1970s cars. It seems that by the mid-1970s the luggage game was over.

Olson with Hans-Werner Aufrecht,
founder of AMG, at factory in Germany

Performance Options

While Mercedes-Benz didn't use a label, their alloy bodied Gullwings were certainly a "factory performance package" for the client that wanted to go racing. Only twenty nine alloy bodied Gullwings were sold new (a few authentic alloy bodies have been installed on other Gullwings... after accidents mostly), and most of them have survived to this day. These cars were delivered with two rear axles (client's choice plus a 4.11:1) and even had plastic windows at the sides and rear to save weight. Also included were "NSL" racing cams with matched fuel injection units, Rudge wheels, sport springs, ventilated brake drums, and racing tires. Everything but the alloy body and plastic windows could be ordered on or for standard 300SLs. While less structured as a package, the 190SL was not left out; it was offered with cut down windowless doors, small windscreen, increased engine output and sport springs, shocks, and tires. Only a few buyers chose these options. And by 1957 the 190SL sports package was dropped from the catalogue. So few all-alloy bodied Gullwings were ordered that alloy Roadsters were not offered, even though one or two may have been made for **Paul O'Shea**'s successful 1957 USA racing campaign. The 300SL Roadster's performance options included a bumperless option, 9.5:1 compression pistons (instead of 8.6:1) continuation of the ventilated brake option, racing windscreen, co-driver's seatcover, and the customary upgrades of springs, shocks and tires. By the late 1960s, sportscar racing was history for Mercedes and performance minded buyers and rallyists were referred to the village of Affalterbach, to an ex-Mercedes employee named **Hans-Werner Aufrecht**. His AMG company has subsequently become world famous for it's high performance options made specifically for Mercedes-Benz cars. During the 1980s AMG retailed a full line of performance items capped by a thirty-two valve V8 "Stage IV" package in 1985. The success of this 400 hp engine, and the 190E 2.3-16, strongly influenced the proliferation of four valve per cylinder engines since then. By 1992 Mercedes-Benz dealers in Europe were selling virtually everything AMG could produce, and the Mercedes Motor Sports Department has asked Mr. Aufrecht to take charge of all running gear and engine tuning of all eight (four teams) Mercedes 190 E Evo-2 racers in the German Touring Car Championships [Mercedes took first place in the 1991 and 1992 manufacturer's title.] Today an SL owner's first step to increasing performance is buying a high performance computer chip from AMG that alters the engine's programed response pattern.

Rudge Wheels

These are a coveted 1950s 300SL option that is found on about 20% of all Gullwings, and 3% of all Roadsters. When 300SLs received disc brakes in 1961, Rudge (a brand name) parts were no longer compatible. While on the subject of wheels, Mercedes has not offered spoke wheels to the public since WWII, even though the 300SLR racers used them in 1954 and 1955.

Show Package

One of the seldom-coded features found on a few SLs is the dress-up given to cars designated for major car show exhibits. This typically entailed chromed engine bay linkages, polished parts and a little more care to paintwork. In the 50's and '60s these tweaked show cars literally backed M-B into having to deliver the same look when some enthusiastic customers requested it. Moreover, floor samples had to be sold, so today there is some interest in these features.

Belly Pans and Undershields

In the beginning a set of three light aluminum "belly pans" enclosed the entire undercarriage of Gullwings for air flow management purposes. As one of the pioneering body designs truly resulting from wind tunnel testing [with small scale models at Stuttgart Technical University in 1952] air turbulence between car and the ground was reduced, and engine heat was relieved out those more efficient and dramatic side vents. 300SL Roadsters received six smaller undershields enabling easier access for service. Heavy gauge protective undershields (and taller springs) were offered for the 100+ countries without a good highway system.

I'm sure some readers will say we forgot the ski racks, fire extinguisher, headrests, first aid kit, Reims short-wave, and so on. The goal here was to select what in my experience appeals to serious SL collectors.

Thanks to Gordon Beck,
Robert Martino, John Brownell,
Mike Egan, John Olson, and
members of MBCA for their assis-
tance on this chapter.

Robert Platz is the owner of Precision Autoworks, East Camden, NJ, and has been professionally restoring Mercedes SLs for over 30 years.

Alloy, finned brake drums of the 300SL are works of art, with 3" wide alloy shoes and steel sleeves. Drum at rear, right has extra ventilation scoops, a performance option.

USA
1957

Paul O'Shea

1933, 1936, 1957
National Champion

SCCA Class D National Championship for 1957 was earned with a team of two factory-prepared 300SLs. This photo was taken at Elkhart Lake in 1957 by SLML subscriber **Gary Stevens**, during his college days.

Before Paul died in 1991, he had the pleasure of witnessing the world-wide revival of the 1950s sportscars which he had raced. Named by **Sports Illustrated** as *Athlete of the Year* in 1955, Paul served as *Honorary Grand Marshal* of several major vintage sports car races in the late 1980s, and raced at Lime Rock as late as Sept, 1990.

SLML became good friends with Paul when **John Olson** restored a 300SL for vintage racing in 1988. The Mercedes

Museum's **Max vonPein** also assisted by providing many archives photos of the original two cars sent to the O'Shea/Tilp Team in 1957. Paul described additional changes made in the USA, such as open brake cooling holes below the grille (seen in the picture above). Paul felt the Roadster's low single-pivot differential made it far easier to maneuver than Gullwings, though he did add stiffer springs during the '57 season. The factory's contributions weren't more h.p. but a whopping 800 lbs. weight loss off the standard car, & improved air drag co-efficients.

SLML's 1959 300SL Roadster equipped with all M-B's performance options, at Elkhart in 1991.

4.
SLs are for
Driving

Why
Rear Wheel Drive?

"Vintage sport car racing experiences have magnified my awareness of a driver's capability to "talk" to the road through both the front and rear wheels..."

Since the first edition of this book was printed, rumors have developed that Mercedes-Benz is working on a new series of vehicles with front wheel drive. Despite that possibility, we think this chapter makes sense.

With all the fanfare about front wheel drive, have you noticed that none of the most costly cars in the world have front wheel drive...Rolls Royce, Ferrari, Lamborghini, or Mercedes-Benz? Aston Martin, Porsche, Lotus, the list goes on. To all of these builders price is not the point; rather it is offering the best possible car. Even in smaller cars, Mercedes-Benz had a new opportunity to introduce front-wheel drive with the 190 series. Why not? Can GM and Saab and Citroen and so many others all be wrong?

There are two issues. One is on-the-road-performance, and the other is manufacturing efficiency (costs). A few years ago during questions at a dinner talk by **Richard Teague**, deceased VP of Styling for American Motors/Renault (a long time collector of historically significant autos), we asked how front wheel drive was justified, when none of the greatest cars in the world offered it. His answer: "It has substantial assembly-line advantages. Front engine, rear drive layouts pose awkward assembly and quality control demands that are simplified with the elimination of a drive shaft and differential. These components require precision parts and alignment at both ends of the car." Front drive permits the engine and drive axles to be assembled entirely separate from the rest of the chassis/body, and dropped in (or pulled out) much quicker. The manufacturing savings per vehicle built, multiplied over a year's production, becomes millions of dollars.

The virtues of front wheel drive to the driver are fewer than we've been led to believe. While greater weight over the driving wheels creates more simple traction in a straight line, i.e. in snow, the actual percentage of improvement is easily erased through minor increases in accelerator application. In snow, once the slipping begins, recovery can be more inelegant than with rear-wheel drive. Living in Minnesota we see an equal number of front and rear-wheel drive cars getting stuck in the snow regardless what the ads say. And once stuck, getting out is about the same.

More important is what is lost when giving up rear wheel drive. Vintage sport car racing experiences have

magnified our awareness of a driver's capability to "talk" to the road through both the front AND rear wheels. For the average motorist this is most apparent in the rain. As cars approach the slipping point (especially slipping sideways) the driver of a rear-wheel power car has several options. 1) *altering front wheel steering direction* , 2) *reducing driving wheel power*, 3) *increasing driving wheel power and secondarily* 4) *applying brakes* .

Of these choices, number 3), applying increased power, defuses sideways motion by shifting it to forward motion ... the direction we wanted to go anyway. It serves a "duty" of sorts by giving the rear wheels and the road something to do together instead of just slipping past each other. With front wheel drive, applying increased power is almost not an option, as it can more easily cause the rear end to swing out further to the side even though the front wheels are retaining some traction.

With front wheel drive the front is expected to steer AND initiate AND terminate power, while the rear merely tags along ... no more help than a trailer! By distributing the driving power and the steering functions to opposite ends of the car, the driver has a greater range of choices for "holding" the front and rear of the car where they are wanted. I think the type of drivers who buy Mercedes-Benz expect & use good handling more than they realize ... in subtle ways, on large curves, in passing situations, and in sudden avoidance maneuvers.

Another haunt as front-wheel drive cars age, is engine resonance transmitted through the steering wheel. "Resonance?, I don't feel anything," the salesperson mused. But it was there. On a three hour drive, slight vibrations can make it seem like six hours!

Mercedes Benz Club of America Tri-Rama Time Trials

Driving Schools
and
High Performance
Driving

"The capacity of most cars is way above the capacity of most drivers. We try to even this out."
— *Robert Bondurant*

Q: Have you ever found yourself driving in the rain and discovering your front wheels want to continue straight when you need to turn? What do you do?

Q: You are driving a car that inherently understeers and therefore you should:

a) Trail the brakes deep into corners.
b) Squeeze the throttle on after braking in a straight line.
c) Use a higher gear than usual in corners.

Fact is both questions have similar answers... lack of front wheel traction from water or inherent understeer requires the same response; shifting weight to the front via deceleration and/or light braking.

There are several excellent schools across the country. Two that stand out are the *Jim Russell Racing School* and the *Bob Bondurant School of High Performance Driving* (which now resides in new facilities 10 miles south of the Phoenix, AZ airport). After listening to graduates and studying cold statistics we decided to attend Bondurant's top-of-the-line 4 day program. Here are some notes on our experience.

DAY 1: After a brief introduction by each student (ages ranged from approx. 25 to late 60s, and 2/3rd were doctors, lawyers & engineers), a welcome and course preview was given personally by Bob Bondurant. Our class had 12 students, and was assigned 4 instructors. We were then given a tour of track training facilities via Ford vans (Ford became enthused about the school a few years ago & now provides all vehicles free to the school, plus other valuable sponsorship). The track introduction was impressive in itself, as the large vans were dispatched around the course at surprising speed with no tire squeal & logic defying smoothness in the numerous corners. We'd just witnessed the impossible and were eager to learn how it had been accomplished. Next we were assigned to 5.0 Liter Ford Mustangs equipped by other sponsors Ronal wheels, Goodyear tires, Recaro driver's seats, Koni shock absorbers. Cars also had roll bars.

Breaking up into small groups, 1 instructor for 3 students, we were asked to follow our instructors in our Mustangs, through the course in parade fashion, to learn where the corners were & following the "line" they took. The first day was only 1/2

over, and we'd already had over an hour on the track. After lunch we brought the Mustangs over to some special skid-track circles where we were given the first ingredient in the high performance driving recipe: The effect of changes in speed (increasing & decreasing) on cornering. With the steering wheel turned into a circle & held in one position, we were told to accelerate until the car began slipping outward in the circle... then we were to decelerate without altering the steering angle. This caused car weight to shift forward, and the car immediately began cutting a tighter circle. Then on the gas again & out the car went. This phenomena is caused by expanding & contracting the outside steering wheel's tire patch size on the ground... driving home the point of how influential the heaviest corner of the car is to steering instructions during turns. Intellectually we may know the logic of this, but it is another matter to feel it

Bondurant's School of High Performance Driving uses "Skid Cars" which allow instructors to alter oversteer & understeer characteristics of the car while riding with the student practising corrective maneuvers.

occurring, and began to trust the knowledge in use. We then returned to a shortened portion of the main track to apply this steering technique into conventional corners... with light braking in the first half of the corners. Our next lesson was found in the adjective "light" braking, or *trailing the brake pedal well into corners* to keep the outward lean of the car slightly toward the front... on that outside front tire. Neither braking or steering can be so sharp as to lift the inside rear wheel to the point that its brake locks up... or the whole car will began sliding. Likewise, reapplying power requires the same finesse for similar reasons. The remainder of the afternoon we practiced these ideas on a variety of corners and speeds. The afternoon ended with a brief classroom critique. *Actual track time, 1st day: 4.5 hours.*

DAY 2: You may have seen press releases on driving school cars with "training wheels" as our photo here on page 120. Bondurant's "Skid-Cars" are much more than mere training wheels to prevent rolling. Each outrigged wheel is on a hydraulic elevator permitting it 4 different heights, controlled by the instructor riding with the student. Driving on a painted oval, a light front end or light rear end can be created to speed up learning about their effects in a safe spin-out area. A light front threatens steering & brake control. A light rear threatens traction and steering. The exercise was done in Skid Cars with both front & rear wheel drive. Up to a point corrective strategy is the same. Progressive braking to shift weight forward cancels front end sliding (under-steer). A light rear invites rear oversteer which required harder straight line braking and sooner on the gas in corners to shift weight back to the rear tire patches... neutralizing the rear's lightness. Steering, and where one arcs the corner are also important, but better saved for presentation in the course. One of the Mercedes owners in the course couldn't resist asking if rear wheel drive or front wheel drive was better in these critical maneuvers. All instructors acknowledged that in the last half of any corner, when acceleration is applied rear wheel drive has an advantage as in those moments weight *always* shifts toward the outside rear wheel, and away from the front wheels. The best traction will always occur where the tire weight patch is heaviest (largest).

Skid Cars also made it clear to us that sudden power was just as bad as abrupt on & off braking... both create unharnessed energy. We knew brake lock-up and wheel spin were bad; what we learned was the terrific potential of gently modulated braking & acceleration during corners.

One of Bondurant's strong points is training aids. After lunch we participated in accident simulation to learn our reactions & options when our lane of traffic is suddenly obstructed. Decision-making, car control, and evasive maneuvers were practised. We only rear-ended 3 of a possible 11 hypothetical cars during our runs. Our instructor gave us a score of 3.2 (2.5 being average).

Bob Bondurant (left) coaching Jorgen Andersen, a student that owns several Mercedes-Benz SLs in Europe.

The remainder of Day 2 we practiced techniques on a shorter loop of the main track. It has left & right corners with negative & positive camber curves with expanding & receding arcs. Each corner has its own best line & apex area. (apex is the area of a corner where the inside wheels are closest to the inside of the curve). Practice included drive & ride-along sessions with our instructors. They also drove behind and in front of us on the track each day to observe our learning. *Actual track time, 2nd day: 5 hours.*

DAY 3: After a chalk talk on the features of more of the track, our instructors again demonstrated the ideal line around the course. These ride-along sessions took place in Ford Taurus Sedans... V-6s with 220 hps. From 10AM to 3PM the 3rd day we turned on the juice on our 5 liter Mustangs, and were even allowed to pass each other at two locations on the track. After lunch most of our laps were timed so we could see how we compared with ourselves and other class members.

Near the end of the day we were introduced to single seat open wheel race cars we would be using the final day. These Formula Fords have no adjustable seats and are essentially built for each size driver (almost). Seating is more inclined as one might look if leaning back hard water skiing. Steering wheel is smaller, and instrumentation reduced. After a "fitting session" we fired up the beasts & followed our instructors around the main track 5 or 6 laps. What a blast! I'd expected to be more nervous about the open wheels, but, when actually behind the wheel, the visibility was so good & steering so precise, that fear disappeared. *Track time, 3rd day: 5 hrs.*

DAY 4: Written test time! The class is recognized by the Sports Car Club of America (SCCA) for 1/2 of its competition driving license so everyone was given a copy of SCCA's General Competition Rules book at the beginning of the course. We were asked about 40 questions on its contents. Everyone passed. Bondurant had their own quiz too. Answers were discussed after the tests. Then out to the Skid Cars again for a reminder of oversteer & understeer corrective maneuvers, and onward to our Formula Racers. For the balance of the day (until graduation session) we were on the main track. It was during this 4th day that the new knowledge we'd dragged through our brains began reaching our automatic reflexes. Everyone was also commenting on how well the individual techniques we'd covered were fitting together. It was reinforcing to experience the same track & corners in two dramatically different vehicles and utilize the *same* adhesion relationships. In retrospect, we'd given too much credit to vehicle differences, and not enough credence to generic principles of how the driver can manipulate weight to a chosen end or corner of any car.

It was more enjoyable at the wheel of the Formula Fords than I expected... carrying nothing along with us as superfluous as windows, extra seats, lights, etc. Just the important stuff in the right places such as mid-engine & rear wheel drive. By mid-afternoon we were all marvelling at what we'd learned in just 19.5 short track hours (28 hours counting classroom time). It is hard to imagine how the facilities or equipment at our disposal could have been better. Each day exactly what was needed was ready for our use. Time was extremely well thought out, as well as use of the grounds by other types of classes.

Finished product that it was, our graduation session even included report cards the instructors kept on each day of our work. Grading categories carry their message too.

We were all graded on:
- *Smoothness*
- *Consistency*
- *Concentration*
- *Attitude*
- *Line Technique*
- *Car Feel*
- *On Track Judgement*
- *Lap Times*
- *Heal & Toe Shifting*
- *Skid Control*
- *Accident Avoidance*
- *Trail Braking*

We also received a nice graduation plaque & a group photograph to remember our new friends. A class act in every respect. Bondurant also has special prices for alumni to take "refresher" sessions occasionally.

Yes, we left Arizona every bit as enthused as when we arrived. We wondered how we could have wait-ed this long to attend a program like Bondurant's. Everyone who likes cars fancies themselves to be at least "above average" drivers. Perhaps we all inhale some driving wisdom intuitively & multiply it irrationally by the years we manage to avoid major accidents. Even in vintage racing a 300SL for ten years I'd never really understood the logic of "trail braking". The Bondurant course teaches why certain consequences *have to occur* as a result of certain conditions... *and how those conditions can be controlled rather than naively tested in a moment of crisis.*
If you love to drive as much as you love your car's engineering and

beauty, a course of this type must go on your "to do" list. It is a rewarding & exciting experience to remember always. And it could save your life!

Convinced of the forgoing, we've arranged with the Bondurant School to conduct special 4 day courses periodically for Mercedes-Benz owners so you can have the experience with like-minded owners (and yours truly).

COSTS
All better known Schools charge between $500 and $700 per day, not always with the school providing vehicles. Bondurant will provide the cars (two types), and helmets when required, and suits, etc. Many schools offer 1, 2 and 3 day programs on various aspects of defensive driving and other basics. SL Market Letter decided Bondurant's best, 4 day program is the "no contest" winner for progressing to expert status without piece-mealing the subject into separate courses. Even if you never put a foot on a race track, the confidence you gain for personal driving, and the pleasure of knowing what professional drivers do know, is forever gratifying. Each class is limited to 12 students, on a first come first serve basis (subject of the school's screening & deposit process). Tuition at press time is $2495. We believe you'll never regret a minute, ...or a cent! Call the *SLML* Business Office if you'd like to sign up for our next Mercedes owner's grouping.

REQUEST FOR ENROLLMENT IN *SLML*'S NEXT 4 DAY COURSE FOR MERCEDES-BENZ OWNERS

•

*(While scheduled for SL Market Letter subscribers for Mercedes-Benz owners.
the course has no legal or operational affiliation with the
SL Market Letter. Inc.. 2020 S. Girard Ave.. Minneapolis. MN 55405 USA)*

• •

I'M CONVINCED. COUNT ME IN! I UNDERSTAND THE SCHOOL'S APPLICATION WILL BE FORWARDED TO ME AND I WILL BE SUBJECT TO THEIR NORMAL CANDIDATE SCREENING CRITERIA & COURSE PAYMENT POLICIES. SEND THIS FORM TO *SLML* IN MINNEAPOLIS.

NAME (PRINT)_____DATE_____

ADDRESS_____

OFFICE PHONE_____

CITY_____

HOME PHONE_____

STATE_____ POSTAGE CODE_____

COUNTRY_____

MERCEDES-BENZ NOW OWNED

_____

Entering the medieval city center of Narni during a "Mille Miglia."

Grand Touring - SL Style

*"Long term Mercedes owners
have all heard
(or are heard saying) that
Mercedes-Benz need to be driven...
that they actually run better if
driven regularly.
It is true that a variety of evils
threaten idle cars."*

One of the worst enemies of unused cars is condensation ...everywhere! In a half filled gas tank (always keep your tank(s) full when parked more than a couple of weeks to keep humidity from attacking the tank's inner walls), inside the brake system, (purge your car's brake fluid by replacing with new fluid every 18 to 24 months), inside the engine and exhaust system. (squirt oil in the spark plug holes). Even a car's smallest underbody scratches & dents take in moisture from the cracks in your garage floor (store cars on, not under, a large piece of plastic).

But wait a minute, the next pages are about using Mercedes-Benz cars on some very extraordinary travels, not pickling them! We've been forever saying that owning a special car is only two dimensional unless we learn how it performs as well as how it looks. Mercedes-Benz cars especially, were built to be used! Putting our action where our mouth is during the past ten years we've entered some of the world's most famous tours, rallies and races, and even equipped one SL with a roll bar and six point safety belts so we could go vintage racing.

It's not necessary to take your car to Italy or Colorado's high country to experience "grand touring." Privately planned trip counts if you treat yourself to your favorite Mercedes and an interesting route, preferably something several days or more in length. Rendezvousing daily with like- minded travelers adds another

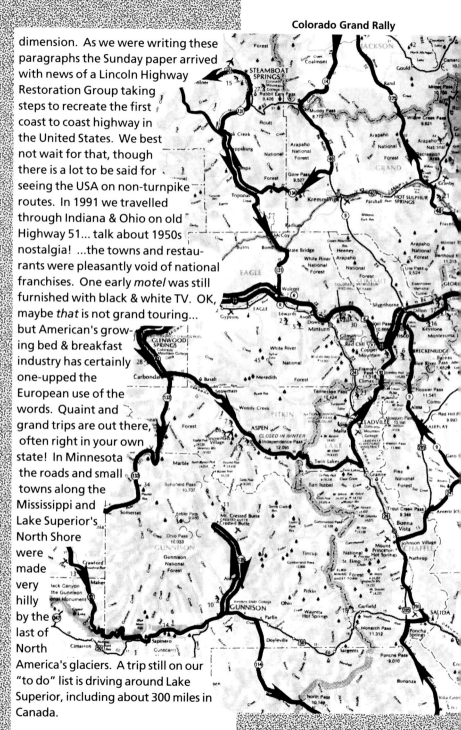

dimension. As we were writing these paragraphs the Sunday paper arrived with news of a Lincoln Highway Restoration Group taking steps to recreate the first coast to coast highway in the United States. We best not wait for that, though there is a lot to be said for seeing the USA on non-turnpike routes. In 1991 we travelled through Indiana & Ohio on old Highway 51... talk about 1950s nostalgia! ...the towns and restaurants were pleasantly void of national franchises. One early *motel* was still furnished with black & white TV. OK, maybe *that* is not grand touring... but American's growing bed & breakfast industry has certainly one-upped the European use of the words. Quaint and grand trips are out there, often right in your own state! In Minnesota the roads and small towns along the Mississippi and Lake Superior's North Shore were made very hilly by the last of North America's glaciers. A trip still on our "to do" list is driving around Lake Superior, including about 300 miles in Canada.

GRAND TOURING IN GROUPS

Car clubs have been sponsoring tours for decades. The Milestone Car Society has an annual Safari, as they call it, even the pre-WW II car clubs have their Glidden Tour. The real old-timers (pre-1905) have their Brighton Run. One of the larger (pun intended) sportscar collectors in the USA, **Bob Sutherland** of Colorado, has kindled fresh interest in American sports-car rallies. A perennial participant in Italy's Mille Miglia (every time with a different old vintage racer), Bob became inspired to reciprocate in 1989 by starting a beautiful "Colorado Grand" that his Italian friends might attend. Knowing Colorado's back roads & highlands from child-hood, many alternatives competed in his head. Colorado's wonderful ski resorts just added to the possibilities, and he found their owners willing to make special off-season deals.

He checked with the Office of State Tourism, the governor's office, and the state police. More people knew of the Mille Miglia than he realized, and all were eager to help. The result is the four & 1/2 day, 1,000 mile rally run every September. It is limited to 85 pre-1962 sportscars (and a few exceptions but no replicas). It has been an overwhelming success, pro-mpting similar events in Arizona (**Copper State 1000** each April), New Mexico (**La Carrera Reale** in May), North Carolina (**The Highland Classics**, through the Blue Ridge & Smokey Mountains each May) and California (**California Mille Miglia**). Some of these events admit sedans & go up to the 1972 model year. Most adopt a charity or two, such as Colorado's State Police Widows and Orphans Fund, M.A.D.D. and other worthwhile causes. Colorado's governor was so enthusiastic that he assigned the state's elite motorcycle troopers to accompany the entire event, provid-ing "an envelope of protection" to use their words. One officer was quoted at the end of the 1990 event video "I've never had so much fun before and been paid for it."

Each of these events has a little dif-ferent personality. Colorado's troopers close off a desolate section of highway for optional high speed radar clocked runs. At 9,000 ft. with 30+ to 50+ year old cars that doesn't result in many ultra-fast times. In a surprise at the final day's banquet the State Troops passed out a summons to every driver in the room, stating the speed they were clocked at, and requiring them to appear for sentenc-ing in exactly one year... at the next Colorado Grand! The 5 day **Copper State 1000** is sponsored by Mecedes-Benz of North America and the Phoenix Museum of Art. It starts at the Museum with a high-test Concours d'Elegance. **California's** route always includes over-night stops in the popular wine country. None of these Rallies are "cheap" ...typically $2,000 to $3,000 for two, includes food, lodging, entry fees, and a daily flow of favors & souvenirs, plus a generous percentage for charity. 90% of the fun is joining it with like minded enthusiasts... some very remarkable enthusiasts and a sprinkling of famous race drivers come out of the woodwork at every event. Some entrants are making the rounds to all of these events; it is an innovative way for sportscar enthusiasts to see America. We've gone to Colorado and Arizona, and Italy and Mexico so far. Here are the latest addresses if you want to obtaining applications!

Colorado Grand for pre-1960 sports & racing car each September:
953 S. Frontage Road W, Suite 222, Vail, CO 81657. Phone: 303-476-4939. FAX 303-476-5740.

Arizona's Copper State 1000 for pre-1961 sports & GT cars each April:
%Phoenix Art Museum, 1625 N. Central Ave., Phoenix. AZ 85004-1685. Phone: 602-952-0380. FAX 602-253-8662.

North Carolina's Highland's Classic for pre-1968 sports cars each May:
NCVM, Inc., P.O. Box 1652. Highland, North Carolina. 28741. Phone: 704-526-5031. FAX : 702-526-9601.

New Mexico's La Carrera Real for significant pre-1966 sports cars:
La Carrera Real, 2442 Cerillos Road, Santa Fe NM 87501. Phone: 1-800-435-8555.

California Mille for pre 1970s sportscars each September:
Amici americani della Mille Miglia, 2300 16th St, San Francisco, CA 94103. Phone 415-626-2300.

Italy's Mille Miglia for pre-1960 sports & GT cars each May:
Mille Miglia, Via Cassala 60, 25126 Brescia, Italy. Phone in Italy: 030-280036.

Mexico's Carrera Panamericana for any 1950s cars (roll bars required) each October: Carrera Panamericana - Mexico, Col. San Refael, Gabino Barreda No. 92, Mexico, D.F. CP-06470. Director: Eduardo Leon Camargo. Phone in Mexico: 535-26-23. FAX: 591-00-60. USA Coordinator: Loyal Truesdale, 3049 Laurel Canyon, Studio City, CA. 91604 Phone: 213-464-5720 FAX: 213-656-7111.

London to Beijing: CarrerVoyages Jules Verne, 10 Glenworth Street, London, England.

Australia Mountain Rally:
Automotion Australia Pty, Ltd. 549 Pittwater Road, Brookvale, NSW 2100, Australia. Contact: Tom Snooks.

Paris to Cape Town Rally:
Thierry Sabine Organization, 71, rue Desnouettes, 75015 Paris, France. Director: Thierry Sabine.

Rallies are a photographer's haven...
the variety of cars and settings is endless.
Here are several 1920's Mercedes during
lunch break of a Mille Miglia.

A Little Summer Excursion

DATES	TRAVELS	IN MILES
Late April	Minneapolis/New York	1,200
Early May	Car shipped to Italy	
May 18/20	Genova to Milan to Brescia, Italy	300
May 25	Brescia to Stuttgart	600
May 21/24	M. Miglia Route + misc. Brescia/Rome/Brescia	1,000
May 26/31	'87 *SL Market Letter* Tour with 17 subscribers in rented SL and SEL cars	1,300
June 1/7	Frankfurt/Rothenburg/ Heidelburg/Ladenburg	450
June 8	To Nurburgring and on to Paris Air Show and 24 hours of LeMans	700
June 13/17	North to Rotterdam via seacoast and backroads of France, Belgium, Netherlands	1,050
Late June	Car Shipped to New York	
Early July	New York to Minneapolis	1,200
SUMMARY:	Total in Europe	4,000
	Total to/from USA seaport	2,400
TRIP TOTAL:		**6,400 miles**

Mille Miglia 1987: A Retrospective

It took several months for us to come down from the incredible "high" of thirty days and 4,000 miles in Europe at the wheel of a 300SL. We met the absolute elite of European motorsports, from the organizers of the prestigious MILLE MIGLIA and its prominent entrants, to Daimler-Benz Museum Director **Max von Pein**, **Hermann Lang** and others.

We successfully completed the *Mille Miglia*, then joined our seventeen participant ten-day *SL Driving Tour* which included the *300SL Convention* (Stuttgart), and went on to the *Annual Mercedes Veteran Car Meet* at Carl Benz's birth place, Ladenburg (near Heidelberg). Next came almost an hour's drive (four laps) on the 14 mile long NURBURGRING race track, accepting a subscriber's invitation to the PARIS AIR SHOW, and concluding with a day at LE MAN's 24 HEURES DU MANS.

During the trip we interviewed **Oliver Gendebein** (winner of many 1950s races including LeMans, Mille Miglia), **Bernhold Ruckwarth**, '86 Mille Miglia winner in a '29 SSK Mercedes, and added fifty new signatures to our 300SL owner's Register. *SL Market Letter* subscribers came out of the woodwork to greet us, ...chance meetings in Modena, Paris and elsewhere. While we go over subscriber records regularly, putting faces with your names is always nice.

We shipped our car in early May to Mercedes-Benz dealer, **Novelli Spa** in Genova, Italy and flew there two weeks later. The following is a detailed description of our Mille Miglia experience.

local octopus and boiled anchovies. We picked up our car, remounted the rearview mirror, fog lights, etc. and drove to Milano to collect MM co-driver **Tom Warth**, and continued toward Monza. After dark, the engine developed unfamiliar clatter,

Warth and Olson descend the starting ramp of the 60th Anniversary Mille Miglia,
Brescia, Italy, May 21, 1987.
This was the second return of this car to Europe since in was built in 1955.

18 MAY: Night's lodging on Mediterranean. Fantasy setting! Eisenhower and Churchill conferred at this address in the 1940's.

19 MAY, TUESDAY - Received lunch invitation from Genova 300SL owner Giovanni Malvicino. His father, Felice, bought 300SL #735 new in 1955! Giovanni and his father participated in two previous Mille-Miglia. Giovanni coached me in the contest's rules over freshly caught

and misfired above 4000 rpm. We re-routed to Brescia.

20 MAY, WEDNESDAY - Brescia Mercedes-Benz Consessionia BONERA Spa. diagnosed two damaged rocker arms caused by adjustment arm nuts coming loose. TWO! MERCEDES ROME told BONERA that they did not have the necessary parts! We started to phone logical sources in West Germany when Mercedes- Benz dealer **Carlos Bonera** turned out to be a 300SL enthusiast himself,

owning both a Gull Wing and Roadster. He and his son had also entered their Gull Wing in the Mille Miglia. He graciously came to our rescue removing the necessary parts from his 300SL Roadster to install on our car and refused to give us a bill!

21 MAY THURSDAY - We were ready for pre-start check-in at the famous *Piazza Vittoria*. Sun was bright and the atmosphere near Mardi Gras pitch. There were hundreds of people with cars from four decades, all in spit-polish condition. 290 entrants were to cross the starting line at twenty-five second intervals starting at 8:00 pm. We made a last minute check list with our sweep car crew, **Paul Robinson** and son **Randy**, from Kansas City. They rented a Porsche 944 and trailed us along the same route (except medieval walled city centers which are restricted to official participant cars). Our #132 departed at 9:54 pm. Throngs of people at the roadside extended *ten miles* out of Brescia from the start. It is said that driving through these crowds causes more engine troubles than open roads. It became dark soon, but even after midnight we saw faces at the roadside of every farm and village. Only in Italy during the MM can you roar through a small community over double the speed limit and be cheered on while doing it.

I was struck particularly by the wide range of spectator ages, from very old-timers who must have stood near the same spots with the same waves thirty or fifty years ago, to mothers with children sitting in high chairs. Also immediately noticeable: Italians, men and women alike, are not capable of waving with one hand or arm. They wave everything! Arms, head, shoulders, hats, the person next to them. The 300SL is not exactly a common sight in Italy and they especially responded at the sight of our "rossa" Mercedes, the Italian racing color.

During the first evening, we passed through Verona, Vicenza, Padova, and Rovigo and arrived at our destination of Ferrara at 2:00 am. All cars were parked and locked bumper to bumper in the town square, and we went straight to bed at the designated hotel (three days food and lodging for drivers and crew were included in the entry fees). MM engine sounds danced in our dreams.

22 MAY FRIDAY - After four hours of sleep came breakfast and an official departure again at 7:54 am. A long drive to ROME with arrival not expected before 10:00 pm. Now cometh our real introduction to Italian driving; it helped to understand the Italian's special arrangement with things legal. Chicago entrant **Joe Marchetti** put it well when he said Italy is the nation of "provisioni", or "rearrangement" to serve the situation at hand. This flexibility extends to driving. For example, it is commonplace for three cars to slip past each other on a two lane road when the center is clearly painted for no passing. Everyone seems fully aware and willing to adapt.

The Mille Miglia is held on two-way, two-lane public roads, with no effort to restrict traffic, be it trucks or the afternoon bicycle race we encountered! Certainly extra accommodation is made for the MM; police are seen admonishing local drivers for not giving priority to entrants. We were asked in particular to stay on the right side of the street in towns, and obey stop lights, though in practice we are waved (by police) through all but two or three red lights and encouraged irresponsibly by enthusiastic crowds. We learned early on NEVER to follow directions from spectators; they have thirty different gestures all of which mean go faster, pass, or stop for some wine.

There is a contest in all of this celebration, including several layers of timed segments within each day's overall average speed goal. We were told not to get too serious about the competition; last year's winner, **Bernhold Ruckwarth**, told us that winning the MM is not a sport; "It is a mathematical science of hundreths of a second," which is unlikely to be won twice by the same team. Our own schedule book called for precisely six hours, 59 minutes and 59 seconds between Rimini and Perugia. We arrived 2.33 minutes late, putting us in 96th place. Concurrently (different stop watch) we were to travel a measured Republic of San Marino course in exactly 11:01 minutes. Another slow section in 6:59 minutes. Then, from Pietralacroce to late lunch at the sea coast town of Numana, came some faster Adriatic Sea roads. Our times were quite good Friday morning, and we arrived within half a second at most check points. At Marina Alta we were in 29th place!

After lunch we left the sea, turning west into heavy mountains. Although the driving was hard on car, tires and driver, it was fun, turn after turn after turn. We noticed that all the shops closed, including gas stations, until 3:00 pm. Luckily, we needed no fuel, though we found Italian gas to be very hard on spark plugs. An engine miss at idle crept up the rpm scale as the plugs deteriorated. One Italian M-B mechanic told us we had a bad coil. We installed our spare, but there was no improvement. Fortunately, the miss disappeared at higher rpm where we spent most of our time.

Gas and oil prices were one of the shockers of our adventure: $4.30 per gallon. Filling our 34 gallon tank meant, yup, $146.20! Then there's that 15 quart oil dry sump oil system at $8.50 per qt. Happily, gas is a mere $2.75 in Germany. From here those big American companies look like saints!

The city of Assisi, important in Catholic history, rolled out its carpet

BRESCIA

Map labels: VICENZA, VERONA, MONTICHIARI, MANTOVA, CREMONA, PARMA, REGGIO EMILIA, MODENA, PADOVA, ROVIGO, FERRARA, BOLOGNA, PASSO DELLA RATICOSA, PASSO DELLA FUTA, FORLI, RAVENNA, RIMINI, CATTOLICA, CASTEL DI MEZZO, PESARO, MUGELLO, FIRENZE, S. MARINO, ANCONA, NUMANA, P. RECANATI, FABRIANO, LORETO, MACERATA, TOLENTINO, GUBBIO, SIENA, PERUGIA, RADICOFANI, FONTI DEL CLITUNNO, TERNI, NARNI, VITERBO, RIGNANO FLAMINIO, **ROMA**

of spectacular ancient buildings, old regional clothing and gifts to each entrant. Toni showed our engine to a curious monk who responded with a special blessing on the machine. Most check points were in the centers of historic villages accessible only through medieval gates, moats, cobblestone streets and grand "piazzas." The charm of it matched fairy tales, as our times schedule eroded. These check points were mandatory to show the organizers we did not short-cut.

The weather was sunny and warm until late afternoon, when the only rain occurred. We were glad our car had a roof as 75% had no tops at all, and 30% were pre-1940 machines. The cars spread out more. We saw broken cars, though the AUTOMOBILE CLUB OF BRESCIA had car transporters picking up casualties promptly. We learned later that over 100 cars do not finish before closing Saturday evening. An occasional C-Type Jaguar or Ferrari blasted past us. It was not that we couldn't keep up; we did follow several for short intervals, but then reminded ourselves that their pace far exceeded the timed aspects of the event. Darkness set in. We were not fed again until 10:00 pm in Rome.

Before leaving the USA we had put in a request to MERCEDES-BENZ ITALIA for two Michelin XWX 215VR 70 x 15 to be installed in Rome. Upon arrival we found no Mercedes

mechanics at the finish area and no instructions at our hotel. We called Rome's M-B ROAD ASSISTANCE number and were told we must drive to the other side of Rome (!) where two mechanics were waiting with four new tires. We said we only requested two. No matter, come and they will be installed. The person on the phone knew nothing about pricing. As on the previous night, cars were parked together, bumper to bumper.

At great inconvenience, after midnight, we found our way across Rome to the designated address. A guard and two workmen (none of

whom spoke English) directed us to the second floor of an enormous service center. They raised the car and loosened the wheels. As we watched, our eyes fell on the new tires. They were the wrong size!!! Work stopped. Frantic phone calls were made. Eventually, the phone was handed to me and an executive said that Michelin does not make XWX in the 215 size and we must take these four tires as they have been purchased for us. I replied we are sorry but Michelin does make 215 and we ordered only two. He claimed that the tires were not returnable, and he must also bill us for two mechanics for two hours over-time. Now, it had been a very long day, but we were not *that* tired. We might at least have been informed of the tire difference before our post midnight drive! We asked to be given back our car and old tires so that we might return to our hotel and get a little sleep. The mechanics got back on the phone and with very straight faces reassembled and released the car (we did at least tip the mechanics). *By Contrast,* the Mercedes-Benz "OLDTIMER'S SERVICE" we found at two subsequent European car events had mobile workshops and mechanics trained in the old models.

23 MAY, SATURDAY - Beautiful sunshine. Everyone fired up their engines. Wonderful sounds. We gassed up (gulp) at what was advertised to be the world's largest gas station (yet they would not take credit cards). Departure was at 7:54:35 am again. We finished a loop around the bottom of Rome and headed north doing the first timed segment 4/10th of a second off prescribed time, putting us in 35th place. That was as good as it got for us. One thing or another made subsequent times worse.

The very next time check was interrupted by our meeting **Oliver Gendebein**. This great racer, now approximately 60 years old, drove a Gull Wing and placed second to John Fitch's 300 in the GT Class of the '55 Mille Miglia. Gendebein explained that he was leading Fitch for all but the final few miles, when he had a tire blow-out. He quickly jacked up his car to switch tires when the jack fell over. People at the road actually picked up one corner of his car to get the spare installed. Fitch rushed by just as the spare was mounted and it was too late to recover the lead. He also said that Fitch's '55 Gull Wing was factory prepared for racing with 300 hp and competition springs, while Gendebein's was his privately purchased 240 hp version offered by M-R dealerships. Gendebein checked our car over closely as he said his was red. He wondered at first if it was his old car, but no such luck. Gendebein co-piloted a silver 300SL that day. He said he had raced faster cars, but the 300SL was the most dependable of them all, and that is why it often won. Suddenly, Tom shouted, "We're late! We're late to the next check point!" We hastily thanked Gendebein and drove on. We arrived 1.49 minutes late, but it was worth it. Proving how small the world is, we next met fellow Minnesotans **Robert Bodin** and **Karl Dedolph** in Bodin's

L-R: Olson, Gendebein, Warth

250 GT Ferrari. Bodin's car was driven by Oliver Gendebein to third place overall in the 1957 MM! After a little 120 mph driving (along with Bodin) before Florence, everything changed to a much slower, scenic mountain ridge run. Italy's answer to the MULHOLAND DRIVE near L.A. but much longer, without *any* residences and very few trees obstructing vision. What a dream! It just doesn't get any better!

Gifts from village mayors and ministers of sport and tourism began filling our car, all with MM inscriptions. Clocks, scrolls, champagne, a 220vt hair dryer, specially cast coins, frequent examples of local craftsmanship. While English is not spoken by many Italians, the towns people were totally dedicated to aiding us everywhere. Before the start in Brescia we asked how to get to our hotel. They led us there even though it turned out to be long distance.

In another fast stretch we were passed aggressively. When each of us drove the other seemed to put on the "drive safely" hat. I guess it always seems safer when you are at the wheel. Tom proved to be a good "co-pilota," alert to things I missed and vice-versa. The problem as often as not was those wonderful spectators. They were everywhere. While we entered one town a truck turned in front of us. We swerved and braked to a standstill. Everyone ran. Too close.

No one knows how many people watch this "happening" each year. For the entire 2.5 day circuit one estimate is 15 million people (25% of the entire Italian population) - clearly a national event. Another estimate is "too many." The original Mille Miglia races were ended in 1957 due to several bad accidents involving spectator and driver deaths. As hard as the current organizers try (and they try very hard) the odds of maintaining sufficient safety are shaky. On the other hand, MM crowds are for the most part veteran crowds. They have been here before and they are showing their kids. They know what is going on as no other audience. They *want* the MM to prevail. Tom expected to see and looked for some public opposition to this uncivilized sport. Nothing appeared. They LOVE it.

Next check point was Bologna. Our gift: a fat 15 inch long bologna of course! From there we came to the second major timing stop of the day, Modena, right in front of the Ferrari factory. Only 3.9 seconds off (early) in a four hour, 51 minute and one second segment. Good for a mere 88th place. These Europeans are good! We had hoped to see Enzo Ferrari, but he is nowhere to be found - at least not while we were there. A European Ferrari Club also held a Convention there on this weekend, and they had not seen him either. We ate a few snacks courtesy of Ferrari and departed for our final four hours, 49 minutes and 59 seconds, zig-zagging through Cremona and Mantova, to Montiichiari (the last official timing point).

The finish in Brescia was merely a physical check point at which we must appear. Our gas supply was running a little low. We probably could have made it, but that is not the kind of a mistake to make so near to the end. It was after 6:00 pm Saturday night in Italy. Everything was closed, but we spotted some people leaving one shop with a pump so we drove in. Of course they re-opened for us.

Entering Brescia was dramatic for two reasons: people again lined the streets from way outside town, and got so thick near the finishing bleachers that no one could see what was happening. That turned out to be a good thing for us because we had our only mechanical failure thirty feet from the finish line! The electrical fuel pump died flat. In slow, hot traffic this pump is mandatory. Thirty feet to go! Tom got out and pushed as I steered us across the finish line. Unbelievable. What a way to end the MM! We were carrying a spare pump, so we steered over along the finish line and installed it in about eight minutes. We roared the engine and waved our doors so that everyone saw that we were moving again under normal power. The crowd cheered as we drove on to our hotel, a welcome shower and dinner. We did it! The drive of a lifetime! So many things to remember!

At dinner with our faithful crew, Paul and Randy, we realized how special the animated Italian spectators were to this colorful madness. Even if a road circuit could be selected in other places like this one (not likely) the overwhelming combination of zest and quaintness of the Italians could not be duplicated anywhere on the globe. Italians really love sports cars and their presence and enthusiasm are integral to this wholly unique summer drive.

Our hats are off to the *MUSICAL WATCH VETERAN CAR CLUB* and the *AUTOMOBILE CLUB OF BRESCIA.* Things certainly ran like a well restored clock! From our original application to food, lodging and overall logistics, all was impressive: 290 starting vehicles meant approximately 580 drivers plus many extra sweep car crews and officials needing room and board for three days in three cities, plus a scoring nightmare that was finished in individually personalized results booklets by breakfast time Sunday morning. And they weren't done yet: Sunday was reserved as "gift-giving" day for the winners with a huge noon banquet. Everyone dug out their white shirts and ties this time, savoring final recollections with everyone together. We have attended many car events in the past 25 years, but this has to take our prize as the biggest, best run, and classiest we have ever joined.

Automobile Club Brescia

Driving Rented SLs In Europe

There are a few rental companies, mostly in Germany and France, that will rent the newest, largest Mercedes models by the day, week, or month. It is great fun is for a group of enthusiasts to rent a dozen autobahn burners together and rendezvous at preselected destinations each night for libation and lodging. The conclusion of the Mille Miglia marked the beginning of a 10 day SL DRIVING TOUR in West Germany, France and Switzerland. Seventeen of us (including six couples) gathered at the MM finish, went by train through Austria to Stuttgart where we had reserved 300SL, 420SL, 500SL and 500SEL rental cars.

During the next week we covered about 1,300 miles, though it always seems like more in Europe due to the number of small towns and curvy two-lane roads. As in some parts of Pennsylvania, you are either making fast tracks on the turnpike or caught up in the quaint, twisting, sometimes mountainous roads. The SLs are a dream for either kind of road.

From Stuttgart we went up the Rhine for overnight in an ancient castle high above the river at Oberwasse. Then down along the French border (some entered France as everyone selected their own routes between hotels), and meeting again at the great Casino and Spas of Baden-Baden. Truly talented chefs are more prevalent in Europe; our meals were always above average, and in many

places exceptional.

Next we used our special Visas [required in '87] to visit the remarkable Schlumpf Brother's car collection (now the French Museum National) in Mulhouse. For starters it boasts the largest gathering of Bugattis in the world, then it becomes apparent how many rare Mercedes-Benz are also present. How did they get them! Actually some were only loaned to the Schlumpfs... but the French don't see it that way. French courts determined that this elaborate, private collection was illegally financed by union pension money before the fall of Schlumpf's textile dynasty. Thus when France took on the pension obligations, they gained the collection.

We left France via a six lane Swiss autobahn to Germany's largest lake, the Bodensee, for more choice dining. Soft tops went up as we

headed toward an annual gathering of 1950s 300SL owners. Wet or not, Stuttgart was a big attraction since the affair would be near and at the factory. There were 100(!) old 300SLs peppered with 300Sc Cabriolets, a 600, a Schultz 300E Convertible, and ...our rented SLs. Knowledgeable owners drove in from many countries. For example an inventor from England, **Ron Cushway**, even had installed ABS brakes on his 300SL Roadster.

Our group was granted permission to participate in the rally because we'd rented SLs. Cameras were busy. A scenic rally even looked beautiful when it rained - fields and forests were lush with vivid greens. This route included stops at Gottlieb Daimler's birth place, the D-B proving grounds, and quiz questions on SL, Mercedes and Benz history.

A cadre of M-B mechanics hovered about. Most of them were students in Daimler-Benz Technician and Master Mechanic programs, which of course include backgrounding on the older cars. The Mercedes-Benz Museum is dutifully passing on the knowledge needed to care for the older models.

Mercedes-Benz hosted several aspects of the meet, the most conspicuous being that Saturday evening's festivities. The Stuttgarter Hotel's main ballroom was aglow with a myriad of flowers, exceptionally fine live music and food served dramatically by the hotel's entire staff. I have yet to attend a banquet executed with such style by any hotel in the USA. Dancing and socializing continued after 2 am! Yours truly received the award for the longest distance travelled with a car.

After the 300SL convention our touring SLs headed toward Frankfurt via Rottenburg, an ancient, walled village on the famous "Romantic Road." Our last supper together was at the Gravenbruch-Kepinski, a grand country hotel near the Frankfurt Airport. We turned in our rental cars at this airport.

Whenever sixteen to twenty like-minded Mercedes enthusiasts put up their hands the SL Market Letter is happy to join in and suggest an itinerary. Leave your name with *Peer Gynt World Ventures* (612-377-0155) if you want to be notified of our next adventure. They usually include some major events such as a Paris Air Show, spectating at a Grand Prix race or the vintage Mille Miglia, and visits to Mercedes-Benz class restaurants. Proper vacations!

PEER GYNT WORLD VENTURES

(612) 377-0155 FAX (612) 377-0157
2020 SOUTH GIRARD
MINNEAPOLIS
5 5 4 0 5
U S A

Peter Helck died in 1988 at 95. It was a special if anticipated loss for us at the SL Market Letter, as we corresponded with Peter many times and saved all his letters. His fascination with racing scenes began in the "brass era"; he saw his first race in 1906 and his work extended into eight decades! This scene is of course Stirling Moss in a 300SLR achieving the fastest (10 hours) win ever recorded in the Mille Miglia, in 1955.

Coast To Coast
In 47 Hours

"In a field of V-12 Ferraris, Porsche Turbos, Maseratis and veteran drivers of the other famous Cannonball runs, a Mercedes-Benz slipped across the nation to win the event 44 minutes ahead of the second place DeTomaso Pantera."

Only two Mercedes-Benz cars were accepted in the starting field of thirty cars for the 3000 mile Boston to San Diego Rally in June 1982, but those two cars got more attention than all the others combined. One was the oldest car to complete the event, our 27 year old 300SL Gull Wing Coupe.

The other Mercedes was the newest entry, a 1982 380SEL sedan entered by **Steve Cook**, Chief Instructor of the *Bob Bondurant School of High Performance Driving*, and **Mike Begley**, his co driver. In a field of V-12 Ferraris, Porsche Turbos, Maseratis and veteran drivers of infamous Cannonball runs, the 380SEL slipped inconspicuously across the nation, without a single speeding ticket at the incredible average speed of 80 m.p.h., winning the event and finishing 44 minutes ahead of the second place DeTomaso Pantera. The elapsed time: 37 hours, 18 minutes! Twenty-one cars finished, including both Mercedes Benzes.

The 300SL Gull Wing, driven by yours truly and **Don Rose** of Salem, MA, also made its passage without surprises, though at the more sedate average speed of 65 m.p.h.. We arrived to flashing cameras and San Diego TV coverage in 47 hours.

The Four Ball Rally, as it was called, was new that year, privately run by members of two Massachusetts families. The object: to drive from Boston to San Diego in the shortest time possible, demonstrating the ability of cars and drivers to do so quickly, yet safely. A $10,000 first prize attracted entrants from fourteen states and Canada. Some participants made extensive modifications to their cars, planning many months ahead. The most common modification was adding fuel capacity. The 380SEL carried 95 gallons, enabling it to cover the entire trip with only one gas stop, in Tulsa, Oklahoma.

Our 1450 mile trip from Minnesota to Massachusetts for the start was a perfect shakedown cruise. With notes from this trip ranging from a loose vent window to tire balancing, the *Paul Russell & Company* put up to five mechanics on the car in a comprehensive inspection and correction procedure covering every part. A pinion seal was found leaking and replaced. Outer sway bar rubbers were replaced. Front brake pivot spacers were binding and replaced. Kingpins were tightened. All fluids were changed and fittings greased. Cylinder head and cam towers were hot torqued and valves adjusted cold. All tires were balanced... and rebalanced.

In between all of this *AVP Restorations* (next door) took the car under their wing for an all night session of cosmetics, so the finished product could as easily have been off to a concours d'elegance as to the starting line of a 3,000 mile endurance run. *Paul Russell & Co.* and AVP Restorations donated a combined total of over sixty hours of pre-rally prep. time and concours detailing, checking over all aspects of the car to ensure a handsome, faultless showing. **Paul Russell** said, "Gull Wings were originally built for exactly this type of major, long distance, express driving. I am pleased to help make the Gull Wing's entry possible." We know its appearance delighted everyone connected with the event, including its competitors.

Banquets were held at the beginning and end of the rally, which aided in getting to know some remarkable people and some of their strategies. Several were father and son teams (two drivers, no more nor less permitted), doctors or business owners. A New Jersey psychiatrist offered second and third place drivers a free couch session. One Ferrari owner brought a mechanic as his co-driver (shades of the era when most racing cars carried driver and mechanic). A Porsche owner had been planning how to win for six months and even interviewed some NASA people on what he should eat. His equipment included a police radio scanner and radar scrambler (highly illegal, of course). Some level of justice prevailed: his engine came apart in the first 800 miles, and he never appeared at the finish line. The cars departed at three minute intervals in downtown Boston traffic. We drew starting number 20 and left at 1:57 PM, Friday June 11th. Everyone picked their own route, which led to over 250 miles difference among the finishers. Some went south early (one actually stopped at the World's Fair in Knoxville), and others went through New York and Buffalo to avoid construction on the Pennsylvania Turnpike. Most went through Indianapolis, St. Louis and Tulsa. After Amarillo, many alternatives ensued. We braved a path off the interstate which became the high point of our trip: Highway 89 south (just west of Flagstaff) through Prescott, through some severe but well maintained mountain roads and down into Congress. From here southwest-ward were unbelievable, ruler-straight 30 mile stretches of perfect, desolate highway, clearly built for one purpose: getting somewhere else. At one spot entering a small town we actually saw a sign that read: "RESUME SPEED LIMIT." That entire 275 miles has to rank as one of the most delightful roads for anyone touring the South west. Our fastest average speed (35 minutes at 130-135 m.p.h.) was logged on this unexpected leg of the rally. Traffic was almost zero, as our southward trek was in early morning with the sun just rising behind us.

Everyone used some form of radar detector, some both front and rear. The 300SL is so conspicuous and inviting to local and state patrols that we would even get shot at with radar when leaving or entering gas stations at 10 m.p.h.. It kept us on our toes. Out on the road, the object is to have long enough range to pick up radar shots at other cars before coming into its range. Rapid deceleration (3.15 m.p.h. per second, the equivalent of dropping from 70 to 55 m.p.h. in 3.8 seconds) reportedly causes erratic inputs which "reject"in a radar unit. Neither Don nor I had ever used a radar detector before this trip, and we found our-selves patting the unit affectionately more than once! After only four stops, thanks to our 34 gallon fuel capacity, we rolled into San Diego at 10:18 am, Pacific time. Breakfast looked good!

It is said that Mercedes-Benz cars last longer and run better when they are used, the logic being that if things are not used, they dry out and become brittle faster than they wear out from use. We can testify that our 7,400 mile trek made the Gull Wing sing more sweetly than ever. Gas mileage actually rose from 17.3 m.p.g. to 19.8 m.p.g. during our coast-to-coast run. Water and oil temperatures sat on a steady 190 degrees no matter what the speed or grade. We certainly have to agree with Paul Russell that our excursion was no more than a normal day's work for our 27 year old car. Routine. And very impressive. We were never bored.

Long Distance Rallies

No sooner did we get home from one our car adventures when we heard **John Johnson** interviewed on WCCO... he'd just finished a book about his 9,450 mile "drive" from London to Beijing, China! Suddenly we were humble again. We hadn't even heard of this Minnesota native so we called him immediately for a lunch date. He'd also driven with his son from London to Cape Town, South Africa, and was planning a trek from Oslo to the Arctic Circle.

John's London-Beijing trip took 53 days, and included seven Mercedes-Benz among the 60 starting cars. The organizers, Voyages Jules Verne of Berkeley and London, took several years to negotiate the governmental permits needed for the expedition. The logistics of moving such an entourage through many primitive regions even involved scheduling gas trucks to meet the travelers when filling stations were non-existent. In a few cases destinations were set by compass!

The seven Mercedes were quite a mix of models, and they all finished. Naturally, we'd have seen to it an earlier decade was represented. Seven other pre-WWII cars were on the entry list, and four more were 30 to 45 years old. Several people participating were in their seventies too. The oldest vehicle was a 1912 Simplex Speedster! We think we'll stick to the comfort of our thirty five year old Mercedes, thank you.

*The Scottish/English team of **Andrew Cowan & Colin Milkin** earn themselves a deep draught in Buenes Aires as winners of the 18,500 mile '78 South American Rally in their 450SLC. Thorough planning for 15,000 ft. mountain passes included oxygen respirators.*

Mercedes in Beijing Rally	Entrants	Nationality
'85 Mercedes 300SE	Rock & Rock	England
'90 Mercedes 230	Vilbig & Langsfield	Germany
'87 Mercedes 300TD	Holley & Holley	USA
'89 Mercedes 190E	Bean & Bean	Great Britain
'89 Mercedes 300FE	Van den Boogaard (2)	Great Britain
'81 Mercedes 230 GE	Frank & Kaufman	Germany
'86 Mercedes 230TE	Emmott & Emmott	Great Britain

Probably the most famous annual auto race in the world is the Paris-Dakar Rally run from Paris through Spain, across the Mediterranean and the Sahara Desert, and eventually to the Atlantic Ocean at Dakar, the capital of Monrovia. The 500SLC above was driven by the well known racer **Jochen Mass** and **Elbert Pfuhl** in the 1984 Paris-Dakar Rally. Except for wheels and roll-bar, this car was largely stock, including air conditioning.

SPORTSCAR VINTAGE
RACING ASSN.

VINTAGE RACING

In December, 1958 nine collectors met in Brookline, Massachusetts to form a new club "for the preservation and operation of vintage sports cars." The charter members, living throughout New England, created an eligibility list of both sports and racing cars built before 1945 ...Alfa, Bentley, Delage, Bugatti, Mercedes-Benz, Stutz, Mercer, etc. Within six months an "Inland Region" was organized in Chicago, and a series of competitive events was scheduled at places like Elkhart Lake, Thompson Raceway, and Roosevelt Raceway.

During the next 15 years membership grew and car eligibility was extended to cars up into the early 1960s. Events included concours, driver's schools, restoration seminars, course racing and hill climbs.

This first club, VSCCA (Vintage Sports Car Club of America) was in large part founded and is still populated by SCCA (Sports Car Club of America) members who feel old sports cars are more fun to drive with other old sports cars - and to drive for the sheer fun of it, without the need to place winning ahead of everything. Today trophies are rare; lists of how cars finished are distributed though most participants would rather lose a place than display bad driving form... or risk their carefully prepared beauty's good health. Careful fun.

One early (1950) SCCA event, the Mount Equinox Hill Climb near Manchester, VT. on a privately owned 6 mile toll road, has become a vintage tradition. Equinox is the highest mountain in southern New England with a summit accessible by automobile. The paved vertical climb is 3,200 feet. Participants at Equinox over the years have been no less than **Briggs Cunningham, John Fitch, Paul O'Shea, Dave Garroway,** and **Max Hoffman.**

During the 1970s and 1980s annual vintage racing week-ends have emerged in many parts of the USA, Europe and Japan. Atlanta, Palm Beach, Sebring, Mospark (Ontario), Lime Rock, Laguna SECA, Sears Point. Europe's big week-ends are at Monte Carlo, Nurburgring, and Donnington in England. There are a dozen excellent vintage racing clubs listed at the end of this chapter.

A profile prepared by **Dick Lewis** characterizes the typical American vintage driver as 42, a family man (there are a few women drivers) who works 45 hours a week at his regular employment, views his car hobby as a necessary retreat from the office, tows his car to events on a trailer, does most of his own maintenance work during the season, but finds for lack of time that he must farm out more serious work to professional restorers.

Following this introduction we've picked three driver's accounts out on the track. We hope a few of you will be inspired to join us!
Alex Dearborn defied the experts choosing a 190SL racer and the results have been extraordinary. Alex learned racing years ago with a Lotus Seven. In 1988 he bought our Gullwing (the same one we took to the Mille Miglia) to enter the vintage racing scene. With it he placed 1st the all-300SL Vintage Race (13 300SLs) conducted by Chicago's *Vintage Sports Car Driver's Club* in 1988 at Elkhart Lake, Wisconsin's four mile long "Road America" course.

The second testimonial is our own at the first all-300SL race (1986) in California, and then, the mother of all races, LaCarrera Panamericana, a 1900 mile six day race across Mexico.

Preparing an SL for Vintage Racing

Clubs across the country have relatively similar requirements for cars and drivers, and some reciprocity of entry privileges if you are in good standing at your home club. Some of the equipment standardization comes from the two or three insurance companies that underwrite virtually all these events. Roll bars are required on all post WWII open cars, though closed cars such as Mercedes Gull Wings frequently get exempted.

Six way seat belts, a driver's suit and helmet, and tire-extinguisher are essential. A fairly fire-proof fuel cell to replace the gas tank and an on board automatic fire extinguisher system can be added temporarily without hurting the car. Even on open cars the roll bars are often designed to remove easily. Ours can telescope downward just enough to let the soft top up. Our small windscreen and cowl uses the same fastening holes as the windshield, and can be changed in 45 minutes. A separate category called "Historic Racing" for 1961-1972 cars has grown during the 1980s, where there would be opportunity for some pioneers to campaign 230/250/280SLs and early 450SLs. Both were raced when new. Vintage organizations by location:

California:	CSRG-	415-948-2857
	HMSA-	805-966-9151
	HRG-	619-436-6477
	SCCA-	510-373-7222
	VARA-	818-845-8980
	VMR-	415-364-8855
Illinois:	CHR-	312-829-7065
	VSCDA-	708-534-7575
	MCSSC-	708-358-8673
Colorado:	MVP-	303-793-0572
	RMVR-	303-586-6366
Michigan:	WHRR-	313-493-3493
	MBHR-	313-373-2500
Minnesota:	VSCR-	612-884-1111
New Englnd:	VSCCA-	516-248-6237
Pennsylvania	VGPA-	215-242-0547
	PVGPA-	412-373-8440
S. Carolina:	SVRA-	803-723-7872
Texas:	CVAR-	214-661-9030
Washington:	SOVREN-	202-232-4644
Brt.Columbia:	VRCBC-	516-248-6237

SLML attends vintage events annually with this rig, a 300SL Roadster and a 15 year old 6.9SEL wagon w/hydropneumatic suspension, a reinforced rear body and Class III hitch.

A Racers View of the 190SL

by Alex Dearborn

I've been having a ball racing my 190SL. I used to race a Gullwing and have some fond memories of those years, but honestly, coming in 3rd or 5th, or even being in the fray in the 190SL has been even more fun. I think it's the improbability of it that makes it so rewarding. Here's what happened at the last outing:

My son Sam & I loaded up the 190SL on the trailer, hitched it to our trusty '66 Bonneville convertible, and headed off for Lime Rock, Connecticut [New England's most famous Race Track with 3 miles of left and right hand corners]. For us the idea of racing a vintage sportscar is to be able to do it for fun, as truly amateur participants. That means we tow it there, we drive it, and bring it home in one piece. The object is never to work on the car at the track. In a perfect world, the car would be beautiful, dead-reliable, fully streetable, and competitive. The Teutonic Tortoise is very close in all departments.

Upon arriving at the track we discover that the Vintage Sports Car Club of America (VSCCA) has us upped a class, running with Jaguars, Ferraris, Astons, Allards, Healeys, etc. C'est la vie. Sam checks the schedule, and I unload and go through tech. Soon, we're out in practice, trying some new tires and getting the cobwebs out of the driver after a winter of less demanding sport.

There are Vintage races around in the USA and Europe almost every weekend. At left, Alex Dearborn takes his 300SL Gullwing through its pace at Lime Rock Race Track.

There are two early practice sessions, and two races in the afternoon. I have the car (and driver) pretty much up to speed by the end of the first practice, so I do only a few laps in the second, to make sure I am qualified. 'Qualification' is for the club to do some timing to see who is fast & who is slow, so they can grid the cars in order of lap times.

The club has us gridded tenth among 33 cars, so I get a real break. Sometimes there's a lot of guesswork in the gridding. In vintage racing we have a rolling start, behind a pace

are great people, too, but this is racing, and I'd rather not come in tenth this time. So I figure out who to tuck behind when the flag drops. It's going to be the guy with the professionally prepared Jag XK120, who's engine builder assures me he has 250 real horsepower. My only other choice is the Allard with the great sounding Cadillac in it, but I figure I might have to follow him through turn one, by which time 4 or 5 cars could get through. In close motor racing, and especially in vintage events, drivers don't want to bash their cars, so there are good

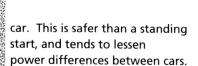

car. This is safer than a standing start, and tends to lessen power differences between cars.

From my vantage point on the outside of the third row, I can see the pace car and all the players. As we cruise around the track on the pace lap, doing the wiggle-woggle to warm up tires, I plan my start. I know some of the drivers, and can rank them anywhere from tigers to pussycats. Mind you the pussycats

and bad times to make a move. One is now, at the start, and one is when we start lapping the field. More about that soon.

As I round the last turn, and the pace car speeds up a little, I strain for a glimpse of the green flag waving, and get into third the sprint to the first turn behind my chosen escort, the Jag. The second row jumps ahead, anticipating the flag fall, so I get on it. My 90 hp doesn't close the resulting gap, so I settle for the Allard, and insinuate my way past in the middle of turn one. Now, I'm about twelfth. Handling is the Teutonic Tortoise's forte, and I make three or four passes in the esses while people are sorting out. As usual, this first lap gets the adrenaline going pretty well if the eternity on the false grid or the pace lap doesn't do it to you.

to sideways in my favorite corner, so I can get by. By this time I'm up to about fifth spot, and have a clear track ahead. It's time to concentrate totally on making lap times, & try to ignore the chaos going on in my mirrors.

I know that soon we will be coming up to lap the slowest cars, and this is a time for more planning. There are a couple of cars having a grand old dice up ahead, and I can only hope they have 20/20 hindsight, and perfect track manners to go with it. If a slower car is about to be lapped, his

As the field starts to spread out, I'm behind an Aston DB4GT, and I remind myself not to make any moves until I study his slow places. Certainly not the straightaway. After a lap of following him around I figure out a corner in which I have the greatest advantage. Two cars behind are doing the same thing with me, so I need to get this done this lap, or risk getting out-powered down the main straight the next lap. I see the Aston get just a little wide and just a little

safest move is to stay on the ideal racing line and not to move over for the faster car. That way the overtaking car knows what to expect, and can choose a way around. If two cars are being overtaken, and they are racing each other, the rules get a little fuzzy. Worse, the overtaken car sometimes doesn't see in his mirrors, and sometimes tries to move out of the way at the last moment. This is white knuckle time.

I choose the outside line on the upcoming corner, use my headlights and pray for early recognition. The dicers seem to hold line, and I figure they must see me. If I go for the inside line, easily the faster of the two, I might lose if they close the door. That would enable my pursuers to get around the outside. If I go on the outside, the dicers will probably crowd to inside, blocking my pursuers' way. It works, and I get a bonus of five car lengths lead since the dicers have slowed my good friends through the corner.

One car gets by me the next lap, and I see one in the grass with steamed engine and driver to match, so I figure I'm still about fifth. I catch a glimpse of the four leaders now, for the first time since lap one. Odd that they would be slower than me? Maybe not... I'm catching them gradually, and try to calculate if I can reel them in before the checquered flag falls. They're dicing with each other, a process which often slows everyone down. On a track with long straights, sometimes drafting can improve collective lap times, but here the effect of a competing gaggle of cars is a net loss of lap time. Also, in most vintage clubs, drivers value their sheetmetal over their competitive libido.

Alas, the flag drops before I can improve my place. But it has been all the agony & ecstasy a man could ask for in one day of sport, and the bonus is being able to loan my trailer to a friend in need with a broken car, and drive my race car home.

Lime Rock is under a special blue law that prohibits racing on Sunday, so all of this has happened on Saturday. Saturday night we repair to the local inns the Connecticut Berkshires offer in abundance, and enjoy a little bench racing. Friends, spouses, and children all participate here, and all seem somehow more ready to enjoy the post-race dinners & camaraderie after participating in such an otherworldly adventure.

Driving home on Sunday, I remember why I restored this 190SL as a dual purpose car. I love to drive it, and a few times a year at the track is just not enough. At many points during the restoration process, I could have jettisoned a little weight (by removing the interior), or improving the handling (by scrapping the rubber mounts) etc. But the car is very user-friendly this way, and, in this trim still more civilized than a stock Austin-Healey or MG. It has synchromesh in low gear, back-up lights, non-glare rear view mirror, power brakes, glove box light, and so on. The SL Market Letter's sport springs leave the car about as firm as it should have been in the first place.

An added benefit to leaving the car fairly close to stock in the chassis department is that the car is able to endure more cornering & bump stress, protecting the chassis & body from cracks & other wear. Same is true of the engine with stock cam & compression. As designed by M-B, it will go up to 6,300rpm many times per lap, for many races & years before needing a rebuild.

I have never had a race car before which I could park after one race, and not even turn a wrench on it before the next one. This year, it has been one oil change and bleed the brakes. Of course we did do a total, ground-up restoration before all of this. If you race a car, you have two choices: Do it all at once or do it a broken piece at a time.

I'd be happy to help any of you inspired to prepare your own 190SL racer. Maybe we can we have a herd of Turtles?

Alex Dearborn, of Topsfield, Massachusetts, has been selling and racing rare post WWII Mercedes-Benz cars for over twenty years.

*Several vintage races sponsored by Kansas City attracted over 100 cars and 20,000 spectators. Right to left: **Rene Shaer**, Kansas, **Russ Moran**, Colorado, **Tom Congleton**, Arizona, and **Olson**, Minnesota.*

The Mercedes-Benz Museum, now responsible for 800 vehicles,
was totally remodeled for the 100th Aniversary
of the company in 1986. It is truly one of the most
spectacular automotive expositions in the world.
The Museum sent a half dozen of its finest race cars to Laguna SECA
for on track demonstrations in 1986.

Racing A 300SL at Laguna Seca

Mercedes-Benz 100th Anniversary Celebration

Picking the high point of the 100th Anniversary Mercedes Celebration at Monterey in 1986 was about as easy as choosing only one Pebble Beach Concours car that we'd like to bring home. From Wednesday and Thursday's Gull Wing Group Sessions, Thursday through Sunday's Historic Auto Races, and the incredible parade of elegance at Pebble Beach, *Mercedes-Benz of North America* (MBNA) peppered everything with favors, careful assistance, and celebration of their 100th birthday. The record crowds "loved every minute" as the headlines reported in Monterey's Sunday Herald newspaper.

Veteran track announcer **Larry Albedi** felt that spectators were more dense than previous Historic Races here, and larger than some IMSA Camel GT races... *Around 25,000 People.* It was a journalist's dream assignment which I'm sure was documented by every car magazine before winter.

Certainly one if the greatest thrills was seeing the world championship Mercedes racing cars driven out onto the track again by the same drivers that brought the awards home with Daimler-Benz in the 1950s, 1930s, and earlier. You will see from the photos here that nearly every-one was on hand... 77 year old **Hermann Lang** was given a 1937 W125, 75 year old **Juan Manuel Fangio** drove an 1954 open wheel W196, **Stirling Moss** pilot the envelope bodied 300SLR, and **John Fitch** rotated among a C111 and 1914 Mercedes racer (a 4 valve design incidentally). All lapped the unusual counter-clock-wise 1.9 mile *Laguna Seca* track a dozen times to the applauding crowd.

These champion cars, impressive enough in a museum, are beyond belief when they burst to life, one after another, and fly off their starting grids. A European tradition (of the past) of allowing too many people to accumulate around the cars prevailed while tower authorities awaited clearance to enter the track.

Lang, 1939 Driving Champion of Europe, happy at the wheel of 570hp 5.6 liter, straight 8.

The machines are not run until the very last instant as their plugs and fuel are not suited to idle speeds. When final clearance is received, three or four factory technicians began to push each car. Whistlers were blown, shouts to clear the way were heard, and dozens of officials, and friends of officials, and journalists opened a narrow path, with one or two cameraman usually the last to get out of the way. The crowd was silenced by a sudden ground shaking roar of each engine's first breaths. And I do mean roar ... louder than unmuffled trucks!

First to depart on Saturday was **Stirling Moss.** His straight eight is red-lined at 11,000 rpm, and from the sound, he hit 8,500 before the first turn. Next was Fangio, followed by Hermann Lang and Fitch, and two

1908 Benz racers. These oldest cars carried a human fuel pump as copilot. **Hermann Lang** was my favorite because he seemed such an improbable sight ... short, old, and a bit over weight, hinting of the appearance of Mr. Magoo. Appearance was where the similarity ended, however, as Lang wielded his steed at very close to the same lap speeds as Fangio and Moss, who were frequently within yards of each other, even in corners. Fangio studied Moss's "line" for about five laps and then took the lead for five more laps ... each a bit faster than the last. Every so often the camera buffs could catch race cars from three decades in one frame. I was surprised how low the RPMs were for the W125; perhaps only 4500 RPM rushing down the main straight.

REPORT FROM THE DRIVER'S SEAT:
Saturday also brought the world's first all 300SL wheel-to-wheel race. This special race was only permitted because 15 cars of one type were registered. Entries in the 12 lap even were:

Californians **Ted Stroscher** has been a top 300SL finisher at vintage races for the past few years. His car was chosen Friday afternoon as people's choice race car for its good appearance. **Paul Russell,** Essex, Massachusetts participated here in his first

California	Massachusetts	Ohio
Roger Glen (GWing)	P. Russell (GWing)	G. Black (GWing)
Hugh Harn (GWing)	J. Tompkin (GWing)	**Kansas**
T. Stroscher (Rdstr)	**New York**	R. Schaer (GWing)
Lou Pavesi (GWing)	Don Narde (Rdstr)	T. Congleton (GW)
Stan Kaufmann (GWing)	**Michigan**	**Minnesota**
Mike Wittman (GWing)	R. Yakel (GWing)	J. Olson (Gwing)
Steve Marx (GWing)		

At least two long distance entries, **Mr. & Mrs. R. Gordon Black** of Ohio, and **Mr. and Mrs. Lynn Yakel,** of Michigan, drove their 300SL Gullwings to Monterey, raced, and toured back home. Well over 50% of the 90+ 300SL attendees drove to and from Monterey. Your editor trailered that year, as we brought our two sons, one of whom started at *Art Center College of Design* in Pasadena in September.

Both Kansas entrants, **Rene Schear** and **Tom Congleton** have considerable race experience and both brought along mechanics for the trip. Tom, in fact, entered a second car, a 1968 Porsche 907 in a later Saturday race and took first place. **Roberta Yakel,** Michigan's entry, has also taken home many awards at previous MBCA and GWG events. Among

vintage sport car race with an all aluminum Gullwing that **Alex Finigen** (and *Automobile Magazine*) drove from Boston for the race.

It is so rare to get a big group of these cars on the same track that at least one conspicuously modified car was admitted; the Gull Wing of **Joe Tompkin** also of Massachusetts, sported non-Mercedes disc brakes, wide wheels and tires and a unique rear stabilizer bar he had designed. **Lou Pavesi** of Los Altos, CA had a very mean looking Gull Wing with roll bar (not required), light weight plastic windows and custom aluminum racing dash.

A five hour track familiarization course on Thursday was given by the *Jim Russell Driver School* which is based at *Laguna Seca* (six miles inland from Monterey). I found this time extremely valuable for acclimating myself to the corkscrew turns, major elevation changes, and two negative camber turns where the pavement tends to fall away from you. We practiced again on Friday.

The green "START" flag fell at 2:55 PM Saturday: 15 300SL charged around the first lap. After the initial shuffling of cars I found myself in third place, with Joe Tompkin's Gull Wing out front, and Ted Stroscher's 300SL Roadster in second. Behind me were Rene Schaer (GW), and Hugh Harn (GW) of Santa Rosa. I tried to stay as close to **Ted** and **Joe** as possible for a few laps to study their line through the course, and to let my brake pads and oil warm up. I eyed my rearview mirror to see which other drivers would show up, but to my pleasant surprise our first three cars drew further away from the others with every lap. Ted's cornering and speeds in the longer straights were very similar to my own. How do you pass a car like that? I did feel he was braking earlier than necessary before corners. The announcer told the crowd that

Stirling Moss, and 300SLR #722 in which he won the 1955 Mille Miglia. Note the stone guard in front of the small windshield. **John Fitch** *placed first in Class in a 300SL in the same event.*

Ted's Roadster had disc brakes which, he said gave Ted an advantage ... wrong on two counts; his car didn't happen to have discs (only started in 1961), and the trick was to use brakes *less*! There are nine turns in the course. By the fifth or sixth lap I was able to go through turn 1 & 2 with no braking at all, and just a late, light tap on turn 3. If I planned a few corners ahead this gave me about 2+ mph more speed than Ted on the hill after turn 3. Ted's natural line after turn 3 was to the right, so I took the inside lane. Approaching the turn 4 braking zone I had inched about half a car's length ahead. As expected Ted began braking earlier than I felt required, and I slipped in front. I knew Ted would not take this sitting down, so to speak, and the next few corners gave the crowds some of their best spectating of the afternoon. Ted and I discovered on this same lap that we began lapping the slowest cars ... two or three were in the next half mile. As we entered the infamous down-hill cork-screw corners I found myself behind a slower car as Ted hunted for a place to repass me and perhaps another car. In the center of the corkscrew I faced the necessity of passing this slower car... choice was not whether to pass, but which side. There was more room on the left, however, the ideal position for entry into the subsequent, larger and final downhill left-hander was the right. I paused briefly looking for a passing signal from the slower car, but he apparently did not envision any passing

until the next straight. As I accelerated to the right, I could see Ted's car in my rear view mirror pulling out to the left. I was pleased, as I was comfortable that I would have enough better position and momentum entering the next corner to stay in second place moving down toward turn 8. I wonder how many passes the crowd saw on the corkscrew that day. Not many, and surely only one by three cars abreast!

I put some distance between myself and Ted during the next couple laps, trying to find Joe Tompkin, *but apparently his car's modifications were pronounced, as he was nowhere in sight.*

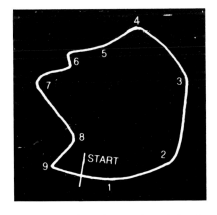

This drawing shows the 1.9 mile track, but does not capture the major elevation changes. The first climb occurs between the "start" and turn 1. Then comes a long run all the way over to just beyond turn 3. Speeds build to over 100 mph. There is a cliff beyond number four, ... the course orientation instructor said if we see any bushes off to the right of that corner, they were actually tree tops.

Turn five is just at the knoll of the highest point on the circuit, leaving cars light on their springs just when braking is required for number six. Answer here is to brake twice, once just before the knoll when full weight of car is on the ground, and then again after resettling before number 6. Turn six is a 90 degree left-handed down a "chute". When you're in a hurry it seems like trying to drive down the center of a short ski-jump scaffold. This is the beginning of the "corkscrew" with "6A", the immediate right-handed smiling just below.

Turn No. 7 and No. 8 continue down hill. Resigning myself to preserving second place I relaxed a bit as Ted crept steadily back in my rearview mirror. In the last two laps we began lapping another group of cars which I knew Ted would utilize if possible. As the Driver School Instructor said, while racing is seen as a sport of brawn, it is in reality a thinkingman's sport. The Fangios and Hermann Langs of this world are typically methodical and very organized. To this day I'm puzzled why 300SLs sold to the public had softer springs than Fangio and Lang were given. It is easy to improve the control and predictability of these cars with sport springs all around and 3 degrees negative camber at the rear wheels (factory specs.).

The Track Marshal signaled for the last lap, and I felt Ted a few car lengths behind. I wondered if he would try the same pass on me before turn No. 4 than I'd used successfully. No, I made it to the corkscrew. Down we both went, about a car's length apart. Moving out toward turn eight, more cars again. At the last turn, a 120 degree left-hander, everyone brakes down to about 25 mph. Already in second gear, I saw an opening on the inside, moved toward it and charged up the main straight toward the checkered flag. I was too busy to look for Ted, though I learned later he was half a car from me at the last turn. As I moved through the finish line I saw **Joe Tompkin's** car about 100 yards ahead. He'd evidently been slowed down lapping some traffic. Wow, that was a thrilling drive! And a thrilling track! We have longer tracks in the Midwest, but not with so many hills or quick succession turns. My helmet off to Ted, Joe, the corner workers, the other drivers, the *Jim Russell Orientation Session*, and **Steven Earle**, the man who has masterminded the Monterey Historic Races at Laguna SECA now for 20 years. As they would say in nearby Carmel, "You made my day!"

FINAL RESULTS: *Group 5A Mercedes-Benz 300SL: First five places: 1. Joe Tompkin, Avg. Speed: 73.566 mph. 2. John Olson, 3. Ted Stroscher, 4. Rene Schaer, 5. Hugh Harm.* No accidents. All cars running at finish.

Fangio, Five time World Driving Champion, sporting a silk shirt and ascot w/ his helmet. Fastest and safest driver from '49 -'57.

And that was just one quarter the fun. While we were racing, nearly 100 of the best restored 300SL cars in the USA lined up in the infield circle in two huge rows ... Roadsters on one side and Gullwings facing them. Over 30 of the 47 colors Daimler-Benz delivered on these cars between 1954 and 1964 (and a few not delivered) were counted. Another section of the display included other rare Mercedes-Benz brought by Mercedes-Benz Club of America (MBCA) members. Judges selected one Gullwing (a fresh frame-up job by *Scott Restoration*), one Roadster, and several "non SLs" for display with the factory race cars at the PEBBLE BEACH *Concours de Elegance* on Sunday. For those of you who have eyed ownership of a 300SL, Gullwing or Roadster, I can't speak enthusiastically enough about the support owners have created for themselves via the *Gull Wing Group International* (GWG). GWG celebrated its 25th anniversary along with M-B's 100th. With one major national meet per year, five "chap-ters" across the country, a monthly newsletter, and many sources of re-manufactured parts, including Daimler-Benz itself, these cars receive more organized survival assistance than any other exotic "oldtimers." This adds to the justification for the stiff price of joining the club... ownership! This last sentence is not technically true, because anyone wanting to learn more about the 300SL is permitted to join GWG as a non-voting "associate" member while scrutinizing ownership. For more details see Gull Wing Chapter in Section Two.

Among MBNA'S favor's were several Friday and Saturday cocktail parties for the friends of Mercedes and miscellaneous private dinners Friday, then copies of the book *The Star and the Laurel* were given to the 325 drivers entered at the Monterey Races; pewter napkin holders from M-B were found by the 600 white tie diners at a joint MBCA/GWG Banquet Saturday, and a free lunch tent at Sunday's Pebble Beach Concours also for MBCA and GWG attendees. Couple this with oceanic transport of factory race cars, drivers and support mechanics and it was clear M-B's event participation is no different

than their car building. MBNA's planning meetings at Monterey with the club, hotel, and track representatives beginning almost a year earlier. **Walter Bodack**, President of MBNA, and **Max von Pein**, Daimler Benz Museum Director, were on hand and served as *Judges at Pebble Beach* Sunday. Focusing on pre-1940 cars of particular elegance, we saw Mercedes of each decade rivaling them all. **Phil Hill** (the ex-race driver and restorer) drove MBNA's beautiful 1905 American Mercedes (built in the USA by Steinway Piano Company). This car's home is the lobby of MBNA'S Montvale, NJ Headquarters.

Rene Schaer's beautifully prepared 300SL racer.

HERMANN LANG
1909-1987

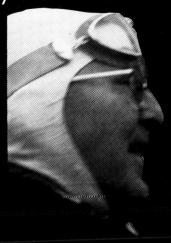

HERMANN LANG, former race driver of Mercedes-Benz, died of cancer October 19, 1987. We first met Lang at the Daimler-Benz 100th anniversary celebration at Monterey/Laguna SECA in 1986, and again during the May 1987 *SLML* Subscriber's Driving Tour in Europe. A treasure in 1986 was the sight of than 75 year old (!) champion Lang willing the 570+ hp open wheel W125 Mercedes racer round Laguna SECA lap after lap, all within an inch of the yellow line of each apex. Ironically, Hitler's battle cheated the world from knowing just how great Germany's top driver had become. After a dutiful apprenticeship as motorcycle racer, Mercedes mechanic, race mechanic, and back-up driver, Hermann won at the Avus track in Berlin in 1935 averaging, repeat, averaging 162.6 mph! This remained a worldwide record for 22 years. The way Neubauer ran the factory team, Hermann was groomed five more years before being "released" to win the 1939 European driver's championship. Just at Lang's prime, European racing ended until the late 1940s. In 1951, Mercedes dug up its 1939 machines and drivers, and Lang took second in the Grand Prix of Argentina. By 1952 the 300SL was ready and Lang won at LeMans and also at Nurburgring, but it was a new kind of driving. Juan Fangio fast became master of 1950s racing, with his series of five annual world driver championships. How many years would Lang have taken home that championship if WWII hadn't broken out? Lang retired from racing in 1954 and continued with DBA as an inspector until age 65. Since then he served an enviable retirement role demonstrating museum race cars at exhibitions in Europe and the USA. Two awesome cocktail table quality books covering Lang's pre and post 1950 years are:

RACING THE SILVER ARROWS
by Nixon and Lang 352 pages,
250 illustrations, $75 from *SLML*.

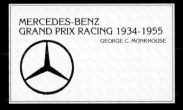

MERCEDES-BENZ GRAND PRIX RACING 1934-1955
by Edward Monkhouse
208 pages, 458 exceptional photos,
$75 from the *SLML* business office.

III. Carrera Panamericana Mexico

Triumphant Double Victory

1st Karl Kling   2nd Hermann Lang

After 3 days of hardest contest supreme victory with a new distance record of
"Type 300 SL" developed out of the custom-built passenger cars of

MERCEDES - BENZ

LA CARRERA:
A RETROSPECTIVE

Fasten your seatbelts! We're off on another trip. Well, an adventure. And *you* don't have to leave the security of your favorite chair.

Our O'Shea-inspired 300SL Roadster was accepted in the 1991 running of **La Carrera Panamericana - Mexico.** If you're old enough to remember, or happened to read SL Market Letter No. 156 on the 1950s Mexican Road Race, or the nine page feature article in the September 1991, **Automobile** magazine titled "Mexican Mayhem," you've got the picture. We didn't know if the anticipation, reality, or remembrance would be best, but now we can give you all three!

During the last six days of October each year a "re-running" of the famous 1950s race takes place, sanctioned by the Mexican government's Department of Tourism, and run from near the Guatemala border 1,900+ miles through Mexico's highest mountain roads, to the American border at Laredo, Texas.

We interviewed a half dozen past entrants... and they all glow with enthusiasm, even those who did not make it to the finish line. **Bruce Turnery** of *Fantasy Junction* fame, had driven in each race since '88, and he said "It's the most fun you can have *with* a car. It's my favorite event bar none." Another *SLML* subscriber **Manfredo Lippmann** of Guatemala, coached us in road conditions, etc. Manfredo drove a Porsche 356 in a Mexican Road Race way back in 1953, and drove again in 1990 in the *same* car. **Bob Anderson**, the President of Carrera Shock Absorbers in Atlanta, has won the Large Touring Car Class several times with a 1954 Lincoln. Lincoln, some of you will recall, was the big winner among American makes in the 1950s, taking 1st & 2nd in its class three years in succession.

An important difference between this and other popular driving events for old cars (Mille Miglia, Colorado Grand) is that it is actually a race. A six day race! Each team requires a driver & co-driver, and a sweep-truck, trailer, & service crew is recommended. Our application for the race was joint with **Jorgen Andersen**, of Denmark, who agreed to pay the bulk of the costs in exchange for us providing the eligible car and orchestrating logistics. A number of our trips have been made possible in this way.

After phone conversations with as many past participants as we could find, we set to work preparing our car, selecting crew and sweep-truck equipment. Much is different about Mexico, from its legal system (French influence) to its "silent policemen" ...the speed-bumps sprinkled plentifully around the entries and exits of the villages and towns. Some are six inches high; an effective way for the inadequately financed police departments to curb over-the-road truckers

& aggressive young Mexicans. Mexican food also had a dubious track record with Americans... so our preparations were diverse. We needed to select a crew including a Mexican who spoke English, locate trailering equipment, prepare the race car, and move everything to the bottom of Mexico. We wrote to everyone we thought could help, including Mercedes-Benz in Germany, MBNA, and Mercedes-Benz Mexico. The response from **M-B Mexico** was very supportive. We were invited to use the fully secured, guarded facilities of M-B's truck dealerships in each city where the race stops at night.

Preparing the car, we learned that the Air-Lift Company in Michigan had experience way back with the original 1950s Mexican Road Races. The winning '52, '53, & '54 Lincolns were equipped with Air Lift products. Their technical department worked with us to identify which of their air bellows would fit in our coil springs. Then our first crew member, **Warren Rauch**, designed an automatic sensor that raises the whole car 2+ inches whenever it dropped below 30 mph... which we would have to do anyway approaching these infamous speed-bumps.

Other LaCarrera safety rules required us to add emergency flashers, and a dual master brake system. As far as we could determine no one has ever before made this change on a 300SL Roadster as our inquiries to all the

The first La Carrera in 1950 *was to promote Mexico's early completion of their portion of the* 12,000 *mile Arctic to Cape Horn Highway. Quality of the roads was good.*

USA

Juarez

Texas

Chihuahua

NuevoLaredo

Saltillo

Gulf
of
Mexico

Zacatecas

San Luis Potosi

Queretaro

MEXICO CITY

Puebla

Oaxaca

Tuxtla

"experts" got us blank stares. We found the necessary parts and in mid-September tested our new brakes on a 2,500 mile drive to & from the 1991 Gull Wing Group Convention in New Jersey. Success.

Next came the two person roll-bar requirement for all open cars. We designed a wonderful telescoping unit that meets SCCA's height requirement but can be lowered enough for street driving that the regular convertible top will go up and down.

By this time fellow Minnesotan **Bruce Kelly** had become our crew chief and was preparing a sweep-truck & trailer. We decided to bring much of the food we'd need in our trailer. 36 gallons of bottled water, much canned food, and a microwave were packed. Even a portable generator and portable welder. And some spare parts.

We hoped to have at least one crew member from Mexico, who knew the language & customs, and would serve as sweep-truck driver in Mexico. We contacted several of our Mexican SL Market Letter subscribers. **Raul Echevarria**, an executive of *Transpac Freight Forwarders (Phone 515-202-1511 in Mexico)*, was extremely helpful lining up essential details in Mexico and getting through the border. At the New Jersey Gull Wing Group Convention we met another Mexican, **Juan A. Lerado de Tejada**. He was also in the

USA for his class reunion at MIT Graduate School of Engineering. Juan insisted on meeting our airplane when we arrived in Mexico City October 18th. Then *Mercedes-Benz Mexico* came through in a most flattering way. **Peter Zell** phoned to suggest "Rather than locate a Mexican driver to serve on your crew, would it help if we sent our truck & two drivers to meet your racecar & trailer at the border and be at your disposal for the entire event?" Well, Yes! ...that would be helpful. Beyond our dreams actually!

Our USA crew members trailered the 300SL to Laredo for reloading at the border & **Powell-Watson Motors**, Laredo's Mercedes-Benz dealer was kind enough to store our state-side rig. We found everyone extremely helpful & enthused to have anything to do with La Carrera. ...that is

except the Mexican Customs folks. Seems they have a fetish for paperwork which delayed some entrants (including the winner) 3 days getting into Mexico! We thought the organizers had alerted the border for the numerous Carrera entries at Laredo's border. Our load sailed through in a mere 3 hours thanks to Raul Echevarria & M-B's Freight Forwarders *(Express Bravo)*. They both called Customs expressing interest in our progress. To listen to crew members **Bruce Kelly & Warren Rauch**, the entry was a sad scene. The file of papers on our single entry is an inch thick!(?) They described their arrival in Nuevo Laredo at 11PM, as an eerie silhouette of damaged buildings, tents, homeless "residents," and night-time camp fires. Warren compared it to scenes from the movie "Escape from New York."

In the next day's sunlight things looked much brighter. More like Maxwell Street, Chicago. As foreigners, they had to remind themselves not to be the pot calling the kettle black. Throughout the trip we saw extremes in everything. Too bad one's eyes grows immune to (these) extremes over time. True at home too! As we would see over the next two weeks, Mexico's people have a "can do" attitude that stretches deep into the countryside. What looked that first night like bombed ruins, by day were partially constructed buildings. Not all those dreams will get finished, but the spark of ideas and self initiative is everywhere. We found no recession in Mexico, only large growth rates. Some Americans are worried about being pulled backwards by freer trade with Mexico...though facilitating private enterprise may be a better alternative than keeping them so poor we end up shipping them free food instead...as we do elsewhere in the world.

The truck M-B Mexico sent to meet us is magnifico! Talk about a roadside service program! Turns out the truck is an experimental diesel w/ over 400hp., 16 forward gears & bunks for two. Built by M-B in Brazil, it has many innovations including some new weight distribution ideas to improve traction & handling. To date there are only three in Mexico and none for sale. From the border, "arriving" is only half over... there is another 1600 miles to the start line,

600 miles south of Mexico City. **Jorgen** and I left the hauling to our crew and flew into Mexico City (called Mexico by residents) a week before the starting flag to get used to the altitude and to a lesser extent, the food. We came directly from a four day *High Performance Driving Course* reserved for *SLML* subscribers at **Bob Bondurant's** wonderful new School at Firebird Raceway near Phoenix (See chapter on Driving Schools).

In Mexico City we relaxed a bit and treated ourselves to what we'd heard was the best hotel in town, the *Camino Real*, now owned by Westin properties. It is in a good location with a 1930's Mexican Bauhaus Modern look, but disappointing. Our rooms had an odor more likely in the Virgin Islands. Hallways went on & on like a maze. We moved after one day to *The Presidente*, now owned by Stouffers. We were given rooms on the 40th floor. Imagine the view at night in what is now the world's largest city. 23 million people! During a two days stay, virtually the only fault in this hotel (and most others in this country) was their utter inability to find guests or even to confirm we were registered. Time after time, even when special phone calls were made to the switchboard *and* front desk, our visitors were left floundering in the lobby. Phone & mail communications proved to be an equal disaster. We were told Mexico's phone monopoly will be opened to competitively marketed services in 1994.

Juan Lerdo de Tejada met our airplane as promised, and gave us a much appreciated driving tour of the City. **Sr. & Sra. Raul Echevarria** treated us to a catered garden party at their home near the US Embassy. It was actually a birthday party for their daughter with several dozen parents also invited, many with a keen interest in cars and La Carrera. When Raul opened his garage we were in for another treat! Five spectacularly perfect machines. A 230SL & a 6.9 sedan w/ only 2,700 miles(!). Then a Porsche 356 Cabriolet. An Alfa Romeo Giulietta Viloce Spyder, and the finale, a BMW M-1! Restoration work where needed, all done in Mexico, was beyond fault. Miraculous paint & leather upholstery work. During this party we received the first successful phone contact from our crew. They'd successfully traversed the border & were about a day north of Mexico [City]. They chose a route outside the City; our plan was to meet them in Pueblo, 120 miles east, on Oct. 21st.

We rented a car to drive along the Carrera route (backwards) to the start line, 600 miles southeast of Mexico City. This proved very valuable. The roads were winding & slow, somewhat like getting off a turnpike in Pennsylvania. We found these roads in a better state of repair than later in northern Mexico. We

quickly met up with the infamous Mexican "tope" ...the silent policemen (photo). Mexican engineers tend to bank curves steeper than I can recall in any other country, which invites faster driving. While guard rails are rare & mountain cliffs common, roads are designed better than we expected. All blacktop construction.

Our destination, *Tuxtla-Gutierrez* is the capital of the eastern state of Chiapas. This portion of Mexico is somewhat conservative (girls & women always wearing dresses or skirts). The influence of a large University is present just blocks from La Carrera headquarters at the Hotel Flamboyant!

All of us absorbed the altitude fluctuations (from 500ft to 11,000ft) well enough, & no one yet had eating problems. We took two Pepto-Bismol tablets daily to insulate our stomachs, and squeezed bottled lime juice on practically everything we ate.

On Technical Inspection Day, October 24, we met the only other Mercedes-Benz entry, a 300SL Gullwing shipped in from Germany by **Rene Herzog**. Our cars were placed in the *Large Sports* Class, with the fastest cars. We had been warned that La Carrera admits some replicars that *look* like cars of the fifties. We were disappointed to see most of them in our Class. 121 cars registered.

Our number: #234. Departure *Assignment:* exactly 7:30:00AM, Friday, October 25. The Herzog/ Kienle Gullwing, #235, to leave 30 seconds later.

Thousands of Mexican car enthusiasts came out for the start of the 9th Carrera. We found elbow to elbow people around the Hotel Flamboyant Headquarters from about 4PM the day before. Driving our rented car back to the hotel at 8PM we would never have reached our parking spot if we hadn't known exactly where the road was under the sea of people. This city is a popular base for serious Mexican tourists ...those going into the Mexico beyond Cancun & Acupolco. Mayan & Olmecs archeology surrounded us here.

DAY 1: Official departure #234 was 7:30:00AM, October 25th.

The Herzog/Kienle Gullwing #235 followed 30 seconds later. Race headed west, then north. 1st day passed through Mexico's narrowest land mass, the 120 miles between the Atlantic & Pacific oceans. The first 200 miles was a mountainous 1,400ft descent, almost a rain forest flush w/ trees, bushes and an occasional elegant cactus. A few loose bulls & donkeys were on the road. This first section has several newly finished, and unfinished, bridges. The estado or state of Chiapas was definitely getting highway funds where they belong. On the other hand, except near Mexico City, budgets don't yet allow luxuries such as roadside shoulders for emergency stopping.

The state of Oaxaca greeted us with one of the worst straight roads of the entire 6 days; the 90 minute lunch stop at Tehuantepec (Elevation: 328ft) was a welcome break!

Weather was cloudy & temperature had dropped 20+ degrees in three hours to 75° as Pacific ocean breezes blew toward us.

Our crew rose each morning at 5AM to beat the road blocks that would prohibit "sweep trucks" from the official route much after 6AM. This also helped them get ideal noon "pit stop" locations. We each used two "carry-on bags" in the car & the rest stayed aboard the truck when possible. All noon food & beverage was pre-planned & purchased in the USA. (Neubauer's team brought their own chef & masseuse, or was it a masseur. Any volunteers for next time?) We had a microwave oven along & 36 gallons of bottled water, canned meats & vegetables. Also 120 gallons of 97 octane USA gas, which

would have been perfect except for a major fuel leak... luckily at a filter gasket! An easy fix. Cautiously we mixed 20% of Mexico's finest, "Magna," for the next few days with no ill effects. The car ran like a champ. We *lived* between 4,000 & 6,500 RPM for 6 days. Music of the gods! Gas mileage actually increased. The automatic altimeter adjustment in our 30+ year old fuel injection worked perfectly though idle & partial load jet changes (below 3,800rpm) were necessary for the large altitude shifts from 300 to 10,000 ft. back to 7,200 ft. at Mexico City & up again before the drop to Laredo. Oil & water stayed at a consistent 180° to 195° no matter how steep the mountain or fast the straight. In villages oil immediately came down to 140° with the oil cooler connected.

Our Route Book graded corners 1, 2, & 3 in severity, so we worked out hand signals.
*Here, **Jorgen Andersen** indicates a #2 curve coming*
up on a poor road before Tehuantepec. Most mountain roads were constructed better.

Afternoon's destination, Oaxaca, was a mile vertical climb. Mixed cliffs & straights. The public everywhere was well informed of our schedule. Locals left whatever they were doing to cheer us by. Children stood outside schools with their teachers. Local police motioned us faster. We gunned our engine & waved our Minnesota TWINS caps. They cheered all the more.

We'd read that smaller cars and hotshots lead the first few days with bigger cars making it up in the long straight of the last two days. Focusing on the long haul we cruised fast but provided no serious resistance to those wanting to pass. A surprisingly fast 1950 Oldsmobile 88 Fastback Coupe steamed past us in the mountains *at least* 20 mph faster than we were traveling. We learned later that it was last year's entry of this year's overall winner... a 400+hp special under the hood. It became clear that what we *saw* wasn't always what we saw.

Oaxaca's capital, also called Oaxaca, is in a pleasant 5,000ft. high valley, not yet over-commercialized. It has pleasant colonial streets and plazas. Typical October temperature:63°. Rain began just as we reached the local Mercedes-Benz [truck] dealer who brought us to the San Fillippe Mission, one of four hotels used by the 550+ LaCarrera travelers. All hotels were excellent. We showered & changed for the nightly driver's meeting & dinner. Our crew set to

work on the car. Brakes were the single greatest problem for all entrants. Our brake pad material was not dissipating heat fast enough which caused variations in pedal travel & pad wear. The cause was not obvious for several evenings, but little else required attention. One noon brake fade caused the "Swift Turtle," a 1954 Ford, to plow into the back of a '53 Oldsmobile 98, and deflect ditchward.

DAY 2: Rain was gone. Starts were usually at each city's center or plaza. Starting order was posted the night before based on accumulating points & penalties. Jon Ward's 1953 Kurtis 500 "Continuation" (we were corrected when calling it a replica) was the 1st day's winner. Mexico City was the 2nd day's goal, via the mountain city of Puebla (7,200ft). Brakes still pulled so we down shifted more often to use brakes less. During short bursts of full speed between mountain passes we found our navigator's windscreen slipping loose. At lunch the portable clamps were trashed & three large bolts added. Roads here were a delight, not many holes & deep banking of corners. Our afternoon's excitement was the left front Michelin XWX blowing out at 120mph. Fate put us on the best highway we would see in all of Mexico, a genuine autobahn quality road 60 miles east of Mexico City. Jorgen was driving when the car moved nearly a whole lane to the left without warning... like a great gust of wind had taken over. Jorgen

had a firm hand on the wheel & fought the car straight without sudden braking. I did not hear a burst, and remained unsure what was happening until we were down nearer 80mph & the lower left front corner was evident. With more luck, traffic was minimal. Once stopped we found the tire's bottom completely gone. The wheel hid behind its loose sidewalls and was not even scratched! Both the front & rear edge of the fender were slightly ripped by the force of the departing tread.

Blow-outs are humbling experiences as they remind us of powerful variables outside our control. The best prepared car & best trained drivers are still at the mercy of many risks, stray animals, other drivers, ...or a tire. We put our spare on quickly & were lapping up the road again within 10 minutes... but there lingered a fear that it could have happened, or would happen again, on one of those two lane roads without a shoulder.

We were expected to arrive at the outskirts of Mexico City by 3:30PM to be escorted into town by motorcycle police before traffic hours began. They led groups of 15 to 20 participants at a time to an enormous cobblestone plaza, filled with thousands of people & encircled by huge old buildings. It felt like arriving in a big piazza in Rome! We were bombarded with autograph seekers as we took off our helmets.

What a welcome! We posed by the car with dozens of extremely polite Mexicans for pictures and autographs. They all understood our inscription:

"Mercedes-Benz - La Carrera
-World Champions in 1952,

Minnesota Twins -
World Champions in 1991."

Adding our name & car number seemed incidental.

La Carrera took 200 rooms at Mexico City's Hotel Presidente, also taking over their underground garage. We skipped evening car service this night so the big M-B truck could by-pass the city entirely.

Results 2nd day (Large Sports Class) :		
1st,Ward/Ward,	**Kurtis500(replica)#207**	
	(2,816pts)	
9th, Herzog/Kienle,	**Mercedes #235**	
	(3,103pts)	
12th, Olson/Andersen,	**Mercedes #234**	
	(3,345pts)	

DAY 3: Destination: San Luis Potasi, another state capital. Altitude 6,157ft. Average October temperature: 63°. News about Mexico's smog is unfortunately true. Serious in the cities. New laws are being passed, but this fight started 10 years behind Los Angeles' efforts & Mexico City is larger than Los Angeles.

Crowds even surrounded toll road gates to wave & cheer as we drove north. In city traffic some drivers were oblivious that a government-approved race was in progress. A few plodded on regardless. We did not see the blatantly reckless driving we'd read about by Mexicans. They do have a more casual attitude than Americans; Mexican no-passing signs are more or less "suggestions," as in Italy. Everyone seems willing to move over when necessary. The 1st party flashing headlights also expects some priority, a custom expanded from negotiating one-way bridges.

A sampling of Mexico's Mayhem; Modified
'54 Corvette, V-8 Henry-J, & 1991 Kurtis 500.

After trying more frequent intervals we settled into driving a half day at a time. Takes too much driver & navigator warm-up time to change too often.

Our Official Route Books (2 volumes totaling 490 pages in 2 languages) are mind-boggling corner-by-corner logs of all 6 days, grading each corner & ear-marking every bridge, speed-bump and village!

We saw our European Gullwing friends daily. They too lost fuel unexpectedly when someone forgot to put the gas cap back on *inside* their trunk. Gas flooded into the trunk & flushed out the lid before it was spotted. They were ahead of us in points starting the 3rd day. Then serious trouble struck their engine, ruining their points for this day. It would have been the end for them but amazingly they brought a spare engine along! That evening while we changed some brake shoes, they changed their engine!

Results 3rd day (Large Sports Class):

1st Ward/Ward,	Kurtis500(replica)#207
	(3,416pts)
5th Olson/Andersen,	Mercedes #234
	(4,130pts)
13th Herzog/Kienle,	Mercedes #235
	(8,203pts)

DAY 4: Destination, Up. Zacatecas. Elevation: 8,147ft. Avg. Oct. Temperature: A cool 56°. This is our shortest day on the road. 253 miles. And the most infamous. It includes LaBufa, a Test Stage of sharp corners just before Zacatecas. Jorgen & I felt the cautions given everyone were overrated. We were careful, but sailed through without a hitch. Then we heard of three mishaps on this most famous of corners, including La Carrera's Chief USA Coordinator, and last year's overall winner, a C- Jaguar [replica] from England. Seems they too thought the section was "overrated." Hmmm. More to think about.

Zacatecas is a charming old city with a strong Spanish look about it. Picturesque old buildings, big & small. Hills everywhere. Won a huge sombrero at the evening's outdoor party. We became brave enough to eat dinners & breakfast at our hotels (as long as Pepto Bismol & lime juice were handy). By now we'd met most of the other teams, though they were dropping out by the dozen, *daily*. Gull Wing Group member **Nicolas Jones** of Connecticut, brought an XK120 for the third year! Canadian **Art Isler's** 190SL included in an early list of entrants was a no-show; car never got back from Europe where it participated in this year's Pirelli Rally (London to Rome). The Herzog/Kienle crew got their 2nd engine (alloy block) running well enough to beat our daily score but their break down had cost them 4500 devastating points for not completing 3rd day stages.

Results thru 4th day (Large Sports Class)

1st Ward/Ward,	Kurtis500(replica) #207	(4,243pts)
5th Olson/Andersen,	Mercedes #234	(5,172pts)
13th Herzog/Kienle,	Mercedes #235	(9,196pts)

DAY 5 & 6: Destination, Saltillo & Nuevo Laredo. Now cometh the long straight roads & a descent of 6,000ft. Unfortunately road maintenance also descended and the quality of road foundations seem to become short-changed. While everyone's average speed improved, especially those with larger engines, conditions did not. Frequent 2" & 3" road surface fluctuations at 125mph required 6 to 10 inch steering corrections... rarely with any shoulders or run-off areas. Sharing our sentiments with veteran participants brought replies like,

DRIVING "STAGES"

Test Stages: Actual racing segments. Federal & local police close down these road segments (up to 35 miles each) and, in the words of our Route Book, "earliness is allowed." Sole criteria is time & distance.

Limited Stages: Up to 135 miles outside population centers. 1 penalty point per second for being over 15 minutes early or *any seconds* late.

Transfer Stages: Segments in or near population centers. Every second of "earliness" penalized & there is no penalty for 1st 15 minutes lateness. Each morning & afternoon included all types of Stages.

"This is La Carrera! Exactly like the 1950s. Like it or leave it." "If its too hot, get out of the kitchen!" "A man's gotta do what a man's gotta do." We know that's mostly macho talk. This awesome event *has* become safer & better managed every year. It is not to be confused with the much shorter, annual Carrera in Baja, which has resulted in several deaths.

Beyond car preparations, the length of La Carrera challenges each team's fortitude & harmony. A special thanks to my 1991 co-pilot **Jorgen Andersen** & crew chief **Bruce Kelly**. La Carrera is called the "Mother of all Road Races." 1,900 miles & 6 days in Ol' Mexico saw one-third of the entries, 40 cars, fail before reaching the finish line. We now understand the pre-race comment that after La Carrera everything else will seem like a picnic!

It was particularly nice & a total surprise to find **Elda & K.B. Pearce** (President of the Gull Wing Group) among those cheering Jorgen and me through the checker flag at Neuvo Laredo! **Richard Brink** was also there (we all got together for a gleeful pose... and of course the photo blurred). La Carrera's Director General, **Eduardo Leon Camargo** was impressed that the Gull Wing Group President showed up at the finish line and awards banquet.

Would we do it again, and again? Bet on it! Unfortunately this is big league entertainment. Transporting a car, crew, and equipment from the USA to the bottom of Mexico and back, food, lodging, entry fee, turn-key, requires $11,000 to $15,000 depending on the number of people invited, and miscellaneous surprises. If you're up to financing such a party, maybe you want to be our next navigator/back-up-driver! One hellava picnic! Viva Carrera!

1991 Results: Large Sports Class

Of 121 starters, 40 cars failed to reach Neuvo Laredo. This is actually a similar survival rate to the Mille Miglia, though the MM is 50% pre-1940 vehicles.

Class/Ovrl Entry		Make	Car No.	Points
1/1:	Ward /Ward	Kurtis 500(rplca)	#207	5,662pts
2/2:	Zumbrana/Berea	Kurtis 500(rplca)	#200	6,020pts
3/5:	Unikel/Strobl	54 Corvette(mdfd)	#209	6,211pts
4/8:	Mason/Lindsay	C-Jaguar(rplca)	#227	6,370pts
5/25:	Olson/Andersen	Mercedes 300SL	#234	6,892pts
6/33:	Frank/Jung	54 Corvette(mdfd)	#212	7,457pts
7/34:	Giese/Giese	55 Corvette(mdfd)	#223	7,476pts
8/36:	N.Jones/Bengola	Jaguar XK120	#208	7,617pts
9/45:	Gillbertson/Jones	Jaguar XK120	#206	8,697pts
10/53:	Veale/Veale	Jaguar XK!20	#231	9,659pts
11/59:	Herzog/Kienle	Mercedes 300SL	#235	10,728pts
12/66:	Quieosa/Lopez	Facel Vega	#204	11,894pts
13/69:	Lewis/Tate	Lstr Jaguar(rplca)	#210	13,008pts
14/74:	Birrane/Craft	Allard J2X(rplca)	#224	14,247pts

Our pedal to the floor for long stretches across northern Mexico's ruler straight, desolate roads brought thoughts of **Nicholas Watt's** painting (below).

Karl Kling had decended the 11,000 ft. mountains and begun he's 1952 victory run to USA border. We wondered if the view from our driver's seat (left) looked much different 30 years later.

The Mexican Road Races have inspired prominent artists such as **Walter Gotschke, Carlos Demand, Dion Pears and Watts**. A limited edition, full color 26" x 17" lithograph by **Nicholas Watts** (below), autographed by **Karl Kling**, is available by mail order($150) from **Jacques Vaucher's** l'art et l'automobile, 20 Arctic Parkway, Trenton, NJ 08638. Ph. 609-392-6197. Mr. Vaucher is a good source for much of the art shown in this book.

NUMMER 7 • 2.JAHRGANG • JUNI 1927 PRE **1.50** MK.

NÜRBURG-RiNG
bei ADENAU (Eifel)

Offizielles Programm
für die
Eröffnungs-Feier des Nürburg-Ring
und die
Eifelrennen 1927 des A.D.A.C.
am 18. u. 19. Juni 1927

5.
Mercedes Art and Memorabilia

MERCEDES ART
AND MEMORABILIA

Even simple sales flyers, especially those concentrating on one specific model, and shop manuals, toy models and posters become scarce and valuable in their second and third decades. Never throw this stuff out when you sell or trade any car. If the car has collector potential, by rights, one set of everything should go to the next owners. If you want to keep a set to muse upon in your old age, buy a second set. Another good retirement investment.

Car sales folders & brochures, free today, some will be worth hundreds of dollars in 30 years. When an older car is purchased, we recommend that a set of all the items printed about the model be acquired. This usually includes several sales pieces, small flyers and hopefully something more fancy. We'd make the following generalizations about this part of the hobby:

1 Reprints are taboo. They are certainly interesting, but they have unproven collector value (ditto for replicars themselves).
2. Virtually any promotional handouts have value, if they really came from the manufacturer; even reprints of magazine reports. However the test report by itself is only significant as a part of the magazine if that is being collected (that's another subject).

3. Single model brochures have the greatest value potiential. Most of the world's more special cars have individual model brochures, separate from the full line catalogs.

4. Even the most homely, obsure catalogs have value. We think of some produced by Nash, and Nash Metropolitan. We have received letters from England offering to buy our Metropolitan folders. Demand for materials on cars that are no longer built weakens as the generation that knew the cars dies off, though the few collectors still needing those items seldom quibble about price.

5. Of course four+ color materials are preferable to black and white. and "Flats" or "flyers," the single sheets and single folds were pre-pared mostly for kids, and those judged by salesman to be non-serious lookers. Even these develop some value as owners begin to accumlate a complete set of everything promoting their model. If a small single page flyer costs $15 and you don't have the item... the price is incidental. The very high prices paid for some flyers result from two things... very few were ever produced, and for some early models only one item was ever produced.

All else being equal, car brochures without any dealer's stamp or other writing are more desirable than ones so marked. If you have or find Mercedes-Benz material beyond the scope of your interests, offer it for sale as someone else is probably hunting for it.

Mercedes-Benz on the other hand has created some spectacular 12 & 14 page portfolios even for the 300Sc, of which only 201 cars were built. This model was given its own personal typeset owner's manual, and shop manuals. The brochure for the 300Sc may take the prize for the finest color drawing and printing quality. Even the binding design is unprecedented to our knowledge; It has three center-fold pictures, and all three have continuous paper across the center fold... The notion that price was no object certainly pre-vailed on everything about that car. Last 300Sc brochure one we saw sold for $400. Same rule applied for the best Grand Mercedes 600 portfolios. In this case... A heavy gauge folder with a series of large (approx. 10"x15") color prints loosely inserted in it, with accompanying technical sheets. Classy! Worth $150 and climbing. More recently the 190E 2.3-16 was given a stiff paper "frame" into which eight descriptive inserts are stacked, each depicting a different aspect of the car; only seven years old, we're sure there's a steady row of buyers at $50 already.

Beware of copies: They've become quite prevalent, sometimes even down to the original code markings. That's outright forgery in our opinion. Colors and papers are the usual give-away, as those used in the 1980s and 1990s seldom have the same hues or feel. If in doubt, be sure who you are dealing with and ask for a descriptive receipt/guaranty.

VINTAGE ART

Intermitently car manufacturers use prominent artists to portray their cars. Riley of England used some wonderful pencil sketches in the 1950s. All German companies, including Tanus (Ford of Germany) contracted superb artists. Even the Volkswagen Microbus was presented in wonderous water colors. Two eminent German automotive artists, **Walter Gotschke** & **Hans Liska** were actually employed by Mercedes-Benz as staff artists, as well as doing free-lance work. Any painting or brochure freaturing their work Is desirable. A frequent contributor to *Road & Track* magazine, Gotschke's original 1950 to 1980 paintings now command $5,000 to $15,000+ depending on the size and tightness

Will Williams' fame doing movie posters, from The King and I to Mutiny on the Bounty, and celebrities from Clarke Gable Marlene Dietrich & John Wayne, brings a new name to automotive art. At the right is 1950s racer Hans Herrmann piloting a 300SL, one in a new three poster series autographed by the three drivers and Williams.

MERCEDES-BENZ

PURSUIT

OF

VICTORY

KARL KLING

with G. MOLTER

Foreword by ALFRED NEUBAUER

GRAND
PRIX
DRIVER

Hermann Lang

Guide to
COMPETITION
DRIVING

by Paul O'Shea

2

MODERN SPORTS CAR SERIES

DICK
SEAMAN
A RACING CHAMPION
by PRINCE CHULA

THE LIFE STORY OF ENGLAND'S GREATEST
ROAD RACING DRIVER . . . .
ONLY ENGLISH MEMBER OF THE FAMOUS
MERCEDES-BENZ RACING TEAM.

Published by
FLOYD CLYMER
LOS ANGELES

$2.00

ADVENTURE
ON
WHEELS

The Autobiography of a Road Racing Champion
JOHN FITCH with William F. Nolan

*Many of Daimler-Benz's leading
race drivers have written books.
None of the books are still
available new, which puts them in
demand with collectors. Specialized topic books are more desirable
than general marque overviews.* **Karl Ludvigsen's**
THE MERCEDES-BENZ RACING CARS, *is considered a classic,
along with all of the books on this page. We've obtained a few of these titles at low-key used book stores,
which is certainly worth an occasional look. Out-of-print books and old Mercedes sales catalogs are offered
to the SLML and advertised in it periodically.*

of the detailing. Each artist seems to capture a style that is uniquely their own.

MERCEDES IN THEIR BLOOD: Of currently active artists **Nicholas Watts, Carlos Demand,** Sweden's **Sune Envall,** America's **Harold Cleworth** and **Don Eddy**, and (recently) German born **Will Williams** have shown a special love for Mercedes-Benz SL subjects. Williams, best known for his Hollywood motion picture posters of the 50's and 60's, has just finished an SL series and consented to do private portraits of owners with their SL in the same theme as his SL series. Original art by these folks are the real prizes, followed by their personally signed, limited edition prints. Choosing the long term survivors, the artists that car enthusiasts will still recognize 20 and 30 years from now, is our challenge. Only a half dozen have met this test from the past. Only a few artists will portray Mercedes subjects so well or for so many years that they are automatically associated with the marque. *Regardless of an artist's personal style, technically accurate detailing quickly separates general subject artists from special subject pros.* For example the same serious error was made by two well known artists working in bronze a few years ago. Independently they decided to do limited edition commemoratives of the 300SLR in which Stirling Moss won the 1955 Mille Miglia. A uniqueness of this car is that the driver straddles the transmission, as is easily seen looking into the cockpit, but both sculptors missed this point. Consequently their otherwise outstanding $10,000+ offerings were seriously flawed. Walter Gotschke or Carlos Demand simply wouldn't make such an error.

POSTERS

Most wall posters distributed to Mercedes-Benz dealerships over the decades become popular artifacts and in some cases art. Particularly posters of specific models, or specific race wins. The large 20+" x 30+" size gets the most attention... big enough to be dramatic, but not too big to display in a private setting. Original Mercedes racing posters from the 1930s in fine condition bring an easy $1,000+, and $500+ for 1950s race announcements. Reproductions of these old dealer materials is a different scene... fun decorations for the garage at $15 to $30 each, but of no true collector value. Some desirable Mercedes paintings and posters are found in this book.

POSTAGE STAMPS

commemorating automobiles are receiving more attention as the numbers of automotive enthusiasts grows. As something of a testimonial, Mercedes-Benz cars appear on more postage stamps world-wide than any other make. Automobile stamps with clearly identifiable makes of cars are few in number.

The United States has only recently printed stamps with identifiable cars, all of American built cars. One of the most valuable auto stamps is American: the 4-cent stamp printed in 1901 in a series of six stamps called the *Pan-American Issue*. The 4-cent example is available by itself, and a "fine" example, unused, has a retail store value of $300+. In determining rareness, age, quantity originally printed and quality of the printing job are the key considerations. Because cars were just becoming recognized as legitimate transportation in 1901, that stamp is especially uncommon. Also, only 5 million of this 4-cent stamp were made, compared to 90 million for the 2-cent and 1-cent stamps in that same Pan-American Issue. That quantity sounds large, but saving/collecting unused stamps was very uncommon at that time.

Thanks to Prince Rainier's keen interest in automobiles, Monoco has done one of the finest jobs in honoring vintage cars and racing victors on commemorative stamps. In a series issues of six, eleven or fourteen stamps, a particular race or era is featured, such as the 75th Anniversary of Grand Prix racing. Naturally, Mercedes-Benz fares well on this basis. It is tempting to put together a collection exclusively of Mercedes-Benz stamps world-wide, as the group issues are often very well done, appealingly documenting a special piece of auto history. Black and white photos do not capture the fine colors which some of them display. It is easy to be taken in by them and the stories behind them.

As a practical matter, some stamp dealers will not break an unused set apart. That is not a problem anyway as most sets are new enough that they can still be purchased for $7 to $10 each. A rather respectable auto stamp collection can be assembled for just a few hundred dollars, all unused, "fine" stamps. Since the whole field of identifiable car stamps is much smaller than, say stamps of ships or even trains, it is both unusual and manageable for a novice collector.

New Zealand has issued an attractive series that includes an early Benz, and the Federal Republic is Islamique recently featured a 1914 Mercedes in a six-stamp group. In 1961 the Deutsche Bundespost saluted Carl Benz (it is spelled with a "C" on the stamp, incidently) and Gottlieb Daimler for the 75th Anniversary of their 1886 inventions. Mercedes-Benz was so delighted that they bought thousands of the two stamp sets to include in an informational folder sent out to Mercedes-Benz owners all over the USA and elsewhere. These stamps themselves are not yet very rare, but the folder with these stamps distributed in the USA by Mercedes-Benz Sales, Inc. of South Bend, Indiana (1961), titled "Stamp of Greatness" (8-1/2" x 8") is quite desirable.

In general, auto stamp collecting is only now gaining attention among automobilia, so it is still possible to become involved at modest prices. The long history of stamp collecting itself, and the fact that authentic stamps are a limited commodity (no replicas) enhance the picture.

THE HOBBY IN MINIATURE

Model or toy collecting is one of the fastest growing areas of the car hobby. In larger cities clubs and annual swap meets are common. Often people receive a gift model of a car they own (or owned, or want). One thing leads to another and they get hooked!

There are Mercedes SL model collectors all over the world. Some, such as **Art Thumwood,** (a helpful collector & trader in SL models in the USA, Scottsdale, AZ, 602-39-SL300), has concentrated mostly on Mercedes SLs. We were astounded to learn he has over 300 different SL models! Art explains that toys are graded, just like stamps or out-of print books.

Symbol	Condition Grading:
MB	Mint boxed
MNB	Mint, no box
E	Excellent, shows evidence of use.
G	Good
P	Poor, Rough or repainted

Note that you should always save the box in which models are sold. Attractively colored boxes add 25% to the value of a toy. Also, the most treasured models are the no-longer made models of the same period as the cars they copy. Most originated as inexpensive toys... children's play things. Those in the photo all sold new for under $5. Collectors often regard tinplate toys to be the most collectible. German examples offer exceptional mechanical quality while the Japanese models are prized for their gimmickry.

Lately, there is a new breed of collector models. These feature exceptional detailing and are priced accordingly. Most new releases hit their lowest prices soon after introduction. That's the time to buy them, ...and don't forget to save that box!

In Europe a popular source for SL models is *Mr. Mercedes Toys & Models,* 39 Nelson Place, Broadstairs, Kent. CT10 1HQ. Their phone is (44) 0843-604795.

The four tinplate models shown below, and their approximate values (MNB) left to right:

Model	Maker	Nationality	Notes	Aprox. Value
300SL Roadster	SHOWA	Japan	"Bump & go" operation	$400
190SL	GAMI	Germany	"Bump & go" operation	$400
230SL	BAMBI	Japan	Friction motor operation	$200
300SL Gullwing	ARNOLD	France (& Germany)	Pwr'd by crank on leash	$400

*These models are from the collections of **Art Thumwood** and **Larry Kay**.*

PHOTOGRAPHY

Photo-journalism came of age during the same years as automobiles. Early action-photographers most associated with Mercedes-Benz are **Edward Monkhouse, Jesse Alexander,** and **Louis Klementaski,** in that order. They are the early masters of cars-in-motion and expressive close-ups of the leading personalitites. Today's best known Mercedes-Benz photgrapers, **Dennis Adler** & **Rich Taylor,** while very good, have concentrated on salon-type staging, devoid of people. Monkhouse's large horizontal format book *Mercedes-Benz Grand- Prix Racing, 1934-1955,* is a masterpiece of 458 photos taken behind the scenes with M-B's blessings, as photo documentation of those successful years (see pg. 171).

Top: Our all time favorite racing photo was taken immediately after **Stirling Moss** won the 1955 Mille Miglia (see painting on page 146). Each person's face is so "telling:" **Rudolf Ulhenhaut,** at left, is the proud father of the winning 300SLR racer, **Denis Jenkinson,** center, the navigator, is mentally still out there somewhere in a corner where he thought they'd crash, and Moss, right, trying to bring Jenkinson into the moment of victory. *Lower Photo:* Ulhenhaut's crowning achievement undressed. 300SLR straight-eights were raced in open & closed wheel versions.

6.
Clubs, Books and
Magazines

CLUBS, BOOKS AND MAGAZINES FOR MERCEDES ENTHUSIASTS

"Mercedes-Benz owners know they've bought something more than a mere luxury car, yet they are not as intense about it as Porsche or Ferrari owners. They don't buy every Mercedes book, or join every owner's group, but they do want to know what's going on. While car clubs can be very useful, realistically, less than 10% take the time to become involved or reap the rewards.

A 230/250/280SL gathering of the German "Pagoda Club" at the fabulous Mercedes-Benz Museum near Stuttgart. Don't miss this stop on any visit to southern Germany.

THE CLUBS

Hyatt Cheek, a colorful Texan suggests that since most old car enthusiasts are a bit soft in the head, they might benefit from joining a support group. It certainly worked for Hyatt. It wasn't long before his groups made him president of the Mercedes-Benz Club of America, and later the the Gull Wing Group. There are a lot of choices on the next few pages. The technical information alone is worth their annual dues.

190SL GROUP: After a false start in Georgia, **Ron Rapp** rekindled the 190SL Group in Maryland, published a regular newsletter and attracted members by the hundreds across the country. A mixture of do-it-yourselfers, professional restorers, and other owners have worked together on many projects from encouraging remanu-facture of unavailable parts to conducting national meets and technical sessions. Celebrating their 10th Anniversary in 1993, they have approximately 860 members. An annual convention typically attracts 100 to 150, for tech sessions, parties, a concours, raffles, vendor displays, and an awards banquet. Annual dues: $30. Car ownership not required. Send checks % *190SL Group, to 16 Theodore Drive, East Brunswick, NJ 08816.*

190SL CLUB e.V.: German 190SL owners group. Meets and newsletter. Contact **Norbert Schneider** for membership application.
% Wetteraustr. 97, W-6360 Friedberg 3. Germany.

GULL WING GROUP INTERNATIONAL (GWG): People seemed to sense the 300SL should be collected almost from day one, 1954. Data in the cars, and who bought them, was tracked carefully by the factory, and even published in some books, almost as a who's who of car owners, before public privacy laws curtailed company disclosures of this type. The GWG was formed over 30 years ago in 1961, initially just for "Gull Wing" Coupe owners. A decade later 300SL Roadster owners (Roadsters share about 60% of the Coupe's parts) were invited to join in on an equal basis. Several other

MBCA National Presidents have presided also as GWG presidents... **(Chad Hunt, Hyatt Cheek)** though the two groups have never seriously considered merging. GWG members have been building a 450+ page *Tech-Tips Manual* from experiences of members that is alone worth the price of membership and price of the Manual. Of the world's ultra-famous and rare cars none have a factory and owner support network to compare with the 300SL. Between Mercedes-Benz and several dozen specialists that duplicate the oddest parts, everything is available. 300SL owners too, have their annual gathering of the faithful. A third of all 300SLs reside in south western United States. Regional chapters are not especially active, but the 700 members are practically a fraternal group, with many having owned

Frank Mallory giving a talk on Solex & Weber Carburetors at a 190SL National Meet.

their cars for over 20 years. Many members (nearly 100) have both a Gullwing and a Roadster though ownership is not required for club membership. Their monthly *300StarLetter* is pipeline to one of the world's most elite car clubs. Dues: $30 per year.
The Gull Wing Group,
15875 Oak Glen Avenue, Morgan Hill, CA 95037. USA.

300SL CLUB e.V.: Factory recognized European owner's group, with excellent network for owners. Quarterly *300SL Bulletin* (In German), a major annual convention and occasional meets with other clubs typify each year. Contact **Robert Bayer** for membership application. % Postfach 1117, 7939 Ehingen (Danau), Germany.

230/250/280SL Clubs: For those of you enthused about 230/250/280SLs, there are several choices.

1. *SL CLUB PAGODA, e.V.* If you speak German this is the most established organization specializing in this series. Excellent factory access to technical details and history on these cars. Month newsletter, meetings & rallies. Contact: **Manfred Luft**, Sonnenbuehl 48, 7000 Stuttgart70, Germany

2. *"PAGODA GROUP" OF THE MERCEDES BENZ CLUB of AMERICA (MBCA):* "Sub-groups" focused on specific Mercedes-Benz models is a new concept for MBCA, serving potentially a half dozen specific models.

201

A "Pagoda Group" for 230/250/280SL enthusiasts, is in its early stages, and eager for members and technical contributors. A quarterly newsletter is budgeted, and increased coverage in the STAR is planned. MBCA membership is a prerequisite for sub group participants.

MBCA is the largest Mercedes club in the world, with roughly 20,000 members. It has over 75 chapters (called sections) across the country, over $500,000 in assets, and even owns its own office building with several permanent salaried employees. The resulting hierarchy of voluntary, elected officials, committees and board members becomes a cast of hundreds. With membership spread widely, only about 15% appear regularly at section events, and 85% of them bring sedans. The club's bi-monthly magazine, the STAR, certainly adds to renewals; its 80+ page color format & prestigious readership attracts enough advertisers to finance internationally known authors, artists, & photography. As a principal voice of such a large club, the magazine has also become a way for the stature of rare models to be publicized (or "legitimized" when claimed provenance isn't verified). These cautions noted, the $35 annual dues is a bargain, especially if the Sub-group for SLs blooms.
Car ownership is not required. Credit card orders can be made via **1-800-637-2360**, or send a check % *MBCA*, 1907 Lelaray St, Colorado Springs, CO 80909.

230/250/280SL Sub-Group Contact: **Peter Lesler**, 4615 Brainard Rd, Chagrin Falls, OH 44022. Phone 216-248-7589.

SL SECTION, THE MERCEDES-BENZ CLUB of ENGLAND: **Gordon Hoey** heads up the SL activities of this 40+ year old Mercedes owners club, ...oldest one in the world. There is no separate SL organization in England, so SL owners tend to find each other through this club's events and "Gazette", an informative 80 page bi-monthly. Annual dues: 26 pound. Initiation fee: 5 pounds. % Mercedes-Benz (UK) Ltd., Deleware Drive, Tongwell, Milton Keynes, Bucks. MK15 8BA. Phone: 0908 668899.

280/350/380/350/500/560SL Club: There's only one to date, again in Germany: *107 SL CLUB. e.V.:* No information about activities or publications. % **Gerhard Spenz**, Schoenauer Bach 11, 5100 Aachen, Germany.

THE MAGAZINES
MERCEDES: (48 DM or $35, 6 times per year, , in ten languages) %Mercedes, Reader's Services, Post Box 111208, W-6000 Frankfurt/Main 11, Germany. In a surprise move during 1992 the Mercedes factory's venerable 30 year old publication *In Aller Welt* was totally revised. Everything about the magazine has become more lavish, including a new policy

to admit selected, high line full page color advertising. Topics range widely from humor to interviews to multi-discipline philosophy of interest to clients in over 160 nations. Each year a 100 page special issue is prepared about the company, its people and products, and is sent out upon request, free to subscribers. In full color for 20 years, it has always been an international magazine bargain.

THE MERCEDES COLLECTOR: ($35, 4 times annually) P.O. Box 4181, Silver Springs, MD 20904. This young magazine focuses on the minutiae of specific models changes to the point of nausea, *unless* the model happens to be yours. Then things get interesting. Contributing editors cover subject like wood refinishing, use of unleaded fuels, merits of synthetic oil and silicone brake fluids, the need for appraisals and other worthy subjects. A continuing treatise is attempting to document *every single change* (it sure seems that way) on both the 190SL and the 230/250/280SL. Other models will probably follow. Nice to read though carefully once, and keep for permanent reference.

JOURNEY: ($36 4 issues annually, $40 outside U.S.) %Journey, 4401 Zephyr Street, Wheat Ridge, Colorado, 80033-3299, USA). Another new quarterly, introduced by a veteran niche magazine publisher **Don Huflin** in Colorado. Featuring personal interviews of significant Mercedes personalities, collectors, private and commercial restorers, and factory representatives. Huflin's reporters often meet with their subjects in their own homes, or with their car collections, filming the interviews and taking extensive pictures. The company does their own printing on three magnificent Heidelberg presses that produce unmatched color photography.

SL MARKET LETTER: ($77 buys 18 issues per year $97 overseas) %SL *Market Letter,* Inc.; published by the nice folks that brought you this book. Typically a 12 page newsletter format, published approximately once every three weeks. Free & quick listings on any M-B subject for private subscribers. Timely collation of SLs and other rare models for sale. Foremost price trends analysis every six months on all SLs and other rare Mercedes models, plus other news about the cars and the company. (Special subscription price offered to readers on last page of this book.)

THE BOOKS
This book includes the fundamental facts about each SL series, but once one buys a specific SL, the quest for further details grows. Unfortunately there are no major books focusing exclusively on the 190SL and the most impressive books about the 113 Body (1960s) and 107 Body (1970s & 1980s) are only printed in German. We have listed them here for those of you who read German. Several

have been done in English for the original 300SLs, our favorite by Lewandowski.

MERCEDES SL SERIES,
by **Brian Laban**. (English text) 7.5" x 10" format, 192 pages, 100 color photos, 20 line drawings. Hrdbd. ISBN:185 223 5950 Evolution of the SLs from 1952 to the high tech 1990s. Each model profiled with history, specifications and features of importance.
Typical Price: $36

MERCEDES 190SL (Auto Classic #3).
by **Stafan Knittel**. (English & German text) 8.25" x 11" soft format 48 pages. 100 b & w photos. Published by Podzun-Pallas. Outstanding accumulation of factory photos and detail on the oroginal design, structure, prototypes, finished versions, and accessories offered. Small but packed with facts.
Orgnl price: $4.
Out of Print.
Typical price now: $30

MERCEDES 300SL (Auto Classic #5).
by **Stafan Knittel**. 8.25" x 11" soft format 48 pages. 100 b & w photos. Sequal to 190SL editon published by Podzun-Pallas. Many early factory photos not found elsewhere, along with design rationale, early history, race experiences, famous owners, and steps taken to switch to a roadster version. Original price: $
Out of Print.
Typical price now: $30

MERCEDES-BENZ 300SL,
by **Jurgen Lewandowski**. (English & German text). 11" x 13" format, 168 pages, Hrdbd. with 160 illustrations, 137 in color with state-of-the-art printing on fine enamel paper. Linen cover with slip-cover and case. Numbered edition (only 3,000 to be sold). ISBN 3-517-01101-0. Published by Sudwest Verlag GmbH, Munchen. English & German text. Companion to matching books on the Ferrari GTO & Porsche 959.
Original price: $250.
3,000 run soldout.
Typical price now: $450

MERCEDES-BENZ 190SL - 280SL,
by **Gunter Engelen**. (German text) 9" x 11" format. 270 pages. Hardbd, w/ 160 50 color photos, 135 b & w. $75. ISBN: Drawn from months in the Mercedes archives by Stuttgarter Engelen, the footnotes and technical appendix alone take over fifty pages. All uncoverable facts are presented without evident judgements of their value to readers; as if to say here's everything we could find, use what you will. This book gave us our first break-down of 190SL and 230SL shipments to the USA during the Studebaker-Packard years, and shipments to MBNA, as distinguished from MBNA sales, which account for how many cars were built in one year and sold in the next.
Typical Price: $75

MERCEDES-BENZ 300SL, by **Michael Riedner** & **Gunter Engelen**. (German text) 9" x 11" format. 270 pages. Hardbd, w/ 160 50 color photos, 135 b & w. ISBN: 3-613-01268-5. Very detailed history, with never before used factory photos and records about original development of the 1952 SLs; creation of the tube frame, engine experiments and results, air tunnel testing for the body shape, and tuning variations for specific races. Then specs of production cars including color & interior combinations, and exact chassis # of each design up-date.
Typical Price: $75

MERCEDES-BENZ 230/250/280SL - 1963-1971, by **R.M. Clarke**. 8" x11" format. Approx 100 pages, 180 illustrations. Reprinted test reports & other articles from major car magazines on these 3 models, their history, introduction, tuning, and specifications.   Typical Price: $16

MERCEDES-BENZ SL & SLC - 1971-1989 (Gold Portfilio Edition), by **R. M. Clarke**. 8" x 11" format. 180 pages. 300+ illustrations. *Brooklands* soft cover compilation of road tests, tech info, and related articles reprinted from magazines. $22

MERCEDES-BENZ SL, by **Bruno Alfieri**. (Text in English, French & Italian). 9.75" x 11" format, 96 pages. 80 color photos, 105 illustrations. Hardbound.   ISBN: 88 85880 55 X.   Devoted to the new #129 Body SL of the 1990s, with a quick look at it's predecessors. Reviews the state-of-the-art rollbar, adaptive dampening suspension, electronic cam shaft adjustment, four valve engines, and more.
Typical Price: $50

A personal adventure with Mercedes-Benz cars

Number 1 • Spring 1993 • $10

SUBSCRIPTION RATES

Subscriptions start with the next issue.

● One year (4 issues) – $36 ($40 U.S. funds outside the U.S.)
● Two years (8 issues) – $68 ($76 U.S. funds outside the U.S.)
● Single issues when available are $10 each

Send orders to:

𝕵𝖔𝖚𝖗𝖓𝖊𝖞

4401 Zephyr Street
Wheat Ridge, Colorado 80033-3299 U.S.A.
Or call for MasterCard, Visa and Discover orders:
(303) 420-2222 or 800-352-5678 7:30 a.m. to 3:30 p.m. Denver time

7. *Leaders in the*
SL Community 1952-94

Robert Bayers

We are pleased to recognize a few of the most well known people in the SL community. Some are private enthusiasts and others are commercially involved. Their help to the SL's original fame or subsequent preservation and to valuable club activities, make them stand out in any summary of the Mercedes-Benz SLs. Inclusion on this list is not an endorsement of any businesses of these people, though many are revered.

	AREAS OF INTEREST			
190SL (121 Body)	300SL (040/042 Body)	#113 (230/250/280SL)	#107 (450/380/560SL)	#129 (300/500/600SL)

Eugen Bohringer

Carlos Bonera

John Burnside

Adams, Bruce. Bolton, **MA**. (508) 779-6513. 190SL Group Authenticity Committee Member. Owner of Sport Leicht, 404 Wattaquadock Hill Rd, 190SL restoration & service company.
— ✔ (190SL)

Andreadis, Alex. Barnes, London, SW13 9JS. **ENGLAND .** 081-748-2942. Pst President of Philpa Car Club of Greece. Runs many concours classics including 300SL, 6.3, 6.9, 500K.
— ✔ (300SL)

Bayer, Robert. Ehingen(Donau), **GERMANY.** 07391-6084 Long-term President of the 300SL Club in Europe. Knows and known by just about every 300SL owner in Europe.
— ✔ (300SL)

Bellamy, Tina. Epping, Essex, CM16 4PX , **ENGLAND.** 0992-573304. 75 Theydon Grove. President of Mercedes-Benz Club of England. Rallies a 300SL & 280SE Cabrio.
— ✔ (300SL)

Bohringer, Eugen. 7000 Stuttgart, **GERMANY** 0711-331293 Neur Berg 44. Very successful rally racer in 1960s and 1970s for Mercedes. Now runs a 300SL at club events.
— ✔ ✔ (300SL, #113)

Bollmeyer, Dieter. 4983 Kieklangern, **GERMANY** (05223-71456) Kiolk-Kampweg 9. Runs Concours GW & Rdstr
— ✔ (300SL)

Bonera, Carlo. Brescia, **ITALY.** ()30-365561 Authorized Mercedes-Benz dealer ; savior to MB entrants in each year's Mille Miglia. Rally's his own 300SL GW and 300SL Rdstr.
— ✔ ✔ ✔ ✔ ✔ (all)

Brockel, Bernd Meyer. 6236 Eschborn 2, **GERMANY.** Haupstrassse 348. Strong supporter of SL Pagoda Clubs & Events.
— ✔ (#107)

Burnside, John . Palos Verdes Estates, **CA.** 213-377-0065. Past Natn'l Pres. of MBCA & long term GWG Bd. Mmbr. Original owner (still) of a Gull Wing and a 300SL Roadster.
— ✔ (#113)

Cheek, Hyatt. Dallas, **TX.** (214) 327-6890. Enthusiastic Mercedes SL owner & personal restorer. Keen knowledge of 300 series, 190SL, the 6.3, and club affairs. Past National President of both Gull Wing Group and MBCA.
— ✔ ✔ (300SL, #113)

Hyatt Cheek

Cox, Vernon. Sunnydale, Berkshire, SL5 0PD , **ENGLAND** (081)748-2942. 13 Sidbury Close. Archivist & Judge for Mercedes-Benz Club of England. Runs with #107 & others. — ✔ (#107)

Cushway, Ron. Loughton, Essex **IG10 2SP ENGLAND.** (081) 508-3839. Trevelan House. Father figure of 40 yr old M-B Clb of England. Prolific inventor (resistance welding) Has 360,000 mi. on '62 300SL which he purchased new. — ✔ (300SL)

Dare, Ollie. Wilton, **CA.** (916) 687-6018. Dare Fitted Luggage, 9902 Mindy Lane. Voice Mail: (916-687-6018). Recreates show quality fitted luggage as offered for 1950s and early 1960s Mercedes-Benz. — ✔ ✔ ✔ (190SL, 300SL, #113)

Dearborn, Alex. Topsfield, **MA.** (508) 887-6644. 16 Maple Street. Buys & sells 1949-71 Mercedes SL, Sc, SE other rare models. Races a 190SL. — ✔ ✔ ✔ (190SL, 300SL, #113)

Demers, John. Kennebunkport, **ME.** (207) 646-4214. Exceptional SL upholsterer. — ✔ ✔ (#107, #129)

Ron Cushway

Drabik, Don. Chicago, **IL.** (312)-222-9238. Central Region V.Pres. of 190SL Group. Host to 1989 Natnl. Convention. — ✔ (190SL)

Frebert, George. Dover, **DE.** (302) 678-1211. Editor and Publisher, Silver Star Restorations (out of print), contents donated 190SL Group Technical Manual. — ✔ ✔ ✔ ✔ (190SL, 300SL, #113, #107)

Frisbie, Stephen. Portland, **OR.** (503) 665-2222. Steve's Restorations. 4440 SE 174th Av. Body-off & ground-up restorations. Pick & file, lead work, & metal fabrication, paint, & upholstery on pre WWII and later Mercedes-Benz. — ✔ (300SL)

Michael Egan

Egan, Michael. Alexandria, **VA.** (703)683-5043. 814 W. Timberbranch Parkway. Prominent international collector of 230/250/280SL history, manuals, and minutiae. — ✔ (#107)

Eicker, Robert. 5600 Wuppertal 2, **GERMANY.** (0202) 466 0406. Elias Ellerstrasse 95. Vry knwldgble & hlpful re 300SL — ✔ (300SL)

Eisenlohr, Bill. Corona, **CA.** (714) 737-3650. Eisenlohr Enterprises. 18600 Quail Hill Dr. Show quality restorer. — ✔ (300SL)

Gannon, Pete. Tempe, **AZ.** (602) 829-7826. 1988 E. 1st St. Over 350 M-B parts cars including SLs. Parts car bought. — ✔ ✔ ✔ (190SL, #107, #129)

Grant, David. Panorama City, **CA.** (818)787-2881. Scott Restorations, Inc. 14661 Lanark Street. Knowledgeable west coast 1950s 300SL advisor and sales specialist. — ✔ (300SL)

Terry Hawirko

Erich Hillgruber

Jerry Hjeltness

Chad Hunt

Gary Jarvis

Hamilton, Tom. E. Rochester, **NY.** (716) 385-2338. Owner of senior award winning 190SL at 1991 190SL Group. National Meeting.

Hatch, Robert. Hudson, **MA.** (508) 562-7355. Hatch & Sons Automotive, Inc., 406 Main St. Restoration & sales of exceptional Mercedes cars. Award for 190SL at 1991 190SL Group National Meeting at Stamford, CT.

Hawirko, Terry. Mississauga, ON, **Canada** (416)670-4901. Classic Car Craft, Ltd. 1312 Britannia Rd, E. Reproducer of numerous 300SL components. Awesome quality.

Hillgruber, Erich K. D2000 Hamburg 1, **GERMANY.** 40-231288. Spaldingstrasse 1. International car club supporter & participant (Mille Miglia, Pebble Beach, M-B Clubs) with remarkable collection of one-of-a-kind Mercedes & SL models.

Hillgruber, Kurt. Pacific Palisades, **CA.** (213)459-4204. Major west coast collector of 300SL Gullwings and Roadsters. Long time Board member of Gull Wing Group.

Hjeltness, Jerry. Escondido, **CA.** (619)746-9966. Hjeltness Restoration, 630 Alpine Way. 300SL restoration & authenticity expert. Popular club tech. speaker.

Hodges, Mike. Hampton, Middx. **England** . (081)979-7180 6 Church Street. Frequent technical writer of #113 and #107 articles for Mercedes-Benz Club of GB.

Hoey, Gordon. .Patcham, Brighton, Sussex, BN1 8NA **U.K.** . (0273-553-694). 11 Carden Ave. Editor of Mercedes-Benz Club Gazette. Drives classics including 190SL and 230SL.

Hunt, Chad. Morgan Hill, **CA.** (408)776-1788. 15875 Oak Glen Ave. Gullwing interior upholstering expert. Large car collection. Past Ntn'l President of GWG & MBCA.

Johnson, Bud. Douglasville, **GA.** (404)942-8444. 9130 Hywy 5. New & used 190/230/250/280/300SL parts.

Jarvis, Gary. La Mesa, **CA.** (619)670-1375. 4308 Alta Mira Drive. Gull Wing Board member. Owns 300SL Roadster with over a dozen 1st & Best of Show trophies.

Kidder, Tim. Sparta, **MI.** (616) 784-4286. K & K Manufacturing. 951 Nine Mile Rd. Mnfrs body floor pans and other essential 190/230/250/280SL rstrtn. parts sold world-wide.

Name	190SL	300SL	#113	#107	#129
Hamilton, Tom	✔				
Hatch, Robert	✔	✔			
Hawirko, Terry		✔			
Hillgruber, Erich K.		✔			
Hillgruber, Kurt		✔			
Hjeltness, Jerry		✔			
Hodges, Mike				✔	
Hoey, Gordon	✔	✔			
Hunt, Chad		✔			
Johnson, Bud	✔	✔	✔		
Jarvis, Gary		✔			
Kidder, Tim	✔	✔			

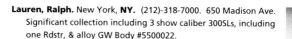

Kienle, Klaus. 7257 Heimerdingen, **GERMANY.** 071 525 2827 Kienle Automobiltechnik, Max Planckstr 4. Showcase restoration facility for in 300, 600, and 111& 112 coupes & cnvrtbls.

Kling, Karl. 7030 Boblingen-Tanenberg, **GERMANY.** Panoramastrasse 36. 1950s Mercedees-Benz Racing Team member. Recently celebrated 80th birthday. Won LaCarrera Panamericana & other major races for M-B in 1952.

Karl Kling

Lauren, Ralph. New York, **NY.** (212)-318-7000. 650 Madison Ave. Significant collection including 3 show caliber 300SLs, including one Rdstr, & alloy GW Body #5500022.

Lesler, Peter. Chagrin Falls, **OH.** (216)248-7589. 4615 Brainard Rd. MBCA Regional VP & Pagoda Group Spksmn.

Lewandowski, Jurgen. Munchen, **GERMANY.** % Sudwest Verlag. Author of best 300SL book available in English and German. 168 pg. ISBN #3-517-01101-0.

Linke, Siegfried. Seattle, **WA.** 206-622-3406. European Mtrs. Major exprt on 1920s thru 1970s M-B, including all SLs. Chrmn. of 1992 Gull Wing Group National Meet. Pebble Beach Judge.

Siegfried Linke

Lorenz, Albrecht . 7012 Fellbach, **GERMANY** 0711-584-658 Hintere Strasse 34/1. Known in the 300SL Club as the "Papst" (the Pope), Albrecht & his father together have worked for M-B 100 years. Worked in the 300SL section training, during 1950s.

Mallory, Frank. Silver Springs, **MD.** (301) 622-4103. Box 4181. Editor & Publisher of *The Mercedes Collector.* Quarterly. $36 per. year. shipped 1st Class anywhere in the world. Technical advisor & supporter of 190SL Group & members.

Marino, Ken. Palm Harbor, **FL.** (813)734-5998. 1500 Chukar Ridge. Technical resource for 230/250/280SLs.

Steve Marx

Marx, Steve. Costa Mesa, **CA.** (714) 548-6273. 1950 Placentia. Marx repair service, especially for older SLs. Gull Wing Group National Board Member.

Marchant, Ken. A. Los Angeles, **CA.** (310)575-0445. Automobile Investment Services. Frequent writer for & supporter of MBCA. On Ntn'l Brd. Specializes in M-B appraisals, inspections.

Miller, Jim. Huntington Beach, **CA.** (714)375-6565. Miller's, Inc. 7391 Prince Dr. Southwestern V. Pres. of 190SL Group. Original Parts for Mercedes from '55 to mid '70s, with emphasis on 190SL, 230/250/280SL and 450SL.

Roberta Nichols

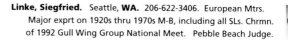

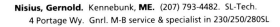
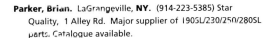

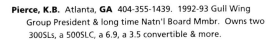
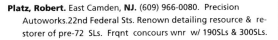
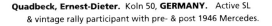
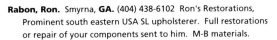

	190SL	300SL	#113	#107	#129

K.B. Pierce

Ron Rapp

Don Ricardo

David Rosales

Narde, Donald. Horseheads, **NY.**   234 Breesport Road. Enthusiastic GW Group supporter and vintage racer. Races a 300SL Roadster and a Daimler SP250.

Nichols (Yakel), Roberta. Plymouth, MI . (313)459-7313. Ford Alternative Fuels Specialist & Speaker. Pst. Pres. of Gull Wing Group, and Club Registrar of 300SL Rdstrs, world-wide.

Nisius, Gernold. Kennebunk, **ME.** (207) 793-4482. SL-Tech. 4 Portage Wy. Gnrl. M-B service & specialist in 230/250/280SL

Parker, Brian. LaGrangeville, **NY.** (914-223-5385) Star Quality, 1 Alley Rd. Major supplier of 190SL/230/250/280SL parts. Catalogue available.

Parker, Sean. Arlington, **TX.** (814) 261-0053. South Central Regional V.Pres. of 190SL Group. Solex 44 carburetor whiz kid. Works for S & S Imports.

Pierce, K.B. Atlanta, **GA** 404-355-1439. 1992-93 Gull Wing Group President & long time Natn'l Board Mmbr. Owns two 300SLs, a 500SLC, a 6.9, a 3.5 convertible & more.

Platz, Robert. East Camden, **NJ.** (609) 966-0080. Precision Autoworks.22nd Federal Sts. Renown detailing resource & re-storer of pre-72 SLs. Frqnt concours wnr w/ 190SLs & 300SLs.

Quadbeck, Ernest-Dieter. Koln 50, **GERMANY.**   Active SL & vintage rally participant with pre- & post 1946 Mercedes.

Rabon, Ron. Smyrna, **GA.** (404) 438-6102 Ron's Restorations, Prominent south eastern USA SL upholsterer. Full restorations or repair of your components sent to him. M-B materials.

Rapp, Ron. Ferndale, **MD.** (410) 760-8716. 3 Westpark Ct. Founder(1983) & 1st Pres. of 190SL Group. Also owns 190SL parts business, SL Auto Haus, which creates & imports needed 190SL parts, i.e. old style tar batteries (from Germany).

Ricardo, Don. Pasadena, **CA.** (213)682-1563. 964 Hillside Terrace. Major collector of significant Mercedes; 300SL back to brass era. Raced Gullwing at Bonneville in '1960s.

Rieger, Tom. Frederick, **MD.** (301) 694-4640. 8412 Rocky Springs Rd. *190SL Group* National Director, and Editor of club's excellent monthly newsletter. Won Best of Show with his Strawberry Red 190SL at '91 190SL Group. Nat'l. Meeting.

Rosales, David. East Brunswick, **NJ.** (908) 257-7549. 16 Theodore Dr. 1991/93 Presidentof the 190SL Group. Also owns 300SL. Frequent concours participant.

	190SL	300SL	#113	#107	#129

Rosales, Susan. East Brunswick, NJ. (908) 257-7549. 16 Theodore Dr. Treasurer & Office Mgr. of the 190SL Group. Frequent concours participant. ✔

Russell, Paul. Essex, **MA.** (508)768-6919. Paul Russell & Co 106 Western Avenue. Internationally famous for Pebble Beach winning restorations. Frequent club tech subject speaker. ✔ ✔ ✔

Paul Russell

Sacco, Bruno. 7032 Sindelfingen, **GERMANY.** Postfach 2 26 Chief of Design at Mercedes, employed there since 1950s. Owner of production 300SL Gullwing #4500001. ✔ ✔ ✔ ✔ ✔

Sachs, Peter G. Stamford, **CT.** 203-968-2970 % Klemantaski Collection, 65 High Ridge Rd. Major New England multi-marque sportscar enthusist. Rallys an alloy bodied 300SL GW. ✔

Samples, Jr. Will. Dallas, **TX.** (214) 521-8875. Ntn'ly recognized resource @ SL authenticity. Thru S & S Imports restores major components, engines, transmissions, differentials, Solex carbs, soft tops. Rglr. tech spkr at clubs, i.e. StarTech '93. ✔ ✔ ✔

Schneider, Norbert. W-6360 Friedberg, **GERMANY.** 06061-13901. Wetterau St. 97, Pres of 190SL Club e.V., in Grmny ✔

Bruno Sacco

Sattelberger, Hermann. Nurnberg, **GERMANY.** Koller and Schwemmer GmbH. 0911-36-10-30. FAX 0911 361-0321. Rothensteig 21. M-B & Bosch apprv'd SL fuel injectn rebldr. ✔ ✔ ✔ ✔

Schneider, Norbert. W-6360 Friedberg, **GERMANY.** 06061-13901. Wetterau St. 97, Pres of 190SL Club e.V., in Grmny ✔

Siech, Peter. 7519 Walzbachal 2, **GERMANY.** Phone (011-49) 07203-8181. Officer of 190SL Club e.V. in Germany. ✔

Shaw, Charlie. Nokesville, **VA.** (703) 594-3448. 11917 Cowne Court. Eastern Regional Vice Pres, 190SL Group. ✔

Will Samples

Splaine, Rich. Grand Rapids, **MI.** (616) 243-0220. Precious Metal Automotive Investment Co. 1601 College Av, SE. Restored sixty 190SLs since 1959. ✔

Sockol, Allan. Rumson, **NJ.** (201) 842-5353. Strong 190SL Group & Gull Wing Group supporter. Owns senior concours 190SL and 300SL. Also is M-B Dealer: Contemporary Motor Cars, Inc. Little Silver, NJ. ✔ ✔ ✔ ✔

Sommers, Dave. Castro Valley, CA. (510) 886-3234. 4512 Lawrence Dr. Northern California VP of 190SL Group and '92 190SL Group Nat'l. Meeting Chairman. ✔

Alan Sockel

212

Karl Weigl

Ozzie vomOrde

Max-Gerrit vonPein

Lynn Yakel

Sonnier, Lee. Marina del Ray, **CA.** (310) 823-0903. 4335 Marina City Drive. Serious student of the 230/250/280SL.

Stroscher, Ted. San Juan Capistrano, **CA.** (714)661-7337. 32101 Cook Ln. Gull Wing Gp Bd mbr and twice Chrmn to Ntn'l Cnvntn. Enthusiastic vintage racer w/ his 300SL Ro.

Thumwood, Art. Scottsdale, **AZ.** (602)397-SL300. SL 300 Parts. 6358 E. Kathleen Rd. Specializes in new & used 1950s 300SL parts. Strong club supporter. Major SL models collection.

Thomas, Peter. Scottsdale, **AZ.** (602)858-6556 . 9901 East Foothills Dr. Largest single exporter of 300SL cars from the USA during the last ten years. Active rally & club supporter.

Toblan, Martin. D-7899 Freiberg, **GERMANY.** Sundgaullee 43. Internationally active 300SL enthusiast and owner.

vomOrde, Ozzie. Reno, **NV.** (702)747-5125. 4235 Ross Dr. Pres. of Gull Wing Group for 8 yrs. through 1991. Exceptional knowlege on 300SL. Also owns 280SL. Has twice driven over 1,000 miles to a concours & still won 1st place.

vonCramm, Stephan. San Diego, **CA.** (619)521-9088. Automobile Appraisal Service. 8767 Ginger Snap Ln. Popular SL appraisal resource in California. Knowledgable on DOT/EPA.

vonPein, Max-Gerrit. 7000 Stuttgart, **GERMANY.** 0711-17-55532. Postfach 600202. Director of Mercedes-Benz Museum. vonPein championed "Oldtimer" training of M-B mechanics, supports M-B Clbs. world-wide with speakers, tech. data, and provenance varification. Rstrtn. shop also available to public.

Weigl, Karl. 7312 Kirchheim, **GERMANY.** 07021-49644 In der Warth 5. Instructor in M-B Oldtimer's Classes on 190/300SL. German 190SL Club Pres. Popular club tech speaker.

Willott, John. Bolder Creek, **CA.** (408)338-3707. Rebuilds 300SL fuel pumps, fuel & oil tubes, and other components. Long time Gull Wing Group Natn'l Board member.

Wright, Marcus. Long Branch, **NJ.** (908)870-1432 (April/Nov). (407) 694-0821 (Dec/Mar) 1950s 300SL engine rebuilder. Also a driving instructor for MBNA's salesman trng.

Wuerther, Ted. Los Altos, **CA.** (415) 941-4110. 24874 Olive Tree Lane. Knowledgeable M-B collector and club supporter.

Yakel, Lynn. Plymouth, **MI.** 313-459-7313. Lyco Engnrg. 8645 North Terrritorial Rd. New & used 300SL /S/Sc & 600 parts. Past Gull Wing Group Natn'l Pres. Frequent club tech. resource. Has raced 300SLs at Bonneville.

214

8. Official M-B Technical Information

Mercedes-Benz cars are always enhanced by a full set of factory manuals, parts books, and operating booklets ... not to mention maybe even reading them! As the cars get older -and more special - even M-B mechanics get out of practice working on them. It is wise to gradually become your own best expert. Getting advice on routine maintenance, trouble shooting and emergency repairs is a lot easier with official factory directions. Being able to solve just one emergency service could justify their cost. Some owners buy two sets, one to use and one for the next generation.

Many Mercedes-Benz Workshop Manuals are "generic," covering several years, engines or body types. A typical car may be covered by four or five books ... one for General Maintenance, one for Electrical Trouble Shooting, one for Chassis & Body, another for the engine, and yet another for air conditioning. Some books are used more than others, but each car deserves a full set. MERCEDES-BENZ AG, and/or MERCEDES-BENZ OF NORTH AMERICA have prepared the publications listed on the next few pages, all in English. Some newer versions such as the 300/500/600SL are so far only presented in microfiche for dealers. If service manuals aren't printed then some other form of repair instruc-

tions and parts schematics will be provided. Mercedes-Benz prefers that you order through your nearest authorized Mercede-Benz dealer. Bring this book with you and the parts department should be able to enter an order via their network computer. If there is no dealer near you, obtain copies by mail or toll-free with Visa or MasterCard (minimum with card, $15).

Service & Parts Literature
Mercedes-Benz of North America, Inc.
Three Mercedes Drive
Montvale, New Jersey 07645
Phone: 1-800-222-0100

Ordering Instructions

1. **Before making inquiries or orders locate your Model Designation, complete with Chassis No. (fourteen digits), and the *Original Registration Year*.**
2. **When ordering, specify the item number, title, quantity, and price of each item.**
3. **If ordering by mail residents of CA, FL, IL, MD & TX please add sales tax.**
4. **If ordering by mail add $5 per order for postage and handling.**
5. **If ordering by mail prepare and include a check to:**
   MERCEDES-BENZ OF NORTH AMERICA
6. **Clearly print your return address and zip code with your order. You must send a check (no CODs), and allow four weeks for delivery.**

Dealer ordering is faster, and they will be able to alert you to newly released manuals & price changes.

No.	Title and Description	Price
OM	**Owner's Manual**	**$4.50**
OM	**Owner's Manual for European Models, in English**	**$15.00**
MB	**Maintenance Booklet**	**$3.50**
MB	**Maintenance Booklet for European Models**	**$10.00**
WD	**Wiring Diagram** Available for many models & years '72 to present. For model years 1980 and newer see ETM item #25.	**$1.00**
1	**170, Service Manual** Order No. S-1204-000. This manual covers cars from 1946 to 1952 and includes models 170V, 170Va, 170S, 170D, 170Da and 170DS. It covers the gasoline engine, all chassis. **For Diesel** engines see item #7.	**$50.00**
2	**220 Service Manual** Order No. S-2200-885. Covers cars produced from 1951 to 1956. The coverage is limited to the engine, clutch, transmission, axle, driveshaft, steering components and maintenance. *The brakes, electrical, body and heating systems are not included.*	**$15.00**
3	**190 Service Manual** Order No. S-1207-000. Covers cars produced from 1956 to 1961, and includes models 190 and 190b. It covers the gasoline engine, all chassis and body maintenance.	**$35.00**
3a	**190SL Supplement to Service Manual** Order No. S-1204-111. Covers cars produced from 1952 to 1963, and is limited to those repairs and maintenance procedures wich differ from the 190. *This supplement together with #3 above provides comprehensive repair information for the **190SL**.*	**$5.00**

4   180 to 220SE, Service Manual   **$35.00**
Order No. S-1201-000. Covers cars from 1953 to 1962,
including 180, 180a, 180b, 180c, 180D, 180D, 190D,
190Db, 219, 220a, 220S and 220SE. Only repairs
and maintenance procedures which differ from the
190SL. Together with #3 gives comprehensive repair
information for 180 to 220SE. M136 fuel injection
of 220SE and hydraulic automatic transmission &
rear axles of 180 and 180D are not here. For diesels
see item 7.

5   300, Service Manual   **$21.00**
Order No. S-1209-000. Covers cars produced from
1951 to 1962, including 300, 300S, 300b, 300C
and 300Sc. Limited to engine, automatic transmission,
steering components and maintenance.

6   300SL, Service Manual   **$50.00**
Order No. S-6510-1408. Covers cars from 1954
to 1963, including the **300SL** Gullwing & Roadster.
Covered are engine, clutch, transmission, all chassis
and body components, the electrical system and
maintenance. Body repairs, removal of interior trim
and heating system not included.

7   Diesel Engines 621 and 622, Service Manual   **$35.00**
Order no. S-6540-2166. This manual covers all
4 cylinder passenger car diesels through 1967.

8   1959-1968 Passenger Cars (post 7/59)   **$35.00**
Order No. S-6510-1402-13. Covers cars produced
from 1959 1968, including 190c, 190Dc, 200,200D,
220b, 220Sb, 220SEb, 220SEb/C, 230, 230S, **230SL,**
250S, 250SE, 250SE/C, **250SL,** 300SE, 300SE/C,
300SEb, and 300SEL. Limited to minor repairs, unit
replacements, body/interior trim assembly jobs, and
maintenance. For automatic transmission see #8a.

No.	Title and Description	Price

8a   **Automatic Transmissions (with 2 planetary gear sets)**   **$15.00**
Order No. S-1200-000. Covers the assembly,
service, and repair of the automatic transmissions
used in the models outlined in #8.

9   **1968 and later Series 108, 109, 111, and 113**   **$35.00**
Order No. S-16510-1404-13. Covers 1968 to 1973,
including 280S, 280SE, 280SE 4.5, 280SE/C, 280SE/C
3.5, 280SEL, 280SEL 4.5, 300SEL, 300SEL 3.5,
300SEL 4.5, and 300SEL 6.3. All systems and
components included, however is limited to minor
repairs, unit replacement, and maintenance. 2.8
liter engine also included. *For 3.5 & 4.5 V8 engines
see #13. For 6.3 V8 see #10.*

10   **600 Service Manual**   **$75.00**
Order No. S-6510-1407-02. Covers cars
produced from 1964 through 1970s. Assembly,
adjustment, test procedures and maintenance of
the engine, tranmission, chassis and body. *Also
useful for repair of 6.3 engine in 300SEL 6.3.*

11   **114/115 Chassis & Body, Service Manual**   **$50.00**
Order No. S-2378-000. Covers cars from '68 to '76,
including 220, 220D, 230/8, 230, 240D, 250, 250C,
280, 280C, 300D. For engines, refer to respective
engine manual. Engine manuals for models 230/8,
250 and 250C are not available.

12   **107 Chassis & Body, Service Manual**   **$50.00**
Order No. S-6510-1930-13. Covers 1972 to 1989
350SL, 380SL, 450SL, 560SL and same SLC models,
plus much useful help on **280SL**/SLC & **500 SL**/SLC
vehicles. *For engine and climate controls, refer to
respective manuals.*

13   **116 (3.5) & 117 (4.5) Engines, Service Manual**   **$35.00**
Order No. S-6510-1916-13. Covers the 8 cylinder
engines (1971 to 1980) for models 280SE 4.5,
280 SE/C 3.5, 280SEL 4.5, 300SEL 3.5, 300SEL 4.5,
350SL, 450SL/SLC, 450SE, and 450SEL. The 6.9
engine is not referred to specifically, but of the
assembly and disassembly are applicable.

14   **115 Engine, Service Manual**   **$50.00**
Order No. S-2390-000. Covers 4 cylinder gas
engines of 220 ('68/73) and 230 ('74/78). Carburetor
coverage is limited to '74/78 models. For earlier
carburetors inquire about a supplement when ordering.
The 115.920 is not referred to specifically, but much
of the assembly & disassembly are applicable.

15   **615, 616, 617.91 Engine, Service Manual**   **$35.00**
Order No. S-2481-000. Covers 4 and 5 cylinder
diesel engines ('68 to 81) for models 220D, 240D,
300D, 300CD, and 300TD.

16   **110 Engine, Service Manual**   **$35.00**
Order No. S-6510-1914-13. Covers 6 cylinder gas
engines for 280, 280C, 280S, ('75 to 76), 280E,
280CE and 280SE ('77 to 81).

17   **116 Chassis & Body, Service Manual**   **$50.00**
Order No. S-6510-1918-13. Covers cars produced
from '73 to 80, including the 280S, 280SE, 300SD,
450SE, 450SEL, and 450SEL 6.9. *For engine and
climate controls refer to respective manuals. The only
6.9 engine manual is available from the M-100 Group.*

18   **123 Chassis & Body Service Manual**   ***$50.00***
*Order No. S-2432-123. Covers '77 to '85 including
230, 240D, 280E, 280CE,300CD, 300TD, 300D Turbo,
300CE Turbo, and 300TD Turbo. For engine & climate
controls refer to respect manuals.*

No.	Title and Description	Price

19 Maintenance Manual
Describes all necessary maintenance and specified
intervals. Illustrated discriptions of maintenance jobs,
with checking and adjustment data & filling capacities.
Information about special tools & torquing specifications.
Indicate:

For 1972-1980	No. S-1288-000	$28.00
For 1982-1986	No. S-1285-000	$28.00
For 1981-1989	No. 128.000	$33.00
For 1990-1992 (expt #140)	No. S-2388	$25.00

20 124 Chassis & Body, Service Manual   **$50.00**
Order No. S-2350-124. Covers cars produced since
1989, and includes the 300D Turbo, 300TD Turbo,
260E and 300E/CE/TE. Does not include suspension
system, rear axle, wheels/chassis measurments or
propeller shaft.

23 617.95 Engine, Service Manual   **$35.00**
Order No. S-6510-1927. Covers the 5 cylinder Turbo
diesel engine (1982-1985) for models 300D Turbo,
300CD Turbo, 300TD Turbo, and 300SD Turbo.

24 Automotive English/Metric Convertor   **$6.00**
Order No. S-2451-000. A universal slide-rule to provide
quick conversions of technical specifications (e.g. torque
engine power, pressure, miles (KM), fuel consumption, etc.,
between English and metric measurements.

25 Electronic Troubleshooting Manuals
Covers repair of electrical systems, and includes schematic
symbols, wiring conversions, basic troubleshooting
procedures, test tools, testing schematics, fuse circuit list,
electric circuit index, power distribution, component
locations and photographs. Please specify:

-1974, available by chassis type (107,114,116)	$15.00
-1979 Edition (covers all 1975 to 1979 models) - S-2379-000	$40.00
-1980 Edition (covers all 1980 models) - S-1222-000	$25.00
-1981 Edition (covers all 1981 models) - S-1223-000	$25.00
-1982 Editon (covers all 1982 models) - S-1230-000	$25.00
-1983 up to 1989 issues available by model & year	$15.00

No.	Title and Description	Price

26   **116 (3.8) & 117 (5.0), Service Manual**   **$35.00**
Order No. S-2467-000. Covers V8 engines
(1980-85) for USA 380SL/SLC, 380SE/SEL/SEC
and 500SEL/SEC.

27   **126 Chassis & Body, Service Manual**   **$50.00**
Order No. S-2350-126. Covers cars produced
1980-1991, including 300SD, 300SDL, 300SE/SEL,
350SD/SDL, 380SE/SEL/SEC, 420SEL, 500SEL/
SEC, and 560SEL/SEC. For engine & climate
control refer to respective manuals.

28   **201 Chassis & Body, Service Manual**   **$50.00**
Order No. S-2348-000. Covers cars produced since
1984, inlcuding 190D 2.2, 190D 2.5, 190D 2.5
Turbo, 190E 2.3, 190E .3-16, and 190E 2.6.
For engine and a/c refer to respective manuals.

29   **102 Engine, Service Manual**   **$35.00**
Order S-2347-000. Covers the 4 cylinder gas
engines (1984-1988) for models 190E 2.3 and
190E 2.3-16.

30   **601 Engine, Service Manual**   **$35.00**
Oder No. S-6510-1821-13
Covers 4 cylinder diesel ('84-85) for 190D 2.2

31   **107 Series Heating, A/C Automatic A/C Service Manual**   **$25.00**
Order No. S-2479-000. Covers climate control
systems for *350/450/380SL/SLC and 560SL*

32   **126 Series Automatic A/C Controls, Service Manual**   **$25.00**
Order No. S-2340-000. Covers the automatic a/c
controls systems for 300SD, 300SDL, 300SE/SEL
350SD/SDL, 380SEL/SEC, 420SEL, 500SEL/SEC

33   **201 Series Tempmatic A/C Controls, Service Manual**   **$25.00**
Order No. S-6510-1931-13. Covers air conditioning
of 190D2.2, 190D 2.5, 190D 2.5 Turbo, 190E 2.3,
190E 2.3-16, and 190E 2.6.

No.	Title and Description	Price
34	**116 Series Heating & Air Conditioning, Service Manual** Order No. S-6510-1924-13. Covers climate controls for 280S, 280SE, 300SD, 450SE/SEL & 450SEL 6.9.	**$25.00**
35	**123 Series Heating & Air Conditioning, Service Manual** Order No. S-2339-000. Covers a/c systems for 230, 240D, 280E, 280SCE, 300D, 300CD, 300TD, 300D Turbo, 300CD Turbo, 300TD Turbo(1977-1985)	**$25.00**
36	**124 Series *Automatic* Climate Control, Service Manual** Order No. S-2380-000. Covers automatic a/c sytem of 300D Turbo, 300TD Turbo, 300D 2.5 Turbo, 260E, 300E, 300CE, 300TE and E 2.6.	**$25.00**
37	**103 Engine, Service Manual** Order No. S-2421-103. Covers 6 cylinder gas engine (1986) of 190E 2.6, 260E, 300E, 300CE, 300TE, 300E 3.6	**$35.00**
38	**116 (4.2) & 117 (5.6) Engine, Service Manual** Order No. S-2466-000. Covers V8 engines (1986 to 1991) for 420SEL, **560SL**, 560SEL/SEC	**$35.00**
	Parts Picture Catologs are available by model year.	*Inquire*

Manuals cannot be returned without advance authorization, and there is a
10% restocking fee on all returned items.

PHOTO CREDITS

We gratefully recognize the following people and organizations for the of the photos and charts in this book.

190SL Group, East Brunswick, NJ: *4, 200, 201*
Dearborn, Alex, Topsfield, MA: *156, 158, 159*
Cleworth, Harold, Los Angeles, CA: *65*
Gotschke, Walter, Germany: *61*
Chicago Historic, Chicago, IL: *113*
Hatch & Sons, Hudson, MA : *32*
Holck, Peter: *146*
Mercedes-Benz (Stuttgart & Montvale): *29, 31, 41, 42, 43, 46, 47, 48, 49, 50, 55, 57, 62, 66, 70, 72, 75, 76, 108, 114, 162, 198*
Moran, Russ, Denver, CO: *61*
Mille Miglia Retrospective, Brescia, Italy: *134, 137*
Morehouse, Ed, Atlanta, GA: *150*
Olson, John, Minneapolis, MN: *35, 60, 87, 91, 97, 99, 101, 106, 109, 110, 112, 113, 120, 122, 123, 125, 131, 138, 139, 141, 144, 154, 164, 166, 169, 170, 171, 172, 176, 179, 181, 183, 184, 187, 207-213*
Paul Russell & Co., Essex, MA: *56*
Rivers, Jim, Wayzata, MN: *100*
Robinson, Randy, Kansas City, KS: *126*
Scott Restoration, Fountain City, CA: *71*
SL Market Letter, Minneapolis, MN: *26, 27, 78, 79, 80, 84, 85, 175*
Sports Leicht, Bolton, MA: *95*
Star Quality, LaGrangeville, NY: *52*
Stevens, Gary, Illinois: *113*
Thumwood, Art, Scottsdale, AZ: *59, 196*
Time Magazine: *23*
Vaucher, Jacques, Trenton, NJ: *187*
Vintage Racing: *113*
Volvo: *116*
Yakel, Lynn, Plymouth, MI: *vi*

INDEX

190SL   51,53-55
190SL Club e.V., Germany   200
190SL Group, USA   199
190E 2.3-16   111,190
230/250/280SL   37,39-43,45-51
230/250/280SL Clbs: see Pagoda & MBCA
300S & 300Sc   10, 87,190
300SL Coupe   57-61
300SL Roadster   62-65
300SL Club e.V. (also see GWG)   201
300SLS and O'Shea/Tilp Racers   67-69
300SLR, eight cylinder race car 67,146,
                                      197
280/350/450/380/560SL   25-31,37
107 SL Club e.V.   202
300/500/600SL   72-77
5 Speed Tranmissions   107

ABS brakes   105
ADS, adaptive dampening suspension 34,38
Adams, Bruce, restorer   95-103
Air Bags, SRS   68,104
Air Conditioning   106
Air Horns   106
Alfrieri, Bruno, author   205
Alloy Wheels   109
Aluminum engines   63,87
Alexander, Jesse, photo-journalist   88
American paintings, Pre WWII   19
AMG, performance options   110
Andersen, Jorgen   122,174,180,185
Antennas   107
Art and Mercedes-Benz   189
Audit Trail, of restoration costs   102
Aufrect, Hans-Werner   110
Automobile, the magazine   165,173
Avanti   9
Average annual SL sales   6
Axle Ratios, effect of   49,64,74

Bayer, Robert, 300SL Club e.V.   201
Black, Gordon   165
BMW   47,178
Begley, Mike, Four Ball Rally   147
Bondurant Driving School   119-125
Bondurant, Bob   119,122,17

Books, Out-of-print copies   192,205
Books, Technical Manuals   215-222
British Intellegence   viii
Brakes, ABS   105
Brakes, disc   41,63
Brakes, G-force sensing   76
Brakes, ventilated drums   112
Bugatti Royale   7
Bumper Guards   107
Byron, Howard   106

C 111   164
C 112   76
Car Repairs, Evaluation Chart   84,85
Cadillac   5,25
California Mille Rally   130
Camargo, Edwardo Leon   186
Clubs for SL owners   199-202
Chapman, Colin   40
Chassis Provenance   88
Cheek, Hyatt   199,200
Cushway, Ron, England   144
Chrysler 300 Convertibles   5
Clarke, R.M., author   205
Classic Automotive Investments   22
Cleworth, Harold,artist   65,193
Colorado Grand Rally   128,129,130
Continental Mark I & II   5
Cook, Steve, Four Ball Rally   147
Copper State 1000 Rally (Ariz) 129,130
Corvair Corsa   46

Dearborn, Alex   157-161
DeLorean, automobile   6
Demand, Carlos, artist   193
deTomaso Pantara   5
Dow Jones Average   120
Duesenberg   5

Earle, Steve   168
Echevarria, Raul   175,178
Eddy, Don, artist   193
Equinox Mountain, hill climb   47,153
Engelen, Gunter, author   39,204,205
Engine Switching   86
Envall, Sue, artist   193

Fake convertibles	83
Fangio, Juan Manuel	163,169
Ferrari	5,9,47,86
Ferrari Market Letter	86
Fitch, John	139,164,166,192
Fitted Luggage	109
Flippen, J. Bradley, re insurance	91,93
Fog lights	108
Forbes Magazine	8
Four Ball Rally	147-149
Front Wheel Drive, a case against	115
Fuel Injection origins	8,57
Genebein, Oliver	133,139
Gotschke, Walter, artist	61,191
Gull Wing Group, International	200
Hardtop	108
Hatch and Sons	32
Helck, Peter, artist	146
Herrmann, Hans	191
Herzog, Rene	178
Highlands Classic Rally (N. C.)	129,130
Hill, Phil	170
Hoffman, Max	57,154
Hunt, Chadwick	200,209
Inflation, adjusting for	20,21
Insurance, pitfalls	90-93
Investors	19
Jaguar	64
Jim Russell Driver's School	119
Johnson, John, author	151
Jones, Nicholas	185
Journey (Magazine)	203,206
Jump Seat, or 3rd seat for SLs	108
Kelly, Bruce, restorer	175
Kienle, Klaus, restorer	179
Kling, Karl	60,70,187,192
Knittel, Stafan, author	204
Laban, Brian, author	204
LaCarrera - Mexico	130,172-187
LaCarrera Reale Rally (NewMexico)	130
Laguna SECA	163-170
Lamp, Norbert	106

Lang, Hermann	163,164,171,192
Leather Interiors	109
Leaders, in the SL Community	207-213
Lerado de Tejada, Juan A.	175-178
Light Alloy Wheels	109
Lippmann, Manfredo	173
Liska, Hans, artist	191
Lowendowski, Jurgen, author	204
Luft, Manfred, German Pagoda Clb.	201
Ludvigsen, Karl, author	68,192
MBCA Pagoda Sub-Group	201
Maintenance, and records	89-90
Marx, Steve	165,210
Mercedes-Benz Club-England	202
Mercedes Collector (Magazine)	203
Mercedes (Magazine)	202
MG, TD	51
Mille Miglia Retrospective, Italy	132-142
Moss, Stirling	166
Most Collectible Mercedes	12-13
Mulholland Drive	140
Mueller, Peter	20
Museum, of Mercedes-Benz, Stuttgart	58,145,162,198
Naul, G. Marshall	3
Nomad, Chevrolet	5
Non-matching engine numbers	86
Nuebauer, Alfred	67,70
Nurburgring	188
O'Shea, Paul	66,67,68,69,113,192
Oldsmobile	43
Oldtimer's Service, of Mercedes-Benz	144
Olson, Art J.	33,35
Olson, Eric J.	iv,165
Paint, and color changes	107
Parks, Michael	46
Paul Russell and Company	56
Panzerwagens	ix,25
Pagoda SL Clubs	198,201
Pebble Beach, Concours	163,170
Peer Gynt World Ventures	145
Performance Options	110-111,113
Pearce, K.B & Elda	186

Platz, Robert   104-112
Postage Stamps, collecting of   193
Posters, as collectibles   193
Price Trends, SL Market Letter   79
Provenance, of cars   87,88
Prudent Man Investing   19

Radios, desirable options   106
Rally Racers, Scuderia Kassel   10
Rapp, Ron, USA 190SL Group   199,211
Rauch, Warren   174
Roush, Gerald (Ferrari Market Letter)   86
Rear Wheel Drive, the case for   115
Replicas, cars & sales folders   183,191
Restoration, A customer view   95
Road & Track, the magazine   191
Riedner, Michael, author   205
Rogers, Will, author   4
Roll Bars   75,155
Rose, Don, The Four Ball Rally   147
Ruckwarth, Bernhold   133
Rudge Wheels   111
Russell, Paul   59,148,165,212

Sales brochures, collectibility   189
Schaer, Rene   161,165-168,170
SRS, Air bags   68,104
Schlumpf Brothers, Museum   144
Schneider, Norbert, 190SL Clb e.V. 200
SCCA Champion, '55, '56, '57   113
Scott Restorations   71
Show Package   111
SL Market Letter   6,12-13,127,203,214
Soft tops   108
Sotheby's Fine Art Index   19-23
South American Rally, 1978   150
Spa Sofia Liege Rally, 230SL wins   44
Space frame (300SL)   vii
Statistics   Specifications   Quantities
   190SL   51   54
   230SL   51   40
   250SL   51   40
   280SL   51   40
   280SL(TwnCam)   26   26
   300S & Sc   -   9
   300SLGullwing   74   58

300SLRoadster   -   64
300SL-24   74   -
300SE Cp &Cabr   -   9
350SL   26   26
380SL   26   26
420SL   26   26
450SL   26   26
500SL   26   26
5.0SLC   -   9
500SLC Racers   10
560SL   26   26
600SL   74   -
20 Rarest   -   9
World Wide   -   iv
Spenz, Gerhard, German 107 Clb   202
Sports Leicht, A restorations center 94
Star Quality, An SL parts supplier 54
Stevens, Brooks, designer   38
Storage Costs   22
Stroscher, Ted   165
Studebaker Starliner   9
Studebaker-Packard   39
Subscriber's Poll, of collectibles 12-13

Teague, Richard, designer   115
Technical Manuals by M-B   215-222
Tompkin, Joe   165,167,168
Turnery, Bruce   173

Uhlenhaut, Rudolf   vii-ix, 40
Ultracar,   A restoration center   14

V-12,600SL   72-77
Value Guides, i.e. price trends   79
Vintage Racing   153-187
Vintage Racing Clubs   155
von Pein, Max-Gerrit   113,170,213

Warth, Tom   134-140
Watts, Nicholas, artist   187,193
Williams, Will, artist   191,193
Workstatement, in restorations   96

Yakel, Lynn   165,213
Yakel, Roberta (Dr. Nichols)   165,210

Zell, Peter, M-B Mexico   176

The **SL Market Letter** has had sport springs made in the USA for most SL models, based on original options that aren't always available as these models get older.

It is impossible to select a universally suitable spring stiffness for cars; when the wheelbase is short and the power of a car climbs the problem increases. Then, some cars never leave the city while others enjoy frequent jaunts in the country. Is the country road a turnpike or a mountain? Adaptive dampening suspension (ADS) is considered the state-of- the-art solution in the newest SLs, but what about earlier models? The **SL Market Letter** has tested all the factory's "sport spring" options way back to the 1950s. None are really stiff, but they are certainly less "busy," with less body roll in corners and less nose dive in braking. **Rudolf Uhlenhaut's** logic in the 1950s and 1960s was to achieve a soft, pleasant ride *as well as* good grip, via independent suspension and negative cambering in corners. While these objectives were met, the suspension's "busy-ness" can distract the driver's senses when driving fast. There is also a slight rear wheel steering just after off-center bumps. None of this is noticeable in moderate driving, but it becomes apparent as speeds increase. The optional springs addressed this issue for the sportive driver.

The **function of springs** is to carry the car's weight and accept fluctuations in load, ground evenness, and G-forces. Fresh **shock absorbers** are of course desireable, *but they won't* reduce nose dive or sudden rolling motions because all German shock absorbers do 85%+ of their "absorbing" on the rebound stroke, not the compression stroke. Compression resistance is the job of the springs themselves. Likewise, **anti-sway bars** reduce side sway but not nose-dive or rear end squat on acceleration and/or when fully loaded.

A full set of new sport springs costs between $800 and $1,000 ($300 for the 190SL) and the added preciseness and seat-of-the-pants confidence they give, makes pre-1985 SLs more fun every time you take the wheel. On the 300SL Roadster and 230/250/280SL it is possible to start by replacing only the rear center equalizing spring ($179). It mounts cross-ways over the differential. This manages full loads better (luggage, full gas tank and two people) without changing normal standing height. The Gullwing and the SLs after 1971 do not have this 5th spring.

M A R K E *SL* L E T T E R

PUBLISHED AND EDITED
AT 2020 SOUTH GIRARD

MINNEAPOLIS. MN 55405
TELEPHONE 612 377 · 0155

ORDER BY FAX
612-377-0157

ORDER BY PHONE
612-377-0155

SL MARKET LETTER, INC
2020 GIRARD AVENUE SOUTH
MINNEAPOLIS, MN 55405 USA

NAME *Print*_____PHONE:_____

ADDRESS _____

CITY:_____ STATE (OR COUNTRY):_____

ZIP:_____

QUANTITY	SL MARKET LETTER SUBSCRIPTIONS	SPECIAL	
_____	6 MO. TRIAL (9 ISSUES) IN N.AMERICA, $42	$37	$_____
_____	6 MO. TRIAL (9 ISSUES)		
	Air Mail Outside North America, $52	$47	$_____
_____	1 YEAR SUBSCRIPTION IN N. AMERICA, $77	$67	$_____
_____	1 YEAR SUBSCRIPTION (18 ISSUES)		
	AIR MAIL OUTSIDE NORTH AMERICA, $97	$87	$_____
_____	2 YEAR SUBSCRIPTION IN N. AMERICA, $129	$119	$_____
_____	2 YEAR SUBSCRIPTION (18 ISSUES)		
	AIR MAIL OUTSIDE NORTH AMERICA, $169	$159	$_____
_____	3 RING SL MARKET LETTER BINDER		
	ORGANIZES UP TO 50 MARKET LETTERS	$10	$_____

QUANTITY	ITEM AND PRICE WITH AIR POSTAGE	SPECIAL	
_____	COLLECTING THE MERCEDES-BENZ SL (*softcover*), $19	$16	$_____
	(*Add $4 **outside** North America for Air Mail*)		
_____	COLLECTING THE MERCEDES-BENZ SL (*hardcover*), $23	$20	$_____
	(*Add $5 **outside** North America for Air Mail*)		
	TOTAL (ALL POSTAGE & HANDLING INCLUDED):		$_____

Please make check % SL MARKET LETTER, INC.
or authorized credit card below:

☐ VISA   ☐ MASTERCARD   ☐ AMERICAN EXPRESS

EXPIRATION DATE:_____

CHARGE $_____ ON MY CREDIT

CARD #_____

SIGNATURE: _____DATE:_____